Unity 5 Game Optimization

Master performance optimization for Unity3D applications with tips and techniques that cover every aspect of Unity3D Engine

Chris Dickinson

PUBLISHING

BIRMINGHAM - MUMBAI

Unity 5 Game Optimization

First published: November 2015

Production reference: 1281015

Published by Packt Publishing Ltd.
Livery Place
35 Livery Street
Birmingham B3 2PB, UK.

ISBN 978-1-78588-458-0

www.packtpub.com

Credits

Author
Chris Dickinson

Reviewers
Clifford Champion
Dr. Sebastian T. Koenig

Acquisition Editor
Indrajit Das

Content Development Editor
Athira Laji

Technical Editor
Prajakta Mhatre

Copy Editor
Charlotte Carneiro

Project Coordinator
Bijal Patel

Proofreader
Safis Editing

Indexer
Rekha Nair

Graphics
Jason Monteiro

Production Coordinator
Aparna Bhagat

Cover Work
Aparna Bhagat

About the Author

Chris Dickinson grew up in England with a strong passion for science, mathematics, and video games. He received his master's degree in physics with electronics from the University of Leeds in 2005, and immediately traveled to California to work on scientific research in the heart of Silicon Valley. Finding that career path unsuitable, he began working in the software industry.

Over the last decade, he has made a career in software development, becoming a senior software developer. Chris has primarily worked in software automation and internal test tool development, but his passion for video games never fully faded. In 2010, he took the path of discovering the secrets of game development and 3D graphics by completing a second degree—a bachelor's degree in game and simulation programming. He authored a tutorial book on game physics (*Learning Game Physics with Bullet Physics and OpenGL* by Packt Publishing). He continues to work in software development, creating independent game projects in his spare time with tools such as Unity 3D.

Acknowledgments

I've managed to grasp an absolutely ridiculous amount of knowledge in just 5 years. None of this would have been possible without the constant motivation from my coworkers, tutors, friends, and family.

Thanks to my comrades in software development for being so understanding of my erratic schedule while I was learning game development at school.

Thanks also to my college tutors for helping accelerate me past the core material and learn so much about game development so quickly.

Thanks to my friends for always being a constant source of harassment and inquisitiveness about what I've been working on.

Thanks to my family for giving me the opportunity to learn, live, and love so much in such a short time.

And of course, thanks to my wonderful wife and best friend, Jamie, for being so caring and supportive of all the late nights and helping me stay creative.

About the Reviewers

Clifford Champion has a broad background in software engineering, with years of experience spanning 3D games, Internet applications, and artificial intelligence. He holds degrees in mathematics and computer science from UCLA and UCSD, respectively. In the past, Clifford worked for video game technology company Havok (now part of Microsoft), and interactive media and design company PlainJoe Studios. Currently, he leads a software team at zSpace (zspace.com), a VR company specializing in 3D for classrooms and industry.

Clifford can be found on Twitter at @duckmaestro and welcomes discussions on any topic.

Dr. Sebastian T. Koenig received his PhD in human interface technology from the University of Canterbury, New Zealand, developing a framework for individualized virtual reality cognitive rehabilitation. He obtained his diploma in psychology from the University of Regensburg, Germany, in the areas of clinical neuropsychology and virtual reality rehabilitation.

Sebastian is the founder and CEO of Katana Simulations, where he oversees the design, development, and evaluation of cognitive assessment and training simulations. His professional experience spans over 10 years of clinical work in cognitive rehabilitation and over 8 years of virtual reality research, development, and user testing. He has extensive experience as a speaker at international conferences and as a reviewer of scientific publications in the areas of rehabilitation, cognitive psychology, neuropsychology, software engineering, game development, game user research, and virtual reality.

Sebastian has developed numerous software applications for cognitive assessment and training. For his work on the virtual memory task, he was awarded the prestigious Laval Virtual Award in 2011, for the Medicine and Health category. Other applications of his include the virtual reality executive function assessment in collaboration with the Kessler Foundation, New Jersey, USA, and the patent-pending Microsoft Kinect-based motor and cognitive training JewelMine/Mystic Isle at the USC Institute for Creative Technologies, California, USA.

He maintains the website at www.virtualgamelab.com, which features his research and his software development projects. His website also contains a comprehensive list of tutorials for the Unity game engine.

www.PacktPub.com

Support files, eBooks, discount offers, and more

For support files and downloads related to your book, please visit www.PacktPub.com.

Did you know that Packt offers eBook versions of every book published, with PDF and ePub files available? You can upgrade to the eBook version at www.PacktPub.com and as a print book customer, you are entitled to a discount on the eBook copy. Get in touch with us at service@packtpub.com for more details.

At www.PacktPub.com, you can also read a collection of free technical articles, sign up for a range of free newsletters and receive exclusive discounts and offers on Packt books and eBooks.

https://www2.packtpub.com/books/subscription/packtlib

Do you need instant solutions to your IT questions? PacktLib is Packt's online digital book library. Here, you can search, access, and read Packt's entire library of books.

Why subscribe?

- Fully searchable across every book published by Packt
- Copy and paste, print, and bookmark content
- On demand and accessible via a web browser

Free access for Packt account holders

If you have an account with Packt at www.PacktPub.com, you can use this to access PacktLib today and view 9 entirely free books. Simply use your login credentials for immediate access.

Table of Contents

Preface

User experience is a critical component of any game. User experience includes not only our game's story and its gameplay, but also how smoothly the graphics run, how reliably it connects to multiplayer servers, how responsive it is to user input, and even how large the final application file size is due to the prevalence of app stores and cloud downloads. The barrier to entering game development has been lowered considerably thanks to the release of cheap, AAA-industry-level game development tools such as Unity. However, the features and quality of the final product that our players expect us to provide is increasing with every passing day. We should expect that every facet of our game can and will be scrutinized by players and critics alike.

The goals of performance optimization are deeply entwined with user experience. Poorly optimized games can result in low frame rates, freezes, crashes, input lag, long loading times, inconsistent and jittery runtime behavior, physics engine breakdowns, and even excessively high battery power consumption (particularly important in this era of mobile devices). Having just one of these issues can be a game developer's worst nightmare as reviews will tend to focus on the one thing that we did badly, in spite of all the things that we did well.

Performance is all about making the best use of the available resources, which includes the CPU resources such as CPU cycles and main memory space, Graphics Processing Unit (GPU) resources such as memory space (VRAM) and memory bandwidth, and so on. But optimization also means making sure that no single resource causes a bottleneck at an inappropriate time, and that the highest priority tasks get taken care of first. Even small, intermittent hiccups and sluggishness in performance can pull the player out of the experience, breaking immersion and limiting our potential to create the experience we intended.

It is also important to decide when to take a step back and stop making performance enhancements. In a world with infinite time and resources, there would always be another way to make it better, faster, or easier to maintain. There must be a point during development where we decide that the product has reached acceptable levels of quality. If not, we risk dooming ourselves to implementing further changes that result in little or no tangible benefit.

The best way to decide if a performance issue is worth fixing is to answer the question "will the user notice it?". If the answer to this questions is "no", then performance optimization would be a wasted effort. There is an old saying in software development:

> *Premature optimization is the root of all evil*

Premature optimization is the cardinal sin of reworking and refactoring code to enhance performance without any proof that it is necessary. This could mean either making changes without showing that a performance problem even exists (answering the question of whether or not it would be noticeable to the user), or making changes because we only believe a performance issue might stem from a particular area before it has been proven to be true. Making these mistakes has cost software developers, as a collective whole, a depressing number of work hours for nothing.

This book intends to give us the tools, knowledge, and skills we need to both detect and fix performance issues in our application, no matter where they stem from. This could be hardware components such as the CPU, GPU, or RAM, within software subsystems such as Physics, Rendering, or within the Unity Engine itself. In addition, the more resources we save, the more we can do within the Unity Engine with the same hardware system, allowing us to generate more interesting and dynamic gameplay.

This will give our game a better chance of succeeding and standing out from the crowd in a marketplace that is inundated with new, high quality games every single day.

What this book covers

Chapter 1, Detecting Performance Issues, provides an exploration of the Unity Profiler and a series of methods to profile our application, detect performance bottlenecks, and perform root cause analysis.

Chapter 2, Scripting Strategies, deals with the best practices for our Unity C# Script code, minimizing Component overhead, improving inter-object communication, and more.

Chapter 3, The Benefits of Batching, explores Unity's Dynamic and Static Batching systems to ease the burden on the rendering system.

Chapter 4, Kickstart Your Art, helps you understand the underlying technology behind our art assets and learn how to avoid common pitfalls with importing, compression, and encoding.

Chapter 5, Faster Physics, is about investigating the nuances of Unity's physics system for both 3D and 2D games, and how to properly organize our physics objects for improved performance.

Chapter 6, Dynamic Graphics, provides an in-depth exploration of the rendering system, and how to improve applications that suffer rendering bottlenecks in the GPU, or CPU, and specialized techniques for mobile devices.

Chapter 7, Masterful Memory Management, examines the inner workings of the Unity Engine, the Mono Framework, and how memory is managed within these components to protect our application from heap allocations and runtime garbage collection.

Chapter 8, Tactical Tips and Tricks, deals with a multitude of useful techniques used by professionals to improve project workflow and scene management.

What you need for this book

The majority of this book will focus on features within the context of Unity version 5.x. Most of the techniques can be applied to Unity 4.x projects, but may require an upgrade to Unity 4 Pro Edition in order to access some of them (such as Occlusion Culling, Static Batching, and even the Profiler itself).

Who this book is for

This book is intended for intermediate and advanced Unity developers who have experience with most of Unity's feature set, and those who want to maximize the performance of their game or solve particular bottlenecks. Whether the bottleneck is caused by CPU overload, runtime spiking, slow memory access, fragmentation, garbage collection, poor GPU fillrate, or memory bandwidth, this book will teach you the techniques you need to identify the source of the problem and help explore multiple ways of reducing their impact on your application.

Familiarity with the C# language will be needed for sections involving scripting and memory usage, and a basic understanding of cg will be needed for areas involving Shader optimization.

Conventions

In this book, you will find a number of text styles that distinguish between different kinds of information. Here are some examples of these styles and an explanation of their meaning.

Code words in text, database table names, folder names, filenames, file extensions, pathnames, dummy URLs, user input, and Twitter handles are shown as follows: "The main Unity callback for application updates is the Update() function."

A block of code is set as follows:

```
public class TestComponent : MonoBehaviour {
    void Update() {
        if (Input.GetKeyDown(KeyCode.Space)) {
            PerformProfilingTest();
        }
    }
}
```

When we wish to draw your attention to a particular part of a code block, the relevant lines or items are set in bold:

```
public class TestComponent : MonoBehaviour {
    void Update() {
        if (Input.GetKeyDown(KeyCode.Space)) {
            PerformProfilingTest();
        }
    }
}
```

New terms and **important words** are shown in bold. Words that you see on the screen, for example, in menus or dialog boxes, appear in the text like this: "The threshold value for the sleeping state can be modified under **Edit | Project Settings | Physics | Sleep Threshold**."

 Warnings or important notes appear in a box like this.

 Tips and tricks appear like this.

Reader feedback

Feedback from our readers is always welcome. Let us know what you think about this book—what you liked or disliked. Reader feedback is important for us as it helps us develop titles that you will really get the most out of.

To send us general feedback, simply e-mail feedback@packtpub.com, and mention the book's title in the subject of your message.

If there is a topic that you have expertise in and you are interested in either writing or contributing to a book, see our author guide at www.packtpub.com/authors.

Customer support

Now that you are the proud owner of a Packt book, we have a number of things to help you to get the most from your purchase.

Downloading the example code

You can download the example code files from your account at http://www.packtpub.com for all the Packt Publishing books you have purchased. If you purchased this book elsewhere, you can visit http://www.packtpub.com/support and register to have the files e-mailed directly to you.

Errata

Although we have taken every care to ensure the accuracy of our content, mistakes do happen. If you find a mistake in one of our books—maybe a mistake in the text or the code—we would be grateful if you could report this to us. By doing so, you can save other readers from frustration and help us improve subsequent versions of this book. If you find any errata, please report them by visiting http://www.packtpub.com/submit-errata, selecting your book, clicking on the **Errata Submission Form** link, and entering the details of your errata. Once your errata are verified, your submission will be accepted and the errata will be uploaded to our website or added to any list of existing errata under the Errata section of that title.

To view the previously submitted errata, go to https://www.packtpub.com/books/content/support and enter the name of the book in the search field. The required information will appear under the **Errata** section.

Piracy

Piracy of copyrighted material on the Internet is an ongoing problem across all media. At Packt, we take the protection of our copyright and licenses very seriously. If you come across any illegal copies of our works in any form on the Internet, please provide us with the location address or website name immediately so that we can pursue a remedy.

Please contact us at copyright@packtpub.com with a link to the suspected pirated material.

We appreciate your help in protecting our authors and our ability to bring you valuable content.

Questions

If you have a problem with any aspect of this book, you can contact us at questions@packtpub.com, and we will do our best to address the problem.

1
Detecting Performance Issues

Performance evaluation for most software products is a very scientific process: determine the maximum supported performance metrics (number of concurrent users, maximum allowed memory usage, CPU usage, and so on); perform load testing against the application in scenarios that try to simulate real-world behavior; gather instrumentation data from test cases; analyze the data for performance bottlenecks; complete a root-cause analysis; make changes in the configuration or application code to fix the issue; and repeat.

Just because game development is a very artistic process does not mean it should not be treated in equally objective and scientific ways. Our game should have a target audience in mind, who can tell us the hardware limitations our game might be under. We can perform runtime testing of our application, gather data from multiple components (CPU, GPU, memory, physics, rendering, and so on), and compare them against the desired metrics. We can use this data to identify bottlenecks in our application, perform additional instrumentation to determine the root cause of the issue, and approach the problem from a variety of angles.

To give us the tools and knowledge to complete this process, this chapter will introduce a variety of methods that we will use throughout the book to determine whether we have a performance problem, and where the root cause of the performance issue can be found. These skills will give us the techniques we need to detect, analyze, and prove that performance issues are plaguing our **Unity** application, and where we should begin to make changes. In doing so, you will prepare yourselves for the remaining chapters where you will learn what can be done about the problems you're facing.

We will begin with an exploration of the **Unity Profiler** and its myriad of features. We will then explore a handful of scripting techniques to narrow-down our search for the elusive bottleneck and conclude with some tips on making the most of both techniques.

The Unity Profiler

The Unity Profiler is built into the **Unity Editor** itself, and provides an expedient way of narrowing our search for performance bottlenecks by generating usage and statistics reports on a multitude of **Unity3D** components during runtime:

- CPU usage per component of the Unity3D Engine
- Rendering statistics
- GPU usage on several programmable pipeline steps and stages
- Memory usage and statistics
- Audio usage and statistics
- Physics engine usage and statistics

With the release of **Unity 5.0**, Unity Technologies has made the Profiler available to all developers running the Personal Edition (the new name for the Free Edition).

Users running the Free Edition of Unity 4 must either upgrade to Unity 5, or purchase a license for Unity 4 Pro Edition.

This additional reporting comes with a price, however. Additional instrumentation flags will be enabled within the compiler, generating runtime logging events and a different level of automated code optimization while the Profiler is in use, which causes some additional CPU and memory overhead at runtime. This profiling cost is not completely negligible, and is likely to cause inconsistent behavior when the Profiler is toggled on and off.

In addition, we should always avoid using Editor Mode for any kind of profiling and benchmarking purposes due to the overhead costs of the Editor; its interface, and additional memory consumption of various objects and components. It is always better to test our application in a standalone format, on the target device, in order to get a more accurate and realistic data sample.

Users who are already familiar with connecting the Unity Profiler to their applications should skip to the section titled *The Profiler window*

Launching the Profiler

We will begin with a brief tutorial on how to connect our game to the Unity Profiler within a variety of contexts:

- Local instances of the application, either through the Editor or standalone
- Profiling the Editor itself
- Local instances of the application in **Unity Webplayer**
- Remote instances of the application on an iOS device (the iPad tablet or the iPhone device)
- Remote instances of the application on an Android device (a tablet or phone device running Android OS)
- We will briefly cover the requirements for setting up the Profiler in each of these contexts.

Editor or standalone instances

The only way to access the Profiler is to launch it through the Unity Editor and connect it to a running instance of our application. This is the case whether we're running our game within the Editor, running a standalone application on the local or remote device, or when we wish to profile the Editor itself.

To open the Profiler, navigate to **Window** | **Profiler** within the Editor. If the Editor is already running in Play Mode, then we may see reporting data gathering in the Profiler Window:

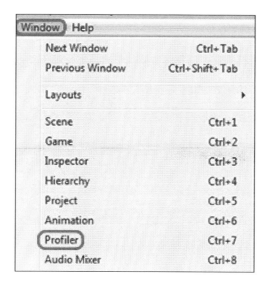

To profile standalone projects, ensure that the **Use Development Mode** and **Autoconnect Profiler** flags are enabled when the application is built.

Selecting whether to profile an Editor-based instance (through the Editor's Play Mode) or a standalone instance (separately built and running in the background) can be achieved through the **Active Profiler** option in the Profiler window.

The Unity Profiler

Editor profiling

Profiling the Editor itself, such as profiling custom Editor Scripts, can be enabled with the **Profile Editor** option in the Profiler window as shown in the following screenshot. Note that this requires the **Active Profiler** option to be configured to **Editor**.

The Unity Webplayer connection

The Profiler can also connect to an instance of the Unity Webplayer that is currently running in a browser. This enables us to profile our web-based application in a more real-world scenario through the target browser, and test multiple browser types for inconsistencies in behavior.

1. Ensure that the **Use Development Mode** flag is enabled when the Webplayer application is built.

2. Launch the compiled Webplayer application in a browser and, while it is active in the browser window, hold the *Alt* key (*Option* key on a Mac) and right-click on the Webplayer object within the browser to open the **Release Channel Selection** menu. Then select the **Development** channel, as shown in the following screenshot:

> Note that changing the **Release Channel** option will restart the Webplayer application.

3. As shown in the following screenshot, open the Profiler in the Unity Editor within the **Profiler** window, and then navigate to **Active Profiler | WindowsWebPlayer(COMPUTERNAME)** or **Active Profiler | OSXWebPlayer(COMPUTERNAME)**, depending on the Operating System:

You should now see reporting data collecting in the Profiler window.

Remote connection to an iOS device

The Profiler can also be connected to an active instance of the application running remotely on an iOS device, such as an iPad or iPhone. This can be achieved through a shared WiFi connection. Follow the given steps to connect the Profiler to an Apple device:

 Note that remote connection to an Apple device is only possible when the Profiler is running on an Apple Mac device.

1. Ensure that the **Use Development Mode** and **Autoconnect Profiler** flags are enabled when the application is built.
2. Connect both the iOS device and Mac to a local or ADHOC WiFi network.
3. Attach the iOS device to the Mac via the USB or the Lightning cable.
4. Begin building the application with the **Build & Run** option as normal.
5. Open the Profiler window in the Unity Editor and select the device under **Active Profiler**.

You should now see the iOS device's profiling data gathering in the Profiler window.

 The Profiler uses ports 54998 to 55511 to broadcast profiling data. Make sure these ports are available for outbound traffic if there is a firewall on the network

Remote connection to an Android device

There are two different methods for connecting an Android device to the Unity Profiler: either through a WiFi connection or using the **Android Debug Bridge (ADB)** tool. ADB is a suite of debugging tools that comes bundled with the Android SDK.

Follow the given steps for profiling over a WiFi connection:

1. Ensure that the **Use Development Mode** and **Autoconnect Profiler** flags are enabled when the application is built.
2. Connect both the Android and desktop devices to a local WiFi network.
3. Attach the Android device to the desktop device via the USB cable.
4. Begin building the application with the **Build & Run** option as normal.
5. Open the Profiler window in the Unity Editor and select the device under **Active Profiler**.

You should now see the Android device's profiling data gathering in the Profiler Window.

For ADB profiling, follow the given steps:

1. From the Windows command prompt, run the `adb devices` command, which checks if the device is recognized by ADB (if not, then the specific device drivers for the device may need to be installed and/or USB debugging needs to be enabled on the target device).

     Note that, if the `adb devices` command isn't found when it is run from the command prompt, then the Android SDK folder may need to be appended onto the Environment's `PATH` variable.

2. Ensure that the **Use Development Mode** and **Autoconnect Profiler** flags are enabled when the application is built.

3. Attach the Android device to the desktop device via the cable (for example, USB).

4. Begin building the application with the **Build & Run** option as normal.

5. Open the Profiler Window in the Unity Editor and select the device under **Active Profiler**.

You should now see the Android device's profiling data gathering in the Profiler window.

The Profiler window

We will now cover the essential features of the Profiler as they can be found within the interface.

 Note that this section covers features as they appear in the Unity Profiler within Unity 5. Additional features were added to the Profiler with the release of Unity 5; these may be different, or not exist, in Unity 4's Profiler.

The Profiler window is split into three main areas:

*   Controls
*   Timeline View
*   Breakdown View

These areas are as shown in the following screenshot:

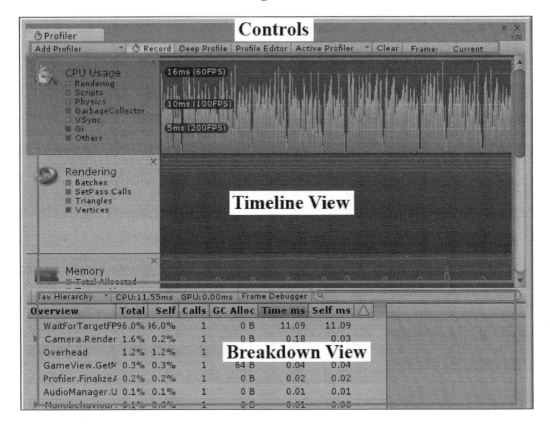

Controls

The top bar contains multiple controls we can use to affect what is being profiled and how deeply in the system data is gathered from. They are:

- **Add Profiler**: By default, the Profiler shows several of Unity's engine components in the Timeline View, but the **Add Profiler** option can be used to add additional items. See the *Timeline View* section for a complete list of components we can profile.

- **Record**: Enabling this option will make the Profiler continuously record profiling data. Note that data can only be recorded if Play Mode is enabled (and not paused) or if **Profile Editor** is enabled.

- **Deep Profile**: Ordinary profiling will only record the time and memory allocations made by any Unity callback methods, such as `Awake()`, `Start()`, `Update()`, `FixedUpdate()`, and so on. Enabling **Deep Profile** recompiles our scripts to measure each and every invoked method. This causes an even greater instrumentation cost during runtime and uses significantly more memory since data is being collected for the entire call stack at runtime. As a consequence, Deep Profiling may not even be possible in large projects running on weak hardware, as Unity may run out of memory before testing can even begin!

> Note that Deep Profiling requires the project to be recompiled before profiling can begin, so it is best to avoid toggling the option during runtime.

Because this option measures all methods across our codebase in a blind fashion, it should not be enabled during most of our profiling tests. This option is best reserved for when default profiling is not providing enough detail, or in small test Scenes, which are used to profile a small subset of game features.

If Deep Profiling is required for larger projects and Scenes, but the **Deep Profile** option is too much of a hindrance during runtime, then there are alternatives that can be found in the upcoming section titled *Targeted Profiling of code segments*.

- **Profile Editor**: This option enables Editor profiling—that is, gathering profiling data for the Unity Editor itself. This is useful in order to profile any custom Editor Scripts we have developed.

> Note that **Active Profiler** must be set to the **Editor** option for this feature to work.

- **Active Profiler**: This drop-down globally offers choices to select the target instance of Unity we wish to profile; this, as we've learned, can be the current Editor application, a local standalone instance of our application, or an instance of our application running on a remote device.

- **Clear**: This clears all profiling data from the Timeline View.

- **Frame Selection**: The **Frame** counter shows how many frames have been profiled, and which frame is currently selected in the Timeline View. There are two buttons to move the currently selected frame forward or backward by one frame, and a third button (the **Current** button) that resets the selected frame to the most recent frame and keeps that position. This will cause the Breakdown View to always show the profiling data for the current frame during runtime profiling.

- **Timeline View**: The Timeline View reveals profiling data that has been collected during runtime, organized by areas depending on which component of the engine was involved.

  Each Area has multiple colored boxes for various subsections of those components. These colored boxes can be toggled to reveal/hide the corresponding data types within the Timeline View.

  Each Area focuses on profiling data for a different component of the Unity engine. When an Area is selected in the Timeline View, essential information for that component will be revealed in the Breakdown View for the currently selected frame.

  The Breakdown View shows very different information, depending on which Area is currently selected.

Areas can be removed from the Timeline View by clicking on the 'X' at the top right of an Area. Areas can be restored to the Timeline View through the **Add Profiler** option in the Controls bar.

CPU Area

This Area shows CPU Usage for multiple Unity subsystems during runtime, such as MonoBehaviour components, cameras, some rendering and physics processes, user interfaces (including the Editor's interface, if we're running through the Editor), audio processing, the Profiler itself, and more.

There are three ways of displaying CPU Usage data in the Breakdown View:

- Hierarchy
- Raw Hierarchy
- Timeline

The **Hierarchy Mode** groups similar data elements and global Unity function calls together for convenience—for instance, rendering delimiters, such as `BeginGUI()` and `EndGUI()` calls are combined together in this Mode.

The **Raw Hierarchy Mode** will separate global Unity function calls into individual lines. This will tend to make the Breakdown View more difficult to read, but may be helpful if we're trying to count how many times a particular global method has been invoked, or determining if one of these calls is costing more CPU/memory than expected. For example, each BeginGUI() and EndGUI() call will be separated into different entries, possibly cluttering the Breakdown View, making it difficult to read.

Perhaps, the most useful mode for the CPU Area is the **Timeline Mode** option (not to be confused with the main Timeline View). This Mode organizes CPU usage during the current frame by how the call stack expanded and contracted during processing. Blocks at the top of this view were directly called by the Unity Engine (such as the Start(), Awake(), or Update() methods), while blocks underneath them are methods that those methods had called, which can include methods on other Components or objects.

Meanwhile, the width of a given CPU Timeline Block gives us the relative time it took to process that method compared to other blocks around it. In addition, method calls that consume relatively little processing time, relative to the more *greedy* methods, are shown as gray boxes to keep them out of sight.

The design of the CPU Timeline Mode offers a very clean and organized way of determining which particular method in the call stack is consuming the most time, and how that processing time measures up against other methods being called during the same frame. This allows us to gauge which method is the biggest culprit with minimal effort.

For example, let's assume that we are looking at a performance problem in the following screenshot. We can tell, with a quick glance, that there are three methods that are causing a problem, and they each consume similar amounts of processing time, due to having similar widths.

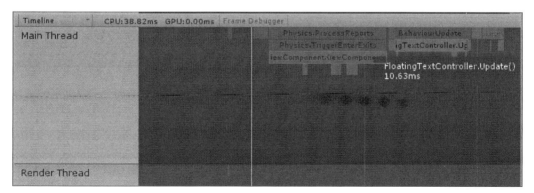

In this example, the good news is that we have three possible methods through which to find performance improvements, which means lots of opportunities to find code that can be improved. The bad news is that increasing the performance of one method will only improve about one-third of the total processing for that frame. Hence, all three methods will need to be examined and improved in order to minimize the amount of processing time during this frame.

The CPU Area will be most useful during *Chapter 2*, *Scripting Strategies*.

The GPU Area

The **GPU Area** is similar to the CPU Area, except that it shows method calls and processing time as it occurs on the GPU. Relevant Unity method calls in this Area will relate to cameras, drawing, opaque and transparent geometry, lighting and shadows, and so on.

The GPU Area will be beneficial during *Chapter 6*, *Dynamic Graphics*.

The Rendering Area

The **Rendering Area** provides rendering statistics, such as the number of SetPass calls, the total number of Batches used to render the scene, the number of Batches saved from Dynamic and Static Batching, memory consumed for Textures, and so on.

The Rendering Area will be useful in *Chapter 3*, *The Benefits of Batching*.

The Memory Area

The **Memory Area** allows us to inspect memory usage of the application in the Breakdown View in two different ways:

- Simple Mode
- Detailed Mode

The **Simple Mode** provides only a high-level overview of memory consumption of components such as Unity's low-level Engine, the Mono framework (total heap size that will be garbage-collected), Graphics, Audio (FMOD), and even memory used to store data collected by the Profiler.

The **Detailed Mode** shows memory consumption of individual game objects and components, for both their native and managed representations. It also has a column explaining the reason for that object consuming memory and when it might be de-allocated.

The Memory Area will be the main focal point of *Chapter 7*, *Masterful Memory Management*.

The Audio Area

The **Audio Area** grants an overview of audio statistics and can be used both to measure CPU usage from the audio system, as well as total memory consumed by **Audio Sources** (for both playing and paused sources) and **Audio Clips**.

The Audio Area will come in handy as we explore art assets in *Chapter 4, Kickstart Your Art*.

Audio is often overlooked when it comes to performance enhancements, but audio can become of the biggest sources of bottlenecks if it is not managed properly. It's worth performing occasional checks on the Audio system's memory and CPU consumption during development.

The Physics 3D/2D Area

There are two different Physics Areas, one for 3D physics (Nvidia's PhysX) and another for the 2D physics system (Box2D) that was integrated into the Unity Engine in version 4.5. This Area provides various physics statistics such as Rigidbody, Collider, and Contact counts.

We will be making use of this Area in *Chapter 5, Faster Physics*.

As of the publication of this text, with Unity v5.2.2f1 as the most recent version, the Physics3D Area only provides a handful of items, while the Physics2D Area provides significantly more information.

Best approaches to performance analysis

Good coding practices and project asset management often make finding the root cause of a performance issue relatively simple, at which point the only real problem is figuring out how to improve the code. For instance, if the method only processes a single gigantic `for` loop, then it will be a pretty safe assumption that the problem is either with the iteration of the loop or how much work is processed each iteration.

Of course, a lot of our code, whether we're working individually or in a group setting, is not always written in the cleanest way possible, and we should expect to have to profile some poor coding work from time to time. Sometimes, *hack-y* solutions are inevitable, and we don't always have the time to go back and refactor everything to keep up with our best coding practices.

It's easy to overlook the obvious when problem solving and performance optimization is just another form of problem solving. The goal is to use Profilers and data analysis to search our codebase for clues about where a problem originates, and how significant it is. It's often very easy to get distracted by invalid data or jump to conclusions because we're being too impatient or missed a subtle clue. Many of us have run into occasions, during software debugging, where we could have found the root cause of the problem much faster if we had simply challenged and verified our earlier assumptions. Always approaching debugging under the belief that the problem is highly complex and technical is a good way to waste valuable time and effort. Performance analysis is no different.

A checklist of tasks would be helpful to keep us focused on the issue, and not waste time chasing "ghosts". Every project is different and has a different set of concerns and design paradigms, but the following checklist is general enough that it should be able to apply to any Unity project:

- Verifying the target Script is present in the Scene
- Verifying the Script appears in the Scene the correct number of times
- Minimizing ongoing code changes
- Minimizing internal distractions
- Minimizing external distractions

Verifying script presence

Sometimes there are things we expect to see, but don't. These are usually easy to note, because the human brain is very good at pattern recognition. If something doesn't match the expected pattern, then it tends to be very obvious. Meanwhile, there are times where we assume something has been happening, but it didn't. These are generally more difficult to notice, because we're often scanning for the first kind of problem. Verification of the intended order of events is critical, or we risk jumping to conclusions, wasting valuable time.

In the context of Unity, this means it is essential to verify that the script we expect to see the event coming from is actually present in the Scene, and that the method calls happen in the order we intended.

Script presence can be quickly verified by typing the following into the **Hierarchy** window textbox:

```
t:<monobehaviour name>
```

For example, typing `t:mytestmonobehaviour` (note: it is not case-sensitive) into the **Hierarchy** textbox will show a shortlist of all GameObjects that currently have a `MyTestMonobehaviour` script attached as a Component.

 Note that this shortlist feature also includes any GameObjects with Components that *derive* from the given script name.

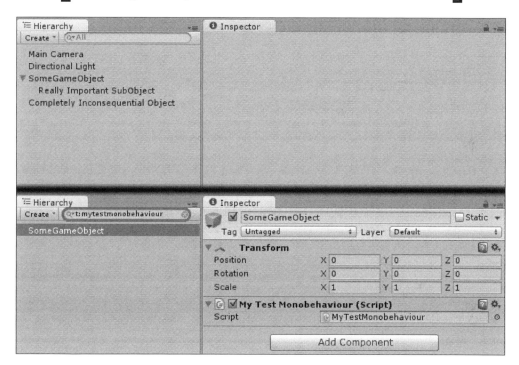

We should also double-check that the GameObjects they are attached to are still enabled, since we may have disabled them during earlier testing, or someone/something has accidentally deactivated the object.

Verifying script count

If we assume that a MonoBehaviour, which is causing performance problems, only appears once in our Scene, then we may ignore the possibility that conflicting method invocations are causing a bottleneck. This is dangerous; what if someone created the object twice or more in the Scene file, or we accidentally instantiated the object more than once from code? What we see in the Profiler can be a consequence of the same expensive method being invoked more than once at the same time. This is something we will want to double-check using the same shortlist method as before.

If we expected only one of the Components to appear in the Scene, but the shortlist revealed more than one, then we may wish to rethink our earlier assumptions about what's causing the bottlenecks. We may wish to write some initialization code that prevents this from ever happening again, and/or write some custom Editor helpers to display warnings to any level designers who might be making this mistake.

Preventing casual mistakes like this is essential for good productivity, since experience tells us that, if we don't explicitly disallow something, then someone, somewhere, at some point, for whatever reason, will do it anyway, and cost us a good deal of analysis work.

Minimizing ongoing code changes

Making code changes to the application in order to hunt down performance issues is not recommended, as the changes are easy to forget as time wears on. Adding debug logging statements to our code can be tempting, but remember that it costs us time to introduce these calls, recompile our code, *and* remove these calls once our analysis is complete. In addition, if we forget to remove them, then they can cost unnecessary runtime overhead in the final build since Unity's Debug logging can be prohibitively expensive in both CPU and memory.

One way to combat this problem is to use a source-control tool to differentiate the contents of any modified files, and/or revert them back to their original state. This is an excellent way to ensure that unnecessary changes don't make it into the final version.

Making use of breakpoints during runtime debugging is the preferred approach, as we can trace the full call stack, variable data, and conditional code paths (for example, if-else blocks), without risking any code changes or wasting time on recompilation.

Minimizing internal distractions

The Unity Editor has its own little quirks and nuances that can leave us confused by certain issues.

Firstly, if a single frame takes a long time to process, such that our game noticeably freezes, then the Profiler may not be capable of picking up the results and recording them in the Profiler window. This can be especially annoying if we wish to catch data during application/Scene initialization. The upcoming section, *Custom CPU Profiling,* will offer some alternatives to explore to solve this problem.

One common mistake (that I have admittedly fallen victim to multiple times during the writing of this book) is: if we are trying to initiate a test with a keystroke and we have the Profiler open, we should not forget to click back into the Editor's Game window before triggering the keystroke! If the Profiler is the most recently clicked window, then the Editor will send keystroke events to that, instead of the runtime application, and hence no GameObject will catch the event for that keystroke.

Vertical Sync (otherwise known as **VSync**) is used to match the application's frame rate to the frame rate of the device it is being displayed on (for example, the monitor). Executing the Profiler with this feature enabled will generate a lot of spikes in the CPU usage area under the heading **WaitForTargetFPS**, as the application intentionally slows itself down to match the frame rate of the display. This will generate unnecessary clutter, making it harder to spot the real issue(s). We should make sure to disable the VSync colored box under the CPU Area when we're on the lookout for CPU spikes during performance tests. We can disable the VSync feature entirely by navigating to **Edit | Project Settings | Quality** and then the subpage for the currently selected build platform.

We should also ensure that a drop in performance isn't a direct result of a massive number of exceptions and error messages appearing in the Editor console. Unity's `Debug.Log()`, and similar methods such as `Debug.LogError()`, `Debug.LogWarning()`, and so on, are notoriously expensive in terms of CPU usage and heap memory consumption, which can then cause garbage collection to occur and even more lost CPU cycles.

This overhead is usually unnoticeable to a human being looking at the project in Editor Mode, where most errors come from the compiler or misconfigured objects. But they can be problematic when used during any kind of runtime process; especially during profiling, where we wish to observe how the game runs in the absence of external disruptions. For example, if we are missing an object reference that we were supposed to assign through the Editor and it is being used in an `Update()` method, then a single MonoBehaviour could be throwing new exceptions every single update. This adds lots of unnecessary noise to our profiling data.

Note that we can disable the **Info** or **Warning** checkboxes (shown in the following screenshot) for the project during Play Mode runtime, but it still costs CPU and memory to execute debug statements, even though they are not being rendered. It is often a good practice to keep all of these options enabled, to verify that we're not missing anything important.

Minimizing external distractions

This one is simple but absolutely necessary. We should double-check that there are no background processes eating away CPU cycles or consuming vast swathes of memory. Being low on available memory will generally interfere with our testing, as it can cause more cache misses, hard-drive access for virtual memory page-file swapping, and generally slow responsiveness of the application.

Targeted profiling of code segments

If our performance problem isn't solved by the above checklist, then we probably have a real issue on our hands that demands further analysis. The task of figuring out exactly where the problem is located still remains. The Profiler window is effective at showing us a broad overview of performance; it can help us find specific frames to investigate and can quickly inform us which MonoBehaviour and/or method may be causing issues. However, we must still determine exactly where the problem exists. We need to figure out if the problem is reproducible, under what circumstances a performance bottleneck arises, and where exactly within the problematic code block the issue is originating from.

To accomplish these, we will need to perform some profiling of targeted sections of our code, and there are a handful of useful techniques we can employ for this task. For Unity projects, they essentially fit into two categories:

- Controlling the Profiler from script code
- Custom timing and logging methods

 Note that the following section mostly focusses on how to investigate Scripting bottlenecks through C# code. Detecting the source of bottlenecks in other engine components will be discussed in their related chapters.

Profiler script control

The Profiler can be controlled in script code through the static Profiler class. There are several useful methods in the Profiler class that we can explore within the Unity documentation, but the most important methods are the delimiter methods that activate and deactivate profiling at runtime: `Profiler.BeginSample()` and `Profiler.EndSample()`.

> Note that the delimiter methods, `BeginSample()` and `EndSample()`, are only compiled in development builds, and as such they cause no overhead in the final build. Therefore, it is safe to leave them in our codebase if we wish to use them for profiling tests at a later date.

The `BeginSample()` method has an overload that allows a custom name for the sample to appear in the CPU Usage Area's Hierarchy Mode view. For example, the following code will profile invocations of this method and make the data appear in the Breakdown View under a custom heading:

```
void DoSomethingCompletelyStupid() {
  Profiler.BeginSample("My Profiler Sample");

  List<int> listOfInts = new List<int>();
  for(int i = 0; i < 1000000; ++i) {
    listOfInts.Add(i);
  }

  Profiler.EndSample();
}
```

> **Downloading the example code**
>
> You can download the example code files from your account at http://www.packtpub.com for all the Packt Publishing books you have purchased. If you purchased this book elsewhere, you can visit http://www.packtpub.com/support and register to have the files e-mailed directly to you.

We should expect that invoking this poorly designed method (it generates a list containing a million integers, and then does absolutely nothing with it) will cause a huge spike in CPU usage, chew up several Megabytes of memory, and appear in the Profiler Breakdown View under the heading *My Profiler Sample* as the following screenshot shows:

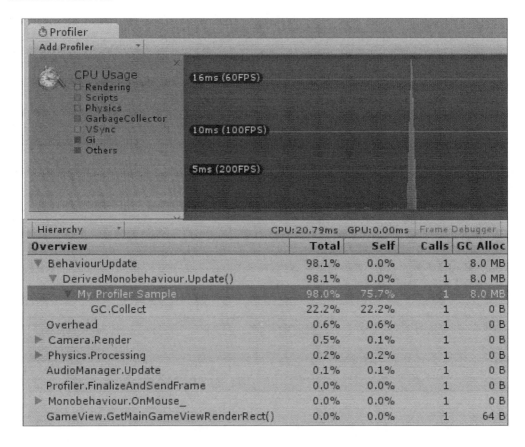

Note that these custom sample names do not appear at the root of the hierarchy when we perform **Deep Profiling**. The following screenshot shows the Breakdown View for the same code under Deep Profiling:

Hierarchy ▼	CPU:115.27ms	GPU:0.00ms	Frame Debugger					
Overview		Total	Self	Calls	GC Alloc	Time ms	Self ms	⚠
▼ BehaviourUpdate		99.5%	0.0%	1	8.0 MB	114.80	0.00	
▼ DerivedMonobehaviour.Update()		99.5%	0.0%	1	8.0 MB	114.79	0.00	
▼ Profiler.BeginSample()		99.5%	0.0%	1	8.0 MB	114.78	0.10	
▼ DerivedMonobehaviour.DoSomething		99.4%	91.3%	1	8.0 MB	114.68	105.36	
▼ List`1.Add()		8.0%	0.1%	1000000	8.0 MB	9.32	0.22	
▼ List`1.GrowIfNeeded()		7.8%	0.0%	19	8.0 MB	9.10	0.00	
▼ List`1.set_Capacity()		7.8%	0.0%	19	8.0 MB	9.09	0.00	
▼ Array.Resize()		7.8%	0.0%	19	8.0 MB	9.09	0.01	
▼ Array.Resize()		7.8%	3.3%	19	8.0 MB	9.08	3.82	
GC.Collect		4.1%	4.1%	1	0 B	4.74	4.74	
▼ Array.Copy()		0.4%	0.0%	19	0 B	0.50	0.00	
▼ Array.Copy()		0.4%	0.0%	19	0 B	0.50	0.00	
Array.FastCopy		0.4%	0.4%	19	0 B	0.49	0.49	
Array.GetLowerBc		0.0%	0.0%	38	0 B	0.00	0.00	
List`1.get_Capacity()		0.0%	0.0%	19	0 B	0.00	0.00	
List`1..ctor()		0.0%	0.0%	1	0 B	0.00	0.00	
▼ Profiler.BeginSampleOnly()		0.0%	0.0%	1	0 B	0.00	0.00	
My Profiler Sample		0.0%	0.0%	1	0 B	0.00	0.00	

Note how the custom name for the sample does not appear at the top of the sample, where we may expect it to. It's unclear what causes this phenomenon, but this can cause some confusion when examining the Deep Profiling data within **Hierarchy** Mode, so it is good to be aware of it.

Custom CPU Profiling

The Profiler is just one tool at our disposal. Sometimes, we may want to perform customized profiling and logging of our code. Maybe we're not confident the Unity Profiler is giving us the right answer, maybe we consider its overhead cost too great, or maybe we just like having complete control of every single aspect of our application. Whatever our motivations, knowing some techniques to perform an independent analysis of our code is a useful skill to have. It's unlikely we'll only be working with Unity for the entirety of our game development careers, after all.

Profiling tools are very complex, so it's unlikely we would be able to generate a comparable solution on our own within a reasonable time frame. When it comes to testing CPU usage, all we need is an accurate timing system, a fast, low-cost way of logging that information, and some piece of code to test against. It just so happens that the .NET library (or, technically, the Mono framework) comes with a `Stopwatch` class under the `System.Diagnostics` namespace. We can stop and start a `Stopwatch` object at any time, and we can easily acquire a measure of how much time has passed since the Stopwatch was started.

Unfortunately, this class is not very accurate—it is accurate only to milliseconds, or tenths of a millisecond at best. Counting high-precision real time with a CPU clock can be a surprisingly difficult task when we start to get into it; so, in order to avoid a detailed discussion of the topic, we should try to find a way for the `Stopwatch` class to satisfy our needs.

Before we get obsessed with the topic of high precision, we should first ask ourselves if we even need it. Most games expect to run at 30 FPS (frames-per-second) or 60 FPS, which means they only have around 33 ms or 16 ms, respectively, to compute everything for the entire frame. So, hypothetically, if we only need to bring the performance of a particular code block under 10ms, then repeating the test thousands of times to get microsecond precision wouldn't really tell us anything useful.

However, if precision is important, then one effective way to increase it is by running the same test multiple times. Assuming that the test code block is both easily repeatable and not exceptionally long, then we should be able to run thousands, or even millions, of tests within a reasonable timeframe and then divide the total elapsed time by the number of tests we just performed to get a more accurate time for a single test.

The following is a class definition for a custom timer that uses a `Stopwatch` to count time for a given number of tests:

```
using UnityEngine;
using System;
using System.Diagnostics;
using System.Collections;

public class CustomTimer : IDisposable {
  private string m_timerName;
  private int m_numTests;
  private Stopwatch m_watch;

  // give the timer a name, and a count of the number of tests we're
running
  public CustomTimer(string timerName, int numTests) {
    m_timerName = timerName;
    m_numTests = numTests;
    if (m_numTests <= 0)
      m_numTests = 1;
    m_watch = Stopwatch.StartNew();
  }

  // called when the 'using' block ends
  public void Dispose() {
```

```
    m_watch.Stop();
    float ms = m_watch.ElapsedMilliseconds;
    UnityEngine.Debug.Log(string.Format("{0} finished: {1:0.00}ms
total, {2:0.000000}ms per test for {3} tests", m_timerName, ms, ms
/ m_numTests, m_numTests));
  }
}
```

The following is an example of the `CustomTimer` class usage:

```
int numTests = 1000;

using (new CustomTimer("My Test", numTests)) {
  for(int i = 0; i < numTests; ++i) {
    TestFunction();
  }
} // the timer's Dispose() method is automatically called here
```

There are three things to note when using this approach. Firstly, we are only making an average of multiple method invocations. If processing time varies enormously between invocations, then that will not be well-represented in the final average. Secondly, if memory access is common, then repeatedly requesting the same blocks of memory will result in an artificially higher cache hit rate, which will bring the average time down when compared to a typical invocation. Thirdly, the effects of JIT compilation will be effectively hidden for similarly artificial reasons as it only affects the first invocation of the method. JIT compilation is something that will be covered in more detail in *Chapter 7, Masterful Memory Management.*

The `using` block is typically used to safely ensure that unmanaged resources are properly destroyed when they go out of scope. When the `using` block ends, it will automatically invoke the object's `Dispose()` method to handle any cleanup operations. In order to achieve this, the object must implement the `IDisposable` interface, which forces it to define the `Dispose()` method.

However, the same language feature can be used to create a distinct code block, which creates a short-term object, which then automatically processes something useful when the code block ends.

> Note that the `using` block should not be confused with the `using` statement, which is used at the start of a script file to pull in additional namespaces. It's extremely ironic that the keyword for managing namespaces in C# has a naming conflict with another keyword.

As a result, the `using` block and the `CustomTimer` class give us a clean way of wrapping our target test code in a way which makes it obvious when and where it is being used.

Another concern to worry about is application warm up. Unity has a significant startup cost when a Scene begins, given the number of calls to various GameObjects' `Awake()` and `Start()` methods, as well as initialization of other components such as the Physics and Rendering systems. This early overhead might only last a second, but that can have a significant effect on the results of our testing. This makes it crucial that any runtime testing begins after the application has reached a steady state.

If possible, it would be wise to wrap the target code block in an `Input.GetKeyDown()` method check in order to have control over when it is invoked. For example, the following code will only execute our test method when the *Space Bar* is pressed:

```
if (Input.GetKeyDown(KeyCode.Space)) {
  int numTests = 1000;

  using (new CustomTimer("Controlled Test", numTests)) {
    for(int i = 0; i < numTests; ++i) {
      TestFunction();
    }
  }
}
```

There are three important design features of the `CustomTimer` class: it only prints a single log message for the entire test, only reads the value from the `Stopwatch` after it has been stopped, and uses `string.Format()` for generating a custom string.

As explained earlier, Unity's console logging mechanism is prohibitively expensive. As a result, we should never use these logging methods in the middle of a profiling test (or even gameplay, for that matter). If we find ourselves absolutely needing detailed profiling data that prints out lots of individual messages (such as performing a timing test on each iteration of a loop, to find which iteration is costing more time than the rest), then it would be wiser to cache the logging data and print it all at the end, as the `CustomTimer` class does. This will reduce runtime overhead, at the cost of some memory consumption. The alternative is that many milliseconds are lost to printing each `Debug.Log()` message in the middle of the test, which pollutes the results.

The second feature is that the `Stopwatch` is stopped before the value is read. This is fairly obvious; reading the value while it is still counting might give us a slightly different value than stopping it first. Unless we dive deep into the Mono project source code (and the specific version Unity uses), we might not know the exact implementation of how `Stopwatch` counts time, at what points CPU ticks are counted, and at what moments any application context switching is triggered by the OS. So, it is often better to err on the side of caution and prevent any more counting before we attempt to access the value.

Finally, there's the usage of `string.Format()`. This will be covered in more detail in *Chapter 7, Masterful Memory Management*, but the short explanation is that this method is used because generating custom strings using the `+operator` results in a surprisingly large amount of memory consumption, which attracts the attention of the garbage collector. This would conflict with our goal of achieving accurate timing and analysis.

Saving and loading Profiler data

The Unity Profiler currently has a few fairly significant pitfalls when it comes to saving and loading Profiler data:

- Only 300 frames are visible in the Profiler window at once
- There is no way to save Profiler data through the user interface
- Profiler binary data can be saved into a file the Script code, but there is no built-in way to view this data

These issues make it very tricky to perform large-scale or long-term testing with the Unity Profiler. They have been raised in Unity's Issue Tracker tool for several years, and there doesn't appear to be any salvation in sight. So, we must rely on our own ingenuity to solve this problem.

Fortunately, the Profiler class exposes a few methods that we can use to control how the Profiler logs information:

1. The `Profiler.enabled` method can be used to enable/disable the Profiler, which is the equivalent of clicking on the **Record** button in the **Control** View of the Profiler.

 Note that changing `Profiler.enabled` does not change the visible state of the Record button in the Profiler's Controls bar. This will cause some confusing conflicts if we're controlling the Profiler through both code and the user interface at the same time.

2. The `Profiler.logFile` method sets the current path of the log file that the Profiler prints data out to. Be aware that this file only contains a printout of the application's frame rate over time, and none of the useful data we normally find in the Profiler's Timeline View. To save that kind of data as a binary file, we must use the options that follow.

3. The `Profiler.enableBinaryLog` method will enable/disable logging of an additional file filled with binary data, which includes all of the important values we want to save from the Timeline and Breakdown Views. The file location and name will be the same as the value of `Profiler.logFile`, but with `.data` appended to the end.

With these methods, we can generate a simple data-saving tool that will generate large amounts of Profiler data separated into multiple files. With these files, we will be able to peruse them at a later date.

Saving Profiler data

In order to create a tool that can save our Profiler data, we can make use of a **Coroutine**. A typical method will be executed from beginning to end in one sitting. However, Coroutines are useful constructs that allow us write methods that can pause execution until a later time, or an event takes place. This is known as yielding, and is accomplished with the `yield` statement. The type of yield determines when execution will resume, which could be one of the following types (the object that must be passed into the `yield` statement is also given):

- After a specific amount of time (`WaitForSeconds`)
- After the next Update (`WaitForEndOfFrame`)
- After the next Fixed Update (`WaitForFixedUpdate`)
- Just prior to the next Late Update (`null`)
- After a `WWW` object completes its current task, such as downloading a file (`WWW`)
- After another Coroutine has finished (a reference to another Coroutine)

The Unity Documentation on Coroutines and Execution Order provides more information on how these useful tools function within the Unity Engine:

- http://docs.unity3d.com/Manual/Coroutines.html
- http://docs.unity3d.com/Manual/ExecutionOrder.html

Coroutines should not be confused with threads, which execute independently of the main Unity thread. Coroutines always run on the main thread with the rest of our code, and simply pause and resume at certain moments, depending on the object passed into the `yield` statement.

Getting back to the task at hand, the following is the class definition for our `ProfilerDataSaverComponent`, which makes use of a Coroutine to repeat an action every 300 frames:

```
using UnityEngine;
using System.Text;
using System.Collections;

public class ProfilerDataSaverComponent : MonoBehaviour {

  int _count = 0;

  void Start() {
    Profiler.logFile = "";
  }

  void Update () {
    if (Input.GetKey (KeyCode.LeftControl) && Input.GetKeyDown
(KeyCode.H)) {
      StopAllCoroutines();
      _count = 0;
      StartCoroutine(SaveProfilerData());
    }
  }

  IEnumerator SaveProfilerData() {
    // keep calling this method until Play Mode stops
    while (true) {

      // generate the file path
      string filepath = Application.persistentDataPath +
"/profilerLog" + _count;

      // set the log file and enable the profiler
      Profiler.logFile = filepath;
      Profiler.enableBinaryLog = true;
      Profiler.enabled = true;
```

```
        // count 300 frames
        for(int i = 0; i < 300; ++i) {

          yield return new WaitForEndOfFrame();

          // workaround to keep the Profiler working
          if (!Profiler.enabled)
            Profiler.enabled = true;
        }

        // start again using the next file name
        _count++;
      }
    }
  }
```

Try attaching this Component to any GameObject in the Scene, and press *Ctrl + H* (OSX users will want to replace the `KeyCode.LeftControl` code with something such as `KeyCode.LeftCommand`). The Profiler will start gathering information (whether or not the Profiler Window is open!) and, using a simple Coroutine, will pump the data out into a series of files under wherever `Application.persistantDataPath` is pointing to.

> Note that the location of `Application.persistantDataPath` varies depending on the Operating System. Check the Unity Documentation for more details at `http://docs.unity3d.com/ScriptReference/Application-persistentDataPath.html`.

It would be unwise to send the files to `Application.dataPath`, as it would put them within the Project Workspace. The Profiler does not release the most recent log file handle if we stop the Profiler or even when Play Mode is stopped. Consequently, as files are generated and placed into the Project workspace, there would be a conflict in file accessibility between the Unity Editor trying to read and generate complementary metadata files, and the Profiler keeping a file handle to the most recent log file. This would result in some nasty file access errors, which tend to crash the Unity Editor and lose any Scene changes we've made.

When this Component is recording data, there will be a small overhead in hard disk usage and the overhead cost of `IEnumerator` context switching every 300 frames, which will tend to appear at the start of every file and consume a few milliseconds of CPU (depending on hardware).

Each file pair should contain 300 frames worth of Profiler data, which skirts around the 300 frame limit in the Profiler window. All we need now is a way of presenting the data in the Profiler window.

Here is a screenshot of data files that have been generated by `ProfilerDataSaverComponent`:

Name	Date modified	Type	Size
profilerLog0	5/26/2015 12:23 PM	File	14 KB
profilerLog0.data	5/26/2015 12:23 PM	DATA File	2,481 KB
profilerLog1	5/26/2015 12:23 PM	File	15 KB
profilerLog1.data	5/26/2015 12:23 PM	DATA File	2,142 KB
profilerLog2	5/26/2015 12:23 PM	File	15 KB
profilerLog2.data	5/26/2015 12:23 PM	DATA File	2,144 KB
profilerLog3	5/26/2015 12:23 PM	File	15 KB
profilerLog3.data	5/26/2015 12:23 PM	DATA File	2,135 KB
profilerLog4	5/26/2015 12:23 PM	File	15 KB
profilerLog4.data	5/26/2015 12:23 PM	DATA File	2,141 KB
profilerLog5	5/26/2015 12:23 PM	File	6 KB
profilerLog5.data	5/26/2015 12:23 PM	DATA File	854 KB

Path: « Users ▸ Chris ▸ AppData ▸ LocalLow ▸ DefaultCompany ▸ Unity Performance Optimization by Chris Dickinson

Note that the first file may contain less than 300 frames if some frames were *lost* during Profiler warm up.

Loading Profiler data

The `Profiler.AddFramesFromFile()` method will load a given profiler log file pair (the text and binary files) and append it into the Profiler timeline, pushing existing data further back in time. Since each file will contain 300 frames, this is perfect for our needs, and we just need to create a simple `EditorWindow` class that can provide a list of buttons to load the files into the Profiler.

Note that `AddFramesFromFile()` only requires the name of the original log file. It will automatically find the complimentary binary *.data* file on its own.

The following is the class definition for our `ProfilerDataLoaderWindow`:

```
using UnityEngine;
using UnityEditor;
using System.IO;
using System.Collections;
using System.Collections.Generic;
using System.Text.RegularExpressions;

public class ProfilerDataLoaderWindow : EditorWindow {

  static List<string> s_cachedFilePaths;
  static int s_chosenIndex = -1;

  [MenuItem ("Window/ProfilerDataLoader")]
  static void Init() {
    ProfilerDataLoaderWindow window =
(ProfilerDataLoaderWindow)EditorWindow.GetWindow
(typeof(ProfilerDataLoaderWindow));
    window.Show ();

    ReadProfilerDataFiles ();
  }

  static void ReadProfilerDataFiles() {
    // make sure the profiler releases the file handle
    // to any of the files we're about to load in
    Profiler.logFile = "";

    string[] filePaths = Directory.GetFiles (Application.
persistentDataPath, "profilerLog*");

    s_cachedFilePaths = new List<string> ();

    // we want to ignore all of the binary
    // files that end in .data. The Profiler
    // will figure that part out
    Regex test = new Regex (".data$");

    for (int i = 0; i < filePaths.Length; i++) {
      string thisPath = filePaths [i];

      Match match = test.Match (thisPath);

      if (!match.Success) {
```

```
        // not a binary file, add it to the list
        Debug.Log ("Found file: " + thisPath);
        s_cachedFilePaths.Add (thisPath);
     }
  }

  s_chosenIndex = -1;
}

void OnGUI () {
  if (GUILayout.Button ("Find Files")) {
    ReadProfilerDataFiles();
  }

  if (s_cachedFilePaths == null)
    return;

  EditorGUILayout.Space ();

  EditorGUILayout.LabelField ("Files");

  EditorGUILayout.BeginHorizontal ();

  // create some styles to organize the buttons, and show
  // the most recently-selected button with red text
  GUIStyle defaultStyle = new GUIStyle(GUI.skin.button);
  defaultStyle.fixedWidth = 40f;

  GUIStyle highlightedStyle = new GUIStyle (defaultStyle);
  highlightedStyle.normal.textColor = Color.red;

  for (int i = 0; i < s_cachedFilePaths.Count; ++i) {

    // list 5 items per row
    if (i % 5 == 0) {
      EditorGUILayout.EndHorizontal ();
      EditorGUILayout.BeginHorizontal ();
    }

    GUIStyle thisStyle = null;

    if (s_chosenIndex == i) {
      thisStyle = highlightedStyle;
    } else {
```

```
            thisStyle = defaultStyle;
        }

        if (GUILayout.Button("" + i, thisStyle)) {
            Profiler.AddFramesFromFile(s_cachedFilePaths[i]);

            s_chosenIndex = i;
        }
    }

    EditorGUILayout.EndHorizontal ();
    }
}
```

The first step in creating any custom `EditorWindow` is creating a menu entry point with a `[MenuItem]` attribute and then creating an instance of a `Window` object to control. Both of these occur within the `Init()` method.

We're also calling the `ReadProfilerDataFiles()` method during initialization. This method reads all files found within the `Application.persistantDataPath` folder (the same location our `ProfilerDataSaverComponent` saves data files to) and adds them to a cache of filenames to use later.

Finally, there is the `OnGUI()` method. This method does the bulk of the work. It provides a button to reload the files if needed, verifies that the cached filenames have been read, and provides a series of buttons to load each file into the Profiler. It also highlights the most recently clicked button with red text using a custom `GUIStyle`, making it easy to see which file's contents are visible in the Profiler at the current moment.

The `ProfilerDataLoaderWindow` can be accessed by navigating to **Window | ProfilerDataLoader** in the Editor interface, as show in the following screenshot:

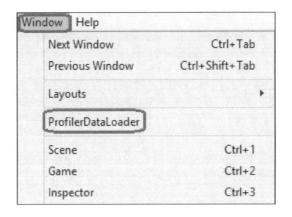

Here is a screenshot of the display with multiple files available to be loaded. Clicking on any of the numbered buttons will push the Profiler data contents of that file into the Profiler.

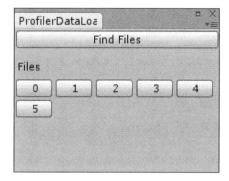

The `ProfilerDataSaverComponent` and `ProfilerDataLoaderWindow` do not pretend to be exhaustive or feature-rich. They simply serve as a springboard to get us started if we wish to take the subject further. For most teams and projects, 300 frames worth of short-term data is enough for developers to acquire what they need to begin making code changes to fix the problem.

Final thoughts on Profiling and Analysis

One way of describing performance optimization is "the act of stripping away unnecessary tasks that spend valuable resources". We can do the same and maximize our own productivity through minimizing wasted effort. Effective use of the tools we have at our disposal is of paramount importance. It would serve us well to optimize our own workflow by keeping aware of some best practices and techniques.

Most, if not all, advice for using any kind of data-gathering tool properly can be summarized into three different strategies:

- Understanding the tool
- Reducing noise
- Focusing on the issue

Understanding the Profiler

The Profiler is an arguably well-designed and intuitive tool, so understanding the majority of its feature set can be gained by simply spending an hour or two exploring its options with a test project and reading its documentation. The more we know about our tool in terms of its benefits, pitfalls, features, and limitations, the more sense we can make of the information it is giving us, so it is worth spending the time to use it in a playground setting. We don't want to be two weeks away from release, with a hundred performance defects to fix, with no idea how to do performance analysis efficiently!

For example, always remain aware of the *relative* nature of the Timeline View's graphical display. Just because a spike or resting state in the Timeline seems large and threatening, does not necessarily mean there is a performance issue. Because the Timeline View does not provide values on its vertical axis, and automatically readjusts this axis based on the content of the last 300 frames, it can make small spikes appear to be a bigger problem than they really are. Several areas in the Timeline provide helpful benchmark bars, giving a glimpse of how the application was performing at that moment. These should be used to determine the magnitude of the problem. Don't let the Profiler trick us into thinking that big spikes are always bad. As always, it's only important if the user will notice it!

As an example, if a large CPU usage spike does not exceed the 60 FPS or 30 FPS benchmark bars (depending on the application's target frame rate), then it would be wise to ignore it and search elsewhere for CPU performance issues, as no matter how much we improve the offending piece of code it will probably never be noticed by the end user, and isn't a critical issue that affects product quality.

Reducing noise

The classical definition of noise in computer science is *meaningless data*, and a batch of profiling data that was blindly captured with no specific target in mind is always full of data which won't interest us. More data takes more time to mentally process and filter, which can be very distracting. One of the best methods to avoid this it to simply reduce the amount of data we need to process, by stripping away any data deemed nonvital to the current situation.

Reducing clutter in the Profiler's graphical interface will make it easier to determine which component is causing a spike in resource usage. Remember to use the colored boxes in each Timeline area to narrow the search. However, these settings are autosaved in the Editor, so be sure to re-enable them for the next profiling session as this might cause us to miss something important next time!

Also, GameObjects can be deactivated to prevent them from generating profiling data, which will also help reduce clutter in our profiling data. This will naturally cause a slight performance boost for each object we deactivate. But, if we're gradually deactivating objects and performance suddenly becomes significantly more acceptable when a specific object is deactivated, then clearly that object is related to the root cause of the problem.

Focusing on the issue

This category may seem redundant, given that we've already covered reducing noise. All we should have left is the issue at hand, right? Not exactly. Focus is the skill of not letting ourselves become distracted by inconsequential tasks and wild goose chases.

Recall that profiling with the Unity Profiler comes with a minor performance cost. This cost is even more severe when using the **Deep Profiling** option. We might even introduce more minor performance costs into our application with additional logging and so on. It's easy to forget when and where we introduced profiling code if the hunt continues for several hours.

We are effectively changing the result by measuring it. Any changes we implement during data sampling can sometimes lead us to chase after nonexistent bugs in the application, when we could have saved ourselves a lot of time by attempting to replicate the scenario under non-profiling conditions. If the bottleneck is reproducible and noticeable without profiling, then it's a candidate to begin an investigation. But if new bottlenecks keep appearing in the middle of an existing investigation, then keep in mind that they could simply be bottlenecks we recently introduced with test code, and not something that's been newly exposed.

Finally, when we have finished profiling, have completed our fixes, and are now ready to move on to the next investigation, we should make sure to profile the application one last time to verify that the changes have had the intended effect.

Summary

You learned a great deal throughout this chapter on how to detect performance issues within your application. You learned about many of the Profiler's features and secrets, you explored a variety of tactics to investigate performance issues with a more hands-on-approach, and you've been introduced to a variety of different tips and strategies to follow. You can use these to improve your productivity immensely, so long as you appreciate the wisdom behind them and remember to exploit them when the situation makes it possible.

This chapter has introduced us to the tips, tactics, and strategies we need find a performance problem that needs improvement. During the remaining chapters, we will explore methods on how to fix issues, and improve performance whenever possible. So, give yourself a pat on the back for getting through the boring part first, and let's move on to learning some strategies to improve our C# scripting practices.

2
Scripting Strategies

Since scripting will consume a great deal of our development time, it will be enormously beneficial to learn some best practices. Scripting is a very broad term, so we will try to limit our exposure in this chapter to situations that are very Unity specific, focusing on problems arising from within the Unity APIs and engine design. We will discuss the nuances and advanced topics of the C# language, .NET library, and Mono Framework, in *Chapter 7, Masterful Memory Management*.

Whether you have some specific problems in mind that you wish to solve or you just want to learn some techniques for future reference, this chapter will introduce you to an array of methods that you can use to improve your scripting efforts now and in the future. In each case, we will explore how and why the performance issue arises, an example situation in which the problem is occurring, and one or more solutions to combat the issue.

Cache Component references

A common mistake when scripting in Unity is to overuse the `GetComponent()` method. For example, the following script code is trying to check a creature's `health` value, and if its health goes below `0`, disable a series of Components to prepare it for a death animation:

```
void TakeDamage() {
  if (GetComponent<HealthComponent>().health < 0) {
    GetComponent<Rigidbody>().enabled = false;
    GetComponent<Collider>().enabled = false;
    GetComponent<AIControllerComponent>().enabled = false;
    GetComponent<Animator>().SetTrigger("death");
  }
}
```

Each time this method executes, it will reacquire five different `Component` references. This is good in terms of heap memory consumption (in that it doesn't cost any), but it is not very friendly on CPU usage. This is particularly problematic if the main method were called during `Update()`. Even if it is not, it still might coincide with other important events, such as creating particle effects, replacing an object with a ragdoll (thus invoking various activity in the physics engine), and so on. This coding style can seem harmless, but it can cause a lot of long-term problems and runtime work for very little benefit.

It costs us very little memory space (only 32 or 64 bits each time; Unity version, platform, and fragmentation permitting) to cache these references for future use. So, unless you're extremely bottlenecked on memory, a better approach would be to acquire the references during initialization and keep them until they are needed:

```
private HealthComponent _healthComponent;
private Rigidbody _rigidbody;
private Collider _collider;
private AIControllerComponent _aiController;
private Animator _animator;

void Awake() {
  _healthComponent = GetComponent<HealthComponent>();
  _rigidbody = GetComponent<Rigidbody>();
  _collider = GetComponent<Collider>();
  _aiController = GetComponent<AIControllerComponent>();
  _animator = GetComponent<Animator>();
}

void TakeDamage() {
  if (_healthComponent.health < 0) {
    _rigidbody.detectCollisions = false;
    _collider.enabled = false;
    _aiController.enabled = false;
    _animator.SetTrigger("death");
  }
}
```

Caching the Component references in this way spares us from reacquiring them each time they're needed, saving us some CPU overhead each time, at the expense of some additional memory consumption.

Obtaining Components using the fastest method

There are several variations of the `GetComponent()` method, and it becomes prudent to call the fastest possible version of this method. The three overloads available are `GetComponent(string)`, `GetComponent<T>()`, and `GetComponent(typeof(T))`. It turns out that the fastest version depends on which version of Unity we are running.

In Unity 4, the `GetComponent(typeof(T))` method is the fastest of the available options by a reasonable margin. Let's prove this with some simple testing:

```
int numTests = 1000000;
TestComponent test;

using (new CustomTimer("GetComponent(string)", numTests)) {
  for (var i = 0; i < numTests; ++i) {
    test = (TestComponent)GetComponent("TestComponent");
  }
}

using (new CustomTimer("GetComponent<ComponentName>", numTests)) {
  for (var i = 0; i < numTests; ++i) {
    test = GetComponent<TestComponent>();
  }
}

using (new CustomTimer("GetComponent(typeof(ComponentName))",
numTests))  {
  for (var i = 0; i < numTests; ++i) {
    test = (TestComponent)GetComponent(typeof(TestComponent));
  }
}
```

This code tests each of the `GetComponent()` overloads a million times. This is far more tests than would be sensible for a typical project, but it is enough tests to prove the point.

Here is the result we get when the tests complete:

```
GetComponent(string) finished: 841.00ms total, 0.000841ms per test for 1000000 tests
UnityEngine.Debug:Log(Object)
GetComponent<ComponentName> finished: 169.00ms total, 0.000169ms per test for 1000000 tests
UnityEngine.Debug:Log(Object)
GetComponent(typeof(ComponentName)) finished: 122.00ms total, 0.000122ms per test for 1000000 tests
UnityEngine.Debug:Log(Object)
```

As you can see, `GetComponent(typeof(T))` is significantly faster than `GetComponent<T>()`, which is around five times faster than `GetComponent(string)`. This test was performed against Unity 4.5.5, but the behavior should be equivalent all the way back to Unity 3.x.

 `GetComponent(string)` should not be used, since it is notoriously slow and is only included for completeness.

These results change when we run the exact same test in Unity 5. Unity Technologies made some performance enhancements to how `System.Type` references are passed around in Unity 5.0, and, as a result, `GetComponent<T>()` and `GetComponent(typeof(T))` become essentially equivalent:

```
GetComponent(string) finished: 2961.00ms total, 0.002961ms per test for 1000000 tests
UnityEngine.Debug:Log(Object)
GetComponent<ComponentName> finished: 113.00ms total, 0.000113ms per test for 1000000 tests
UnityEngine.Debug:Log(Object)
GetComponent(typeof(ComponentName)) finished: 114.00ms total, 0.000114ms per test for 1000000 tests
UnityEngine.Debug:Log(Object)
```

As you can see, the `GetComponent<T>()` method is only a tiny fraction faster than `GetComponent(typeof(T))`, while `GetComponent(string)` is now around 30 times slower than the alternatives (interestingly, it became even slower than it was in Unity 4). Multiple tests will probably yield small variations in these results, but ultimately we can favor either of the type-based versions of `GetComponent()` when we're working in Unity 5, and the outcome will be about the same.

There is one caveat, however. If we're running Unity 4, then we still have access to a variety of quick accessor properties such as `collider`, `rigidbody`, `camera`, and so on. These properties behave like precached Component member variables, which are significantly faster than all of the traditional `GetComponent()` methods:

```
int numTests = 1000000;
Rigidbody test;

using (new CustomTimer("Cached reference", numTests))
{
  for (var i = 0; i < numTests; ++i) {
    test = gameObject.rigidbody;
  }
}
```

Note that this code is intended for Unity 4, and will not compile in Unity 5 due to the removal of the rigidbody property.

Running this test in Unity 4 gives us the following result:

> ① Cached reference finished: 102.00ms total, 0.000102ms per test for 1000000 tests
> UnityEngine.Debug:Log(Object)

In an effort to reduce dependencies and improve code modularization in the engine's backend, Unity Technologies has deprecated all of these quick accessor variables in Unity 5. Only the transform property remains.

> Unity 4 users considering an upgrade to Unity 5 should know that upgrading will automatically modify any of these properties to use the GetComponent<T>() method. However, this will result in uncached GetComponent<T>() calls scattered throughout your code, possibly requiring you to revisit the techniques introduced in the earlier section, entitled *Cache Component References*.

The moral of the story is that if we are running Unity 4, and the required Component is one of GameObject's built-in accessor properties, then we should use that version. If not, then we should favor GetComponent(typeof(T)). Meanwhile, if we're running Unity 5, then we can favor either of the type-based versions: GetComponent<T>() or GetComponent(typeof(T)).

Removing empty callback declarations

When we create new MonoBehaviour script files in Unity, whether we're using Unity 4 or Unity 5, it creates two boilerplate methods for us:

```
// Use this for initialization
void Start () {

}


// Update is called once per frame
void Update () {

}
```

The Unity engine hooks in to these methods during initialization and adds them to a list of methods to call back at key moments. However, if we leave these as empty declarations in our codebase, then they will cost us a small overhead whenever the engine invokes them.

The `Start()` method is only called when the GameObject is instantiated for the first time, which can be whenever the scene is loaded or a new GameObject is instantiated from a Prefab. Therefore, leaving the empty `Start()` declaration may not be particularly noticeable unless there's a lot of GameObjects in the scene invoking them at startup time. However, it also adds unnecessary overhead to any `GameObject.Instantiate()` call, which typically happens during key events, so they can potentially contribute to, and exacerbate, already poor performances situation when lots of events are happening simultaneously.

Meanwhile, the `Update()` method is called every time the scene is rendered. If our scene contains thousands of GameObjects owning components with these empty `Update()` declarations, then we can be wasting a lot of CPU cycles and causing havoc on our frame rate.

Let's prove this with a simple test. Our test scene should have GameObjects with two types of Component, one type with an empty `Update()` declaration, and another with no methods defined:

```
public class CallbackTestComponent : MonoBehaviour {
  void Update () {}
}

public class EmptyTestComponent : MonoBehaviour {
}
```

Here are the test results for `32,768` Components of each type. If we enable all objects with no stub methods during runtime, then nothing interesting happens with CPU usage in the Profiler. We may notice some memory consumption changes and some slightly different VSync activity, but nothing very concerning. However, as soon as we enable all the objects with empty Unity callback declarations, we will observe a huge increase in CPU usage:

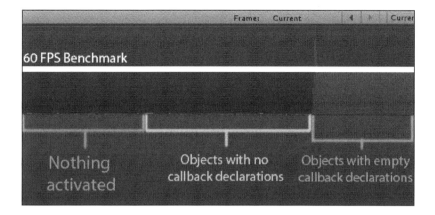

The fix for this is simple; delete the empty declarations. Unity will have nothing to hook into, and nothing will be called. Sometimes, *finding* such empty declarations in an expansive codebase can be difficult, but using some basic regular expressions (regex), we should be able to find what we're looking for relatively easily.

All common code-editing tools for Unity, such as MonoDevelop, Visual Studio, and even Notepad++, provide a way to perform a regex-based search on the entire codebase. Check the tool's documentation for more information, since the method can vary greatly depending on the tool and its version.

The following regex search should find any empty Update() declarations in our code:

```
void\s*Update\s*?\(\s*?\)\s*?\n*?\{\n*?\s*?\}
```

This regex checks for a standard method definition of the Update() method, while including any surplus whitespace and newline characters that can be distributed throughout the method declaration.

Naturally, all of the above is also true for the non-boilerplate Unity callbacks, such as OnGUI(), OnEnable(), OnDestroy(), FixedUpdate(), and so on. Check the MonoBehaviour Unity Documentation page for a complete list of these callbacks at http://docs.unity3d.com/ScriptReference/MonoBehaviour.html.

It might seem unlikely that someone generated empty versions of these callbacks in our codebase, but never say *never*. For example, if we use a common base class MonoBehaviour throughout all of our custom components, then a single empty callback declaration in that base class will permeate the entire game, which can cost us dearly. Be particularly careful of the OnGUI() method, as it can be invoked multiple times within the same frame or user interface (UI) event.

Avoiding the Find() and SendMessage() methods at runtime

The SendMessage() method and family of GameObject.Find() methods are notoriously expensive, and should be avoided at all costs. The SendMessage() method is about 2,000 times slower than a simple function call, and the cost of the Find() method scales very poorly with Scene complexity since it must iterate through every GameObject in the Scene. It is sometimes reasonable to call Find() during initialization of a Scene, such as Awake() and Start(), only for objects that already exists in the Scene. However, using either method for inter-object communication at runtime is likely to generate a very noticeable overhead.

Relying on Find() and SendMessage() type methods is typically symptomatic of poor design, inexperience in programming with C# and Unity, or just plain laziness during prototyping. Their usage has become something of an epidemic among beginner- and intermediate-level projects, such that Unity Technologies feels the need to keep reminding users to avoid using them in a real game, over and over again in their documentation and at their conferences. They only exist as a less *programmer-y* way to introduce new users to inter-object communication, and for some special cases where they can be used in a lazy, but responsible, way.

To be fair, Unity targets a wide demographic of users, from individual hobbyists, students, and those with delusions of grandeur, to small, mid-sized, and large development teams. This results in an incredibly wide range of software development ability. When you're starting out with Unity, it can be difficult to figure out on your own what you *should* be doing differently, especially given how the Unity engine does not adhere to the design paradigms of many other game engines. It has some foreign and quirky concepts surrounding scenes and prefabs, as well as no *god class* entry points, nor any obvious raw-data storage systems to work with.

Since we're talking about scripting optimization in this section, let's explore the subject in some detail, discussing some alternative methods for inter-object communication.

Let's start by examining a worst-case example, which uses both Find() and SendMessage() methods, and discover some ways to improve upon it. The following example method attempts to instantiate a given number of enemies from a prefab, and then notifies an EnemyManager object of their existence:

```
public void SpawnEnemies(int numEnemies) {
  for(int i = 0; i < numEnemies; ++i) {
    GameObject enemy =
(GameObject)GameObject.Instantiate(_enemyPrefab, Vector3.zero,
Quaternion.identity);
```

```
        GameObject enemyManagerObj = GameObject.Find("EnemyManager");
        enemyManagerObj.SendMessage("AddEnemy", enemy,
        SendMessageOptions.DontRequireReceiver);
    }
}
```

Putting method calls inside a loop, which always output to the same result, is a big red flag for poor performance, and when we're dealing with expensive methods such as `Find()`, we should always look for ways to call them as few times as possible. Ergo, one improvement we can make is to move the `Find()` call outside of the `for` loop and cache the result in a local variable to be used within the loop.

We can also optimize our usage of the `SendMessage()` method by replacing it with a `GetComponent()` call. This replaces a very costly method with a much gentler variation, achieving effectively the same result.

This gives us the following:

```
public void SpawnEnemies(int numEnemies) {

    GameObject enemyManagerObj = GameObject.Find("EnemyManager");
    EnemyManagerComponent enemyMgr =
    enemyManagerObj.GetComponent<EnemyManagerComponent>();

    for(int i = 0; i < numEnemies; ++i) {
        GameObject enemyIcon =
    (GameObject)GameObject.Instantiate(_enemyPrefab, Vector3.zero,
    Quaternion.identity);
        enemyMgr.AddEnemy(enemy);
    }
}
```

If this method is called during the initialization of the Scene, and we're not overly concerned with loading time, then we can probably consider ourselves finished with our optimization work.

However, we often need new objects that are instantiated at runtime to find an existing object to communicate with. In this example, we want new enemy objects to register with our `EnemyManagerComponent` so that it can do whatever it needs to do to control the enemy objects in our Scene. We would like a reliable and fast way for new objects to find existing objects without unnecessary usage of the `Find()` method, due to the overhead involved.

There are multiple approaches we can take to solving this problem, each with their own benefits and pitfalls:

- Static classes
- Singleton Components
- Assign references to pre-existing objects
- A global messaging system

Static classes

This approach involves creating a class that is globally accessible to the entire codebase at any time. The object stays alive from the moment the application starts, to the moment it is closed. Global `manager` classes are often frowned upon, since the name doesn't say much about what it's meant to do, and they can be difficult to debug since changes can occur from anywhere, at any point during runtime. In addition, it is probably the least robust approach when it comes to changing or replacing it at a future date. Despite all of these drawbacks, it is by far the easiest solution to implement, and so we will cover it first.

The Singleton design pattern is a common way of ensuring that we have a globally-accessible object, and that only one instance ever exists in memory. However, the way that Singletons are *primarily* used (note the qualifier) in Unity projects, can be easily replaced with a simple C# Static class without the need to implement `private` constructors, and the unnecessary property access of an `Instance` variable. Essentially, implementing a typical Singleton design pattern in C# just takes more code, and time, to achieve the same result as a `static` class.

A `static` class that functions in much the same way as our `EnemyManagerComponent` is used in the previous example can be defined as follows:

```csharp
using System.Collections.Generic;

public static class EnemyManager {
  static List<GameObject> _enemies;

  public static void AddEnemy(GameObject enemy) {
    _enemies.Add (enemy);
  }

  public static void RollCall() {
    for(int i = 0; i < _enemies.Count; ++i) {
```

```
      Debug.Log (string.Format("Enemy \"{0}\" reporting in...", _
    enemies[i].name));
      }
    }
  }
```

Note that every member and method has the `static` keyword attached, which implies that only one instance of this object will ever reside in memory. Static classes, by definition, do not allow any nonstatic instance members to be defined, as that would imply that we could somehow duplicate the object.

Static classes can be given a `static` constructor, which can be used to initialize member data. A `static` constructor can be defined like so, and it is called the moment the class is first accessed (either through a member variable or a member function):

```
static EnemyManager() {
  _enemies = new List<GameObject>();
}
```

This type of global class is generally considered to be a cleaner and easier-to-use version of the typical Singleton design pattern in the world of C# development.

Singleton Components

The disadvantage of the `static` class approach is that they must inherit from the lowest form of class—Object. This means that static classes cannot inherit from `MonoBehaviour` and therefore we cannot make use of any of its Unity-related functionality, including the all-important event callbacks, as well as Coroutines. Also, since there's no object to select, we lose the ability to inspect the object's data at runtime through the Inspector. These are features that we may wish to make use of in our global Singleton classes.

A common solution to this problem is to implement a *"Singleton as a Component"* class that spawns a GameObject containing itself, and providing static methods to grant global access. Note that, in this case, we must essentially implement the typical Singleton design pattern, with private static instance variables, and a global `Instance` method for global access.

Here is the definition for a `SingletonAsComponent` class:

```
public class SingletonAsComponent<T> : MonoBehaviour where T :
SingletonAsComponent<T> {

  private static T __Instance;

  protected static SingletonAsComponent<T> _Instance {
```

```
get {
  if(!__Instance) {
        T [] managers =
        GameObject.FindObjectsOfType(typeof(T)) as T[];
        if (managers != null) {
            if(managers.Length == 1) {
                __Instance = managers[0];
                return __Instance;
            } else if (managers.Length > 1) {
                Debug.LogError("You have more than one " +
                typeof(T).Name + " in the scene. You only
                need 1, it's a singleton!");
                for(int i = 0; i < managers.Length; ++i) {
                    T manager = managers[i];
                    Destroy(manager.gameObject);
                }
            }
        }

        GameObject go = new GameObject(typeof(T).Name,
        typeof(T));
        __Instance = go.GetComponent<T>();
        DontDestroyOnLoad(__Instance.gameObject);
  }
  return __Instance;
}
set {
    __Instance = value as T;
}
    }
}
```

Since we wish this to be a global and persistent object, we need to call
DontDestroyOnLoad() shortly after the GameObject is created. This is a special
function that tells Unity that we wish the object to persist between Scenes for as long
as the application is running. From that point onward, when a new scene is loaded,
the object will not be destroyed and will retain all of its data.

This class definition assumes two things. Firstly, because it is using generics to define
its behavior, it must be derived from in order to create a concrete class. Secondly,
a method will be defined to assign the _Instance variable and cast it to/from the
correct Type.

For example, the following is all that is needed to successfully generate a new `SingletonAsComponent` derived class called `MySingletonComponent`:

```
public class MySingletonComponent : SingletonAsComponent<MySingletonC
omponent> {
  public static MySingletonComponent Instance {
    get { return ((MySingletonComponent)_Instance); }
    set { _Instance = value; }
  }
}
```

This class can be used at runtime by having any other object access the `Instance` property at any time. If the Component does not already exist in our Scene, then the `SingletonAsComponent` base class will instantiate its own GameObject and attach an instance of the derived class to it as a Component. From that point forward, access through the `Instance` property will reference the Component that was created.

 While it is possible, we should not place our `SingletonAsComponent` derived class in a **Scene** Hierarchy. This is because the `DontDestroyOnLoad()` method will never be called! This would prevent the Singleton Component's GameObject from persisting when the next Scene is loaded.

Proper cleanup of a Singleton Component can be a little convoluted because of how Unity tears down Scenes. An object's `OnDestroy()` method is called whenever it is destroyed during runtime. The same method is called during application shutdown, whereby every Component on every GameObject has its `OnDestroy()` method called by Unity. Application shutdown also takes place when we end Play Mode in the Editor and return to Edit Mode. However, destruction of objects occurs in a random order, and we cannot assume that the Singleton Component will be the last object destroyed.

Consequently, if any object attempts to do anything with the Singleton in the middle of their `OnDestroy()` method, then they will be calling the `Instance` property. If the Singleton has already been destroyed prior to this moment, then calling `Instance` during another object's destruction would create a new instance of the Singleton Component in the middle of application shutdown! This can corrupt our Scene files, as instances of our Singleton Components will be left behind in the Scene. If this happens, then Unity will throw the following error message at us:

Some objects were not cleaned up when closing the scene. (Did you spawn new GameObjects from OnDestroy?)

The reason some objects may wish to call into our Singleton during destruction is that Singletons often make use of the Observer pattern. This design pattern allows other objects to register/deregister with them for certain tasks, similar to how Unity latches onto callback methods, but in a less automated fashion. We will see an example of this in the upcoming section *A global messaging system*. Objects that are registered with the system during construction will want to deregister with the system during their own shutdown, and the most convenient place to do this is within its OnDestroy() method. Consequently, such objects are likely to run into the aforementioned problem, where Singletons are accidentally created during application shutdown.

To solve this problem, we need to make three changes. Firstly, we need to add an additional flag to the Singleton Component, which keeps track of its active state, and disable it at the appropriate times. This includes the Singleton's own destruction, as well as application shutdown (OnApplicationQuit() is another useful Unity callback for MonoBehaviours, which is called during this time):

```
private bool _alive = true;
void OnDestroy() { _alive = false; }
void OnApplicationQuit() { _alive = false; }
```

Secondly, we should implement a way for external objects to verify the Singleton's current state:

```
public static bool IsAlive {
  get {
    if (__Instance == null)
      return false;
    return __Instance._alive;
  }
}
```

Finally, any object that attempts to call into the Singleton during its own OnDestroy() method, must first verify the state using the IsAlive property before calling Instance. For example:

```
public class SomeComponent : MonoBehaviour {
    void OnDestroy() {
    if (MySingletonComponent.IsAlive) {
        MySingletonComponent.Instance.SomeMethod();
    }
  }
}
```

This will ensure that nobody attempts to access `Instance` during destruction. If we don't follow this rule, then we will run into problems where instances of our Singleton object will be left behind in the Scene after returning to Edit Mode.

The irony of the Singleton Component approach is that we are using one of Unity's `Find()` methods to determine whether or not one of these Singleton Components already exists in the Scene before we attempt to assign the `_Instance` reference variable. Fortunately, this will only happen when the Singleton Component is first accessed, but it's possible that the initialization of the Singleton would not necessarily occur during Scene initialization and can therefore cost us a performance spike at a bad moment during gameplay, when this object is first instantiated and `Find()` gets called. The workaround for this is to have some god class confirm that the important Singletons are instantiated during Scene initialization by simply calling `Instance` on each one.

The downside to this approach is that if we later decide that we want more than one of these manager classes executing at once, or we wish to separate its behavior to be more modular, then there would be a *lot* of code that needs to change.

There are further alternatives that we can explore, such as making use of Unity's built-in bridge between script code and the Inspector interface.

Assigning references to pre-existing objects

Another approach to the problem of inter-object communication is to use Unity's built-in serialization systems. Software design purists tend to get a little combative about this feature, since it breaks encapsulation; it makes variables marked `private` act in a way that treats them as `public`. Even though the value only becomes public with respect to the Unity Inspector and nothing else, this is still enough to wave some red flags.

However, it is a very effective tool for improving development workflow. This is particularly true when artists, designers, and programmers are all tinkering with the same product, where each has wildly varying levels of computer science and software programming knowledge. Sometimes it's worth bending a few rules in the name of productivity.

Whenever we create a `public` variable, Unity automatically serializes and exposes the value in the Inspector interface when the Component is selected. However, `public` variables are dangerous from a software design perspective—these variables can be changed through code at any time, which can make it hard to keep track of the variable, and introduce a lot of unexpected bugs.

As an alternative, we can take any `private` or `protected` member variable of a class and expose it to the Unity Editor Inspector interface with the `[SerializeField]` attribute. This approach is preferred over `public` variables, as it gives us more control of the situation. This way, at least we know the variables cannot be changed at runtime via code outside the class (or derived class), and therefore maintain encapsulation from the perspective of script code.

For example, the following class exposes three `private` variables to the Inspector:

```
public class EnemySpawnerComponent : MonoBehaviour {

  [SerializeField] private int _numEnemies;
  [SerializeField] private GameObject _enemyPrefab;
  [SerializeField] private EnemyManagerComponent _enemyManager;

  void Start() {
    SpawnEnemies(_numEnemies);
  }

    void SpawnEnemies(int _numEnemies) {
      for(int i = 0; i < _numEnemies; ++i) {
        GameObject enemy = (GameObject)GameObject.Instantiate
                            (_enemyPrefab, Vector3.zero,
                             Quaternion.identity);
        _enemyManager.AddEnemy(enemy);
      }
    }
}
```

 Note that the `private` access specifiers shown in the preceding code are redundant keywords in C#, as member variables are always `private` unless specified otherwise, but these access specifiers are included for completeness.

Looking at this Component in the **Inspector** view reveals three values, initially given default values of 0, or null, which can be modified through the Inspector interface:

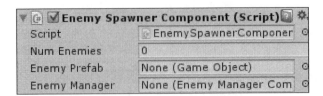

We can drag and drop a Prefab reference from the Projects window into the **Enemy Prefab** field, or, if we felt so inclined, even a reference to another GameObject that is present in the Scene. Although, given that it's being used like a Prefab in the code, it would be unwise to do this, since we would be cloning a GameObject that might have already undergone changes in the Scene. Prefabs serve the purpose of a blueprint from which to instantiate new GameObjects and should be used as such.

The **Enemy Manager** field is interesting because it is a Component reference and not a GameObject reference. If a GameObject is dropped into this field, then it will refer to the *Component* on the given object, as opposed to the GameObject that we dragged and dropped into the field. If the given object does not have the expected Component, then nothing will be assigned.

> A common usage of the Component reference technique is to obtain references to Components attached to the same GameObject it is attached to. This is an alternative approach to the topic discussed in the section entitled *Cache Component References*, earlier in this chapter.

The danger here is that since Prefabs are essentially GameObjects, Prefabs with the required Component *can* be assigned to these fields, even though we might not wish them to be. Unity loads Prefabs into memory much like GameObjects, and assumes they'll be used in Prefab-like ways; that is, treated as nothing more than blueprints to be instantiated from on an as-needed basis. However, they still count as data stored in memory and can therefore be edited on a whim, making them susceptible to changes that directly affect all future GameObjects instantiated from them.

To make matters worse, these changes become permanent even if they are made during Play Mode, since Prefabs occupy the same memory space whether Play Mode is active or not. This means that we can accidentally corrupt our Prefabs, if we assign them to the wrong fields. Consequently, this approach is a more team-friendly way of solving the original problem of inter-object communication, but it is not ideal due to all of the risks involved with team members accidentally breaking things or leaving `null` references in place.

It is also important to note that not all objects can be serialized by the Inspector view. Unity can serialize all primitive data types (`ints`, `floats`, `strings`, and `bools`), various built-in types such as (`Vector3`, `Quaternion`, and so on) enums, classes, and structs, as well as arrays and lists of other serializable types. However, it is unable to serialize static fields, read-only values, properties, and dictionaries.

Some Unity developers like to implement pseudo-serialization of dictionaries via two separate lists for keys and values, along with a Custom Editor script, or via a single list of objects, which contain both keys and values. Both of these solutions are a little clumsy, but perfectly valid.

The last solution we will look at will provide a way to hopefully get the best of both worlds by combining ease of implementation, ease of extension, and strict usage that avoids too much human error.

A global messaging system

The final suggested approach to the problem of inter-object communication is to implement a global messaging system that any object can access and send messages through to any object that may be interested in listening to that specific type of message. Objects either send messages or listen for them, and the responsibility is on the listener to decide what messages it is interested in. The message sender can broadcast the message without caring at all who is listening. This approach is excellent for keeping our code modular and decoupled.

The kinds of message we wish to send can take many forms, such as including data values, references, instructions for listeners, and more, but they should all have a common, basic declaration that our messaging system can use to determine what the message is, and who it is intended for.

The following is a simple class definition for a `Message` object:

```
public class BaseMessage {
  public string name;
  public BaseMessage() { name = this.GetType().Name; }
}
```

The `BaseMessage` class's constructor caches the Type in a local string property to be used later for cataloguing and distribution purposes. Caching this value is important as each call to `GetType().Name` will result in a new string being allocated on the heap, and we want to minimize this as much as possible. Our custom messages must derive from this class, which allows them to add whatever superfluous data they wish, while still maintaining the ability to be sent through our messaging system. Take note that, despite acquiring the Type name during the base class constructor, the `name` property will still contain the name of the derived class, not the base class.

Moving on to our `MessagingSystem` class, we should define its features by what kind of requirements we need it to fulfill:

- It should be globally accessible
- Any object (`MonoBehaviour` or not) should be able to register/deregister as listeners, to receive specific message types (that is, the Observer pattern)
- Registering objects should provide a method to call when the given message is broadcast
- The system should send the message to all listeners within a reasonable timeframe, but not choke on too many requests at once

A globally accessible object

The first requirement makes the messaging system an excellent candidate for a Singleton object, since we should only ever need one instance of the system. Although, it is wise to think long and hard if this is truly the case before committing to implementing a Singleton. If we later decide that we want multiple instances of this object to exist, then it can be difficult to refactor due to all of the dependencies we will gradually introduce to our codebase as we use the system more and more.

For this example, we will assume that we are absolutely positive that we will only need one of these systems, and design it accordingly.

Registration

Meeting the second and third requirements can be achieved by offering some public methods that allow registration with the messaging system. If we force the listening object to provide us a delegate function to call when the message is broadcast, then this allows listeners to customize which method is called for which message. This can make our codebase much easier to understand, if we name the delegate after the message it is intended to process.

 Delegate functions are incredibly useful constructs in C# that allows us to pass local methods around as arguments to other methods, and are typically used for callbacks. Check the MSDN C# Programming Guide for more information on delegates at https://msdn.microsoft.com/en-us/library/ms173171.aspx.

In some cases, we might wish to broadcast a general notification message and have all listeners do something in response, such as an *"Enemy Spawned"* message. Other times, we might be sending a message that specifically targets a single listener amongst a group. For example, we might wish to send an *"Enemy Health Value Changed"* message that is intended for a specific health bar object that is attached to the enemy that was damaged. If we implement a way for listeners to stop message processing early, then we can save a significant number of CPU cycles, if there are many listeners waiting for the same message type.

The delegate we define should therefore provide a way of retrieving the message via an argument, and return a response that determines whether or not processing for the message should stop when the listener is done with it. The decision on whether to stop processing or not can be achieved by returning a simple Boolean, where `true` implies that this listener has handled the message, and processing for the message must stop.

Here is the definition for the delegate:

```
public delegate bool MessageHandlerDelegate(BaseMessage message);
```

Listeners must define a method of this form and pass a reference to it when it registers with the `MessagingSystem`, thus providing an entry point for the messaging system to call when the message is broadcast.

Message processing

The final requirement for our messaging system is that this object has some kind of timing-based mechanism built in to prevent it from choking on too many messages at once. This means that, somewhere in the process, we will need to make use of `MonoBehaviour` event callbacks in order to work during Unity's `Update()` and be able to count time.

This can be achieved with the `static` class-based Singleton (which we defined earlier), which would require some other `MonoBehaviour`-based god class to call into it, informing it that the Scene has updated. Alternatively, we can use the `SingletonAsComponent` to achieve the same thing, but do so independently of any god class. The only difference between the two is whether or not the system is dependent on the control of other objects.

The `SingletonAsComponent` approach is probably the best, since there aren't too many occasions where we wouldn't want this system acting independently, even if much of our game logic depends upon it. For example, even if the game was paused, we wouldn't want the game logic to pause our messaging system. We still want the messaging system to continue receiving and processing messages so that we can, for example, keep UI-related Components communicating with one another while the gameplay is in a paused state.

Implementing the messaging system

Let's define our messaging system by deriving from the `SingletonAsComponent` class, and provide a method for objects to register with it:

```
using System.Collections.Generic;

public class MessagingSystem : SingletonAsComponent<MessagingSystem> {

  public static MessagingSystem Instance {
    get { return ((MessagingSystem)_Instance); }
    set { _Instance = value; }
  }

  private Dictionary<string,List<MessageHandlerDelegate>>
_listenerDict = new Dictionary<string,List<MessageHandlerDelegate>>();

  public bool AttachListener(System.Type type,
MessageHandlerDelegate handler) {
    if (type == null) {
      Debug.Log("MessagingSystem: AttachListener failed due to no
message type specified");
      return false;
    }

    string msgName = type.Name;

    if (!_listenerDict.ContainsKey(msgName)) {
      _listenerDict.Add(msgName, new
List<MessageHandlerDelegate>());
    }

    List<MessageHandlerDelegate> listenerList =
_listenerDict[msgName];
    if (listenerList.Contains(handler)) {
      return false; // listener already in list
    }

    listenerList.Add(handler);
    return true;
  }
}
```

The `_listenerDict` variable is a dictionary of strings mapped to lists of `MessageHandlerDelegates`. This dictionary organizes our listener delegates into lists by which message type they wish to listen to. Thus, if we know what message type is being sent, then we can quickly retrieve a list of all delegates that have been registered for that message type. We can then iterate through the list, querying each listener to see if one of them wants to handle it.

The `AttachListener()` method requires two parameters; a message type in the form of a `System.Type`, and a `MessageHandlerDelegate` to send the message to when it comes through the system.

Message queuing and processing

In order to process messages, our `MessagingSystem` should maintain a queue of incoming message objects so that we can process them in the order they are broadcasted:

```
private Queue<BaseMessage> _messageQueue = new
Queue<BaseMessage>();

public bool QueueMessage(BaseMessage msg) {
  if (!_listenerDict.ContainsKey(msg.name)) {
    return false;
  }
  _messageQueue.Enqueue(msg);
  return true;
}
```

The method simply checks if the given message type is present in our dictionary before adding it to the queue. This effectively tests whether or not an object actually cares to listen to the message before we queue it to be processed later. We have introduced a new `private` member variable, `_messageQueue`, for this purpose.

Next, we'll add a definition for `Update()`. This method will be called regularly by the Unity Engine. Its purpose is to iterate through the current contents of the message queue, one message a time, verify whether or not too much time has passed since we began processing, and if not, pass them along to the next stage in the process:

```
private float maxQueueProcessingTime = 0.16667f;

void Update() {
  float timer = 0.0f;
  while (_messageQueue.Count > 0) {
    if (maxQueueProcessingTime > 0.0f) {
      if (timer > maxQueueProcessingTime)
```

```
        return;
    }

    BaseMessage msg = _messageQueue.Dequeue();
    if (!TriggerMessage(msg))
      Debug.Log("Error when processing message: " + msg.name);

    if (maxQueueProcessingTime > 0.0f)
      timer += Time.deltaTime;
  }
}
```

The time-based safeguard is in place to make sure that it does not exceed a processing time limit threshold. This prevents the messaging system from freezing our game if too many messages get pushed through the system too quickly. If the total time limit is exceeded, then all message processing will stop, leaving any remaining messages to be processed during the next frame.

Lastly, we need to define the `TriggerMessage()` method, which distributes messages to listeners:

```
public bool TriggerMessage(BaseMessage msg) {
   string msgName = msg.name;
   if (!_listenerDict.ContainsKey(msgName)) {
      Debug.Log("MessagingSystem: Message \"" + msgName + "\" has no
listeners!");
      return false; // no listeners for message so ignore it
   }

   List<MessageHandlerDelegate> listenerList =
_listenerDict[msgName];

   for(int i = 0; i < listenerList.Count; ++i) {
      if (listenerList[i](msg))
         return true; // message consumed by the delegate
   }
   return true;
}
```

This method is the main workhorse of the messaging system. The `TriggerEvent()`'s purpose is to obtain the list of listeners for the given message type and give each of them an opportunity to process it. If one of the delegates returns `true`, then processing of the current message ceases and the method exits, allowing the `Update()` method to process the next message.

Normally, we would want to use QueueEvent() to broadcast messages, but TriggerEvent() can be called instead. This method allows message senders to force their messages to be processed immediately without waiting for the next Update() event. This bypasses the throttling mechanism, but this might be necessary for messages that need to be sent during critical moments in gameplay, where waiting one additional frame might result in strange-looking behavior.

Implementing a custom message

We've created the messaging system, but an example of how to use it would help us wrap our heads around the concept. Let's start by defining a simple message class, which we can use to transmit some data:

```
public class MyCustomMessage : BaseMessage {
  public readonly int _intValue;
  public readonly float _floatValue;
  public MyCustomMessage(int intVal, float floatVal {
    _intValue = intVal;
    _floatValue = floatVal;
  }
}
```

Good practice for message objects is to make their member variables readonly. This ensures that the data cannot be changed after the object's construction. This safeguards the content of our messages against being altered, as they're passed between one listener and another.

Message registration

Here's a simple class that registers with the messaging system, requesting to have its HandleMyCustomMessage() method called whenever a MyCustomMessage object is broadcast from anywhere in our codebase:

```
public class TestMessageListener : MonoBehaviour {

  void Start() {
    MessagingSystem.Instance.AttachListener(typeof(MyCustomMessage),
this.HandleMyCustomMessage);
  }

  bool HandleMyCustomMessage(BaseMessage msg) {
    MyCustomMessage castMsg = msg as MyCustomMessage;
    Debug.Log (string.Format("Got the message! {0}, {1}",
castMsg._intValue, castMsg._floatValue));
```

```
        return true;
    }
}
```

Whenever a `MyCustomMessage` object is broadcast (from anywhere!), this listener will retrieve the message through its `HandleMyCustomMessage()` method. It can then typecast it into the appropriate derived message type and handle the message in its own unique way. Other classes can register for the same message, and handle it differently through its own custom delegate method (assuming an earlier object didn't return `true` from its own delegate).

We know what type of message will be provided by the `msg` argument of the `HandleMyCustomMessage()` method, because we defined it during registration through the `AttachListener()` call. Due to this, we can be certain that our typecasting is safe, and we can save time by not having to do a `null` reference check, although, technically, there is nothing stopping us using the same delegate to handle multiple message types! In these cases, though we would need to implement a way of determining which message object is being passed, and treat it accordingly. The best approach is to define a unique method for each message type in order to keep things appropriately decoupled.

Note how the `HandleMyCustomMessage` method definition matches the function signature of `MessageHandlerDelegate`, and that it is being referenced in the `AttachListener()` call. This is how we tell the messaging system what method to call when the given message type is broadcast, and how delegates ensure type safety. If the function signature had a different return value or a different list of arguments, then it would be an invalid delegate for the `AttachListener()` method, and we would get compiler errors.

The beautiful part is that we're free to give the delegate method whatever name we want. The most sensible approach is to name the method after the message which it handles. This makes it clear to anyone reading our code what the method is used for and what message object type is required to call it.

Message sending

Finally, let's implement an example of sending a message so that we can test this system out! Here's a component that will broadcast an instance of our `MyCustomMessage` class through the messaging system when the *Space Bar* is pressed:

```
public class TestMessageSender : MonoBehaviour {

    public void Update() {
        if (Input.GetKeyDown (KeyCode.Space)) {
```

```
        MessagingSystem.Instance.QueueMessage(new MyCustomMessage(5,
    13.355f));
        }
    }
}
```

If we add both the `TestMessageSender` and `TestMessageListener` objects to our Scene and press the *Space bar*, we should see a log message appear in the console, informing us of a successful test:

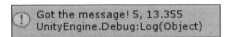

Our `MessagingSystem` Singleton object will be created immediately upon Scene initialization, when the `TestMessageListener`'s `Start()` method is called and it registers the `HandleMyCustomMessage` delegate. No additional effort is required on our part to create the Singleton we need.

Message cleanup

Since message objects are classes, they will be created dynamically in heap memory and will be disposed of shortly afterwards when the message has been processed and distributed amongst all listeners. However, as you will learn in *Chapter 7, Masterful Memory Management*, this will eventually result in a garbage collection as heap memory accumulates over time. If our application runs for long enough, it will eventually result in the occasional garbage collection. Therefore, it is wise to use the messaging system sparingly and avoid spamming messages too frequently on every update.

The more important clean-up operation to consider is deregistration of delegates if an object needs to be destroyed or de-spawned. If we don't handle this properly, then the messaging system will hang on to delegate references that prevent objects from being fully destroyed and freed from memory.

Essentially, we need to pair every `AttachListener()` call with an appropriate `DetachListener()` method when the object is destroyed, disabled, or we otherwise decide that we no longer need it to be queried when messages are being sent.

The following method definition in the MessagingSystem class will detach a listener for a specific event:

```
public bool DetachListener(System.Type type, MessageHandlerDelegate
handler)
  {
    if (type == null) {
      Debug.Log("MessagingSystem: DetachListener failed due to no
message type specified");
      return false;
    }

    string msgName = type.Name;

    if (!_listenerDict.ContainsKey(type.Name)) {
      return false;
    }

    List<MessageHandlerDelegate> listenerList =
_listenerDict[msgName];
    if (!listenerList.Contains (handler)) {
      return false;
    }

    listenerList.Remove(handler);
    return true;
  }
```

Here is an example usage of the DetachListener() method, added to our TestMessageListener class:

```
void OnDestroy() {
  if (MessagingSystem.IsAlive) {
    MessagingSystem.Instance.DetachListener(typeof(MyCustomMessage),
this.HandleMyCustomMessage);
  }
}
```

Note how this definition makes use of the IsAlive property declared in the SingletonAsComponent class. This safeguards us against the aforementioned problems during application shutdown, where we cannot guarantee that the Singleton was destroyed last.

Wrapping up the messaging system

Congratulations are in order, as we have finally built a fully functional global messaging system that any and all objects can interface with, to send messages between one another! A useful feature of this approach is that it is MonoBehaviour-agnostic, meaning that the message senders and listeners do not even need to derive from `MonoBehaviour` to interface with the messaging system; it just needs to be a class that provides a message type and a delegate function of the matching function signature.

As far as benchmarking the `MessagingSystem` class goes, we should find that if it is capable of processing hundreds, if not thousands of messages in a single frame with minimal CPU overhead (depending on the CPU, of course). The CPU usage is essentially the same whether one message is being distributed to 100 different listeners, 100 messages are distributed to just one listener. It costs about the same either way.

Even if we're predominantly sending messages during UI or gameplay events, this is probably far more power than we need. So, if it does seem to be causing performance problems, then it's far more likely to be caused by what the listener delegates are *doing* with the message than the messaging system's ability to process those messages.

There are many ways to enhance the messaging system to provide more useful features we may need in the future, such as:

- Allow message senders to suggest a delay (in time or frame count) before a message is processed and distributed

- Allow message listeners to define a priority for how urgently it should receive messages compared to other listeners waiting for the same message type—a way of skipping to the front of the queue if it registered later than other listeners

- Implement some safety checks to handle situations where a listener gets added to the list of message listeners for a particular message, while a message of that type is still being processed—C# will throw an enumeration exception at us since the delegate list will be changed by `AttachListener()`,while it is still being iterated through in `TriggerEvent()`

At this point, we have probably explored messaging systems enough, so these tasks will be left as an academic exercise for you to undertake, if you become comfortable using this solution in your games.

Let's explore some further techniques that we can use to improve performance through scripting.

Disabling unused scripts and objects

Scenes can get pretty busy sometimes, especially when we're building large, open worlds. The more objects invoking code in an `Update()` method, the worse things will scale and the slower your game becomes. However, much of what is being processed may be completely unnecessary if it is outside of the player's view or simply too far away to matter. This may not be a possibility in large city-building simulation games where the entire simulation must be processed at all times, but it is often possible in first person and racing games, where the player is wandering around a large expansive area, where non-visible objects can be temporarily disabled without having any noticeable effect on gameplay.

Disabling objects by visibility

Sometimes, we want Components or GameObjects to be disabled when they're not visible. Unity comes with built-in rendering features to avoid rendering objects that are not visible by Cameras (**Frustum Culling**, which is automatic in all versions), and to avoid rendering objects that are hidden behind other objects (**Occlusion Culling**, to be discussed in *Chapter 6, Dynamic Graphics*), but this does not affect Components that are non-renderable, such as AI scripts. We must control that behavior ourselves.

This problem can be solved easily by using the `OnBecameVisible()` and `OnBecameInvisible()` MonoBehaviour callbacks. As the names imply, these callback methods are invoked when a renderable object has become visible or invisible with respect to the game view and any Cameras in our Scene. In addition, when there are multiple Cameras in a Scene (for example, a local multiplayer game), the callbacks are only invoked if the object becomes visible to any *one* Camera, and becomes invisible to *all* Cameras. This means the aforementioned callbacks will be called at exactly the right times to implement this feature.

Since the visibility callbacks relate to and communicate with the rendering system, the GameObject must have a renderable object attached, such as a Mesh or SkinnedMesh. We must ensure that the Components we want to receive the visibility callbacks from are attached to the same GameObject as the renderable object and not some parent or sub-object, otherwise they won't be invoked.

 Note that Unity also counts the hidden camera of the Scene View towards the `OnBecameVisible()` and `OnBecameInvisible()` callbacks. If we find that these methods are not being invoked properly during Play Mode testing, make sure to turn the Scene View Camera away from everything.

To enable/disable individual components with the visibility callbacks, we can add the following methods:

```
void OnBecameVisible() { enabled = true; }
void OnBecameInvisible() { enabled = false; }
```

And, to enable/disable the entire GameObject the Component is attached to, we can implement the methods this way instead:

```
void OnBecameVisible() { gameObject.SetActive(true); }
void OnBecameInvisible() { gameObject.SetActive(false); }
```

Disabling objects by distance

In other situations, we want Components or GameObjects to be disabled after they are far enough away from the player, such that they may be barely visible, but too far away to matter. A good candidate for this type of activity is roaming AI creatures that we want to see at a distance, but where we don't need it to process anything.

The following code is a simple Coroutine that periodically checks the total distance from the target object and disables itself if it strays too far away from it:

```
[SerializeField] GameObject _target;
[SerializeField] float _maxDistance;
[SerializeField] int _coroutineFrequency;

void Start() {
  StartCoroutine(DisableAtADistance());
}

IEnumerator DisableAtADistance() {
  while(true) {
    float distSqrd = (Transform.position -
_target.transform.position).sqrMagnitude;

    if (distSqrd < _maxDistance * _maxDistance) {
      enabled = true;
    } else {
      enabled = false;
    }

    for (int i = 0; i < _coroutineFrequency; ++i) {
      yield return new WaitForEndOfFrame();
    }
  }
}
```

We should assign the Player object (or whatever object we want it to compare with) to the _target field in the Inspector, define the maximum distance in _maxDistance, and modify the frequency with which the Coroutine is invoked by using the _coroutineFrequency property. Any time the object goes further than _maxDistance distance away from the object assigned to _target, it will be disabled. It will be re-enabled if it returns within that distance.

A subtle performance-enhancing feature of this implementation is comparing against distance-squared instead of the raw distance. This leads us conveniently to our next tip.

Consider using distance-squared over distance

It is safe to say that CPUs are relatively good at multiplying floating-point numbers together, but relatively dreadful at calculating square roots from them. Every time we ask a Vector3 to calculate a distance with the magnitude property or with the Distance() method, we're asking it to perform a square root calculation (as per the Pythagorean theorem), which can cost a lot of CPU overhead compared to many other types of vector math calculations.

However, the Vector3 class also offers a sqrMagnitude property, which is the same as distance, only squared. This lets us perform essentially the same comparison check without the expensive square root included, so long as we also square the value we're trying to compare it against; or, to describe this mathematically, if the magnitude of A is less than the magnitude of B, then A^2 will be less than B^2.

For example, consider code like the following:

```
float distance = (transform.position -
other.transform.position).Distance();
if (distance < targetDistance) {
  // do stuff
}
```

This can be replaced with the following and achieve a nearly identical result:

```
float distanceSqrd = (transform.position -
other.transform.position).sqrMagnitude;
if (distanceSqrd < targetDistance * targetDistance) {
  // do stuff
}
```

The reason the result is *nearly* identical is because of floating-point precision. We're likely to lose some of the precision that we would have had from using the square-root values, since the value will be adjusted to an area with a different density of representable numbers; it can land exactly on, or closer to, a more accurate representable number, or, more likely, it will land on a number with less accuracy. As a result, the comparison is not *exactly* the same, but in most cases, it is close enough to be unnoticeable, and the performance gain can be quite significant for each instruction we replace in this manner.

If this minor precision loss is not important to you, then this performance trick should be considered. However, if precision is very important to you (such as running an accurate large-scale galactic space simulation), then you might want to look elsewhere for performance improvements.

Note that this technique can be used for *any* square-root calculations; not just for distance. This is simply the most common example you might run across, and bring to light the important `sqrMagnitude` property of the `Vector3` class—a property which Unity Technologies intentionally exposed for us to make use of in this manner.

Avoid retrieving string properties from GameObjects

Ordinarily, retrieving a string property from an object is the same as retrieving any other reference type property in C#; it is acquired with no additional memory cost. However, for whatever arcane reason hidden within the Unity source code, retrieving string properties from GameObjects duplicates the string in memory and results in a heap allocation. This draws the attention of the Garbage Collector, which, if we are not careful, can cause CPU spikes that will affect performance during runtime.

The two properties of GameObject affected by this strange behavior are `tag` and `name`. Retrieving either of these properties for any reason will cause unnecessary heap allocations. Therefore, it is unwise to use either property during gameplay, and you should only use them in *performance-inconsequential* areas such as Editor Scripts. However, the Tag system is commonly used for runtime identification purposes, which can make this a significant problem for some teams.

For example, the following code would cause an additional heap memory allocation during every iteration of the loop:

```
for (int i = 0; i < listOfObjects.Count; ++i) {
  if (listOfObjects[i].tag == "Player") {
    // do something with this object
  }
}
```

It is often better practice to identify objects by their Components, class types, and identifying values that do not involve strings, but sometimes we're forced into a corner. Maybe we didn't know any better when we started, we inherited someone else's codebase, or we're using it as a workaround for something. Let's assume that, for whatever reason, we're stuck with the Tag system, and we want to avoid these heap allocations.

Fortunately, the `tag` property is most often used in comparison situations, and GameObject provides an alternative way to compare `tag` properties, which does not cause a heap allocation—the `CompareTag()` method.

Let's perform a simple test to prove how this simple change can make all the difference in the world:

```
void Update() {
  int numTests = 10000000;
  if (Input.GetKeyDown(KeyCode.Alpha1)) {
    for(int i = 0; i < numTests; ++i) {
      if (gameObject.tag == "Player") {
        // do stuff
      }
    }
  }

  if (Input.GetKeyDown(KeyCode.Alpha2)) {
    for(int i = 0; i < numTests; ++i) {
      if (gameObject.CompareTag ("Player")) {
        // do stuff
      }
    }
  }
}
```

We can execute these tests by pressing the *1* and *2* keys to trigger the respective `for` loop. Here are the results:

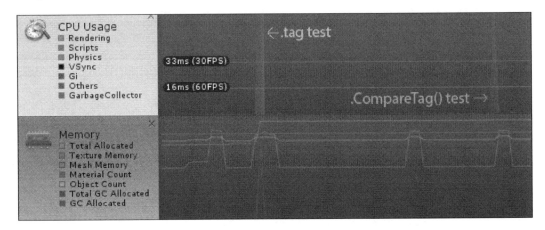

Looking at the Breakdown view for each spike, we can see two completely different situations:

Overview	.tag test	Total	Self	Calls	GC Alloc	Time ms	Self ms
▼ BehaviourUpdate		99.9%	0.0%	1	362.4 MB	2435.13	0.00
▼ StringAllocationTest.Update()		99.9%	79.9%	1	362.4 MB	2435.12	1946.66
GC.Collect		20.0%	20.0%	1	0 B	488.46	488.46

Overview	.CompareTag() test	Total	Self	Calls	GC Alloc	Time ms	Self ms
▼ BehaviourUpdate		99.8%	0.0%	1	0 B	1787.69	0.00
StringAllocationTest.Update()		99.8%	99.8%	1	0 B	1787.69	1787.69
WaitForTargetFPS		0.1%	0.1%	1	0 B	3.11	3.11

Retrieving the `tag` property 10 million times results in about 363 MB of memory being allocated just for strings alone. This takes 2435 milliseconds to process, where 488 milliseconds are spent on garbage collection. Meanwhile, using `CompareTag()` 10 million times costs 1788 milliseconds to process, and causes no heap memory allocations, and hence no Garbage Collection. This should make it abundantly clear that we must avoid using the `name` and `tag` properties. So, if Tag comparison becomes necessary, then we should make use of `CompareTag()`.

Note that passing in a string literal like `"Player"` does not result in a runtime heap allocation, since the application technically allocates this value during initialization and merely references it at runtime. However, if we dynamically generate the comparison string, then we will run into the same heap memory allocation problems, because we're essentially creating a new string object each time.

You will learn more nuances about the Garbage Collector and string usage in *Chapter 7, Masterful Memory Management*.

Update, Coroutines, and InvokeRepeating

Update is called every frame, but sometimes we hack in ways for the Update to be called less frequently than normal, and perhaps, without realizing it, we create a situation where an empty method is called more often than not:

```
void Update() {
  _timer += Time.deltaTime;
  if (_timer > _aiUpdateFrequency) {
    ProcessAI();
    _timer -= _aiUpdateFrequency;
  }
}
```

With this function definition, we are essentially calling an empty function almost every frame. In fact, it is worse than that; we're also performing a Boolean check that almost always returns `false`. This is fine if we don't abuse the concept, but as you've learned, having too many of these unnecessary function calls hiding in our Scene can be a sneaky hit on our performance.

This function is a perfect example of a function we can convert into a Coroutine to make use of their delayed-invocation properties:

```
void Start() {
  StartCoroutine(UpdateAI());
}

IEnumerator UpdateAI() {
  while (true) {
    yield return new WaitForSeconds(_aiUpdateFrequency);
    ProcessAI();
  }
}
```

However, this approach has its drawbacks. For one, a Coroutine comes with an additional overhead cost relative to a standard function call (around twice as slow), as well as some heap memory allocations to store the current state in memory until the next time it is invoked. Secondly, once initialized, Coroutines run independent, of the GameObject's `Update()` process and will be invoked regardless of whether the GameObject has been disabled or not. Care must be taken before deciding to adopt this approach.

However, if the situation is appropriate, the benefits of calling nothing during most frames, often outweighs the additional cost during the frames where it is invoked. Indeed, if we aren't performing too many complex things with `yield` statements, then we can often create an even simpler version of the method using `InvokeRepeating()`, which has a slightly smaller overhead cost (about 1.5 times slower than a standard function call):

```
void Start() {
    InvokeRepeating("ProcessAI", 0f, _aiUpdateFrequency);
}
```

Note that `InvokeRepeating` is also independent of the GameObject's `Update()` method, and will continue to be invoked even if the object is disabled.

Regardless of which approach we pick, there is an additional risk—having too many methods triggering in the same frame simultaneously. Imagine thousands of these objects that initialized together during Scene initialization. Every time `_aiUpdateFrequency` seconds go by, they will all invoke the `ProcessAI()` method within the same frame, and cause a huge spike in CPU usage.

Possible solutions to this problem include:

- Generating a new random time to wait each time the timer expires or Coroutine triggers
- Spread out Coroutine initialization so that only a handful of them are started each frame
- Delegate the responsibility of calling updates to some master class that places a limit on the number of invocations that occur each frame

Reducing excessive Update definitions to a simple Coroutine can potentially save us a lot of unnecessary overhead, so we should consider converting them whenever we feel it is appropriate. However, we might also consider re-evaluating our solution to the original problem in order to prevent lots of timed events all triggering at the same moment.

Another approach to optimizing updates is to not use `Update()` at all, or more accurately, to only use it once. When Unity calls `Update()`, it involves bridging the gap between a GameObject's native and managed representation of the GameObject, which can be a costly task. You will learn more about this native-managed bridge in *Chapter 7, Masterful Memory Management*, but for now, just consider that every callback we rely on Unity to invoke for us comes with a hidden processing cost attached relative to a standard function call.

We can therefore minimize this overhead by limiting how often it needs to cross the bridge. We can do this by having a god class take care of calling our own custom update-style method across all of our custom Components, in its own definition of `Update()`. In fact, many Unity developers prefer this approach right from the start of their projects, as it gives them finer control over when and how updates propagate throughout the system, for things such as menu pausing and cool time manipulation effects.

All objects wanting to integrate with such a system must have a common entry point. We can achieve this through an interface class. Interfaces essentially set up a contract whereby any class that implements the interface must provide a specific series of methods. In other words, if we know the object implements an interface, then we can be certain about what methods are available. In C#, classes can only derive from a single base class, but they can implement any number of interfaces (this avoids the "deadly diamond of death" problem that C++ programmers may be familiar with).

The following interface definition will suffice, which only requires the implementing class to define a single method:

```
public interface IUpdateable {
  void OnUpdate(float dt);
}
```

Next, we'll define a `MonoBehaviour` class, which implements this interface:

```
public class UpdateableMonoBehaviour : MonoBehaviour, IUpdateable
{
  public virtual void OnUpdate(float dt) {}
}
```

Note that we're naming the method `OnUpdate()` rather than `Update()`. We're defining a custom version of the same concept, but we want to avoid name collisions with the standard `Update()` callback.

The `OnUpdate()` method of the `UpdateableMonoBehaviour` class retrieves the current delta time (`dt`), to spare us from a bunch of unnecessary `Time.deltaTime` calls. We've also made the function `virtual`, to allow derived classes to customize it. However, as you know, Unity automatically grabs and invokes methods defined with the name `Update()`, but since we're defining our own custom update with a different name, then we need to implement something that will call this method when the time is appropriate; some kind of "GameLogic" god class.

During the initialization of this Component, we should do something to notify our `GameLogic` object of both its existence and its destruction, so that it knows when to start and stop calling its `OnUpdate()` function.

In the following example, we will assume that our GameLogic class is a Singleton Component, as defined earlier in the section entitled *Singleton Components*, and has appropriate static functions defined for registration and deregistration (although bear in mind that it can just as easily use our messaging system!).

For MonoBehaviours to hook into this system, the most appropriate place is within Start() and OnDestroy():

```
void Start() {
   GameLogic.Instance.RegisterUpdateableObject(this);
}

void OnDestroy() {
   GameLogic.Instance.DeregisterUpdateableObject(this);
}
```

It is best to use the Start() method for this task, since using Start() means that we can be certain all other pre-existing Components will have at least had their Awake() methods called prior to this moment. This way, any critical initialization work will have already been done on the object before we start invoking updates on it.

Note that, because we're using Start() in a MonoBehaviour base class, if we define a Start() method in a derived class, then it will effectively override the base-class definition and Unity will grab the derived Start() method as a callback instead. It would, therefore, be wise to implement a virtual Initialize() method so that derived classes can override it to customize initialization behavior without interfering with the base class's task of notifying the GameLogic object of our component's existence.

For example:

```
void Start() {
   GameLogic.Instance.RegisterUpdateableObject(this);
   Initialize();
}

protected virtual void Initialize() {
   // derived classes should override this method for
initialization code
}
```

We should try to make the process as automatic as possible to spare ourselves having to re-implement these tasks for each new Component we define. As soon as a class inherits from our UpdateableMonoBehaviour class, then should be secure in the knowledge that its OnUpdate() method will be called whenever it is appropriate.

Finally, we need to implement the GameLogic class. The implementation is pretty much the same whether it is a Singleton Component or a standalone Component, and whether or not it uses the MessagingSystem. Either way, our UpdateableMonoBehaviour class must register and deregister as IUpdateableObject objects, and the GameLogic class must use its own Update() callback to iterate through every registered object and call their OnUpdate() function.

Here is the class definition for the GameLogic system:

```
public class GameLogic : SingletonAsComponent<GameLogic> {
  public static GameLogic Instance {
    get { return ((GameLogic)_Instance); }
  set { _Instance = value; }
  }

List<IUpdateableObject> _updateableObjects = new
List<IUpdateableObject>();

  public void RegisterUpdateableObject(IUpdateableObject obj) {
    if (!_Instance._updateableObjects.Contains(obj)) {
      _Instance._updateableObjects.Add(obj);
    }
  }

  public void DeregisterUpdateableObject(IUpdateableObject obj) {
    if (_Instance._updateableObjects.Contains(obj)) {
      _Instance._updateableObjects.Remove(obj);
    }
  }

  void Update() {
    float dt = Time.deltaTime;
    for(int i = 0; i < _Instance._updateableObjects.Count; ++i) {
      _Instance._updateableObjects[i].OnUpdate(dt);
    }
  }

}
```

If we make sure all of our custom MonoBehaviours inherit from the UpdateableMonoBehaviour class, then we've effectively replaced *N* invocations of the Update() callback with just one Update() callback, plus *N* virtual function calls. This can save us a large amount of performance overhead, because even though we're calling virtual functions, we're still keeping the overwhelming majority of update behavior inside managed code, and avoiding the native-managed bridge as much as possible.

Depending on how deep you already are into your current project, such changes can be incredibly daunting, time-consuming, and likely to introduce a lot of bugs as subsystems are updated to make use of a completely different set of dependencies. However, the benefits can outweigh the risks if time is on your side. It would be wise to do some testing on a group of objects in a Scene that is similarly designed to your current Scene files to verify if the benefits outweigh the costs.

Consider caching Transform changes

The Transform Component only stores data relative to its own parent. This means that accessing and modifying a Transform Component's `position`, `rotation`, and `scale` properties can result in a lot of unanticipated matrix multiplication calculations to generate the correct Transform representation for the object through its parents' Transforms. The deeper the object is in the Hierarchy, the more calculations are needed to determine the final result. To make matters worse, changes to a Transform Component also send internal notifications to colliders, rigid bodies, lights, and cameras, which must be processed.

However, this also means that using `localPosition`, `localRotation`, and `localScale` have a relatively trivial cost associated with them, because the values can be retrieved and written as they are passed in. Therefore, these local property values should be used whenever possible. However, changing our mathematical calculations from world space to local space can overcomplicate what were originally simple (and solved!) problems, so making such changes risks breaking our implementation and introducing a lot of unexpected bugs. Sometimes it's worth absorbing a minor performance hit in order to solve a complex 3D mathematical problem more easily!

In addition, it is not uncommon, during some complex event, we replace a Transform's properties multiple times in the same frame (although this is probably a warning sign of over-engineered design). We can consider minimizing the number of times we modify the Transform values by caching them in a member variable and committing them only at the end of the frame, as follows:

```
private bool _positionChanged;
private Vector3 _newPosition;

public void SetPosition(Vector3 position) {
    _newPosition = position;
    _positionChanged = true;
}
```

```
void FixedUpdate() {
  if (_positionChanged) {
    transform.position = _newPosition;
    _positionChanged = false;
  }
}
```

This code will only commit changes to the position in the next `FixedUpdate()` method.

Note that this will *not* result in sluggish-looking behavior during gameplay, since all physics calculations are performed immediately after `FixedUpdate()`. There would not be any frames rendered before the physics engine gets a chance to respond to the Transform change.

Faster GameObject null reference checks

It turns out that performing a `null` reference check against a Unity object invokes a method on the other side of the native-managed bridge (mentioned earlier and explored in more detail in *Chapter 7, Masterful Memory Management*), which, as expected, results in some unnecessary performance overhead:

```
if (gameObject != null) {
  // do stuff with gameObject
}
```

There is a simple alternative that generates a functionally equivalent output, but operates around twice as quickly (although it does obfuscate the purpose of the code a little):

```
if (!System.Object.ReferenceEquals(gameObject, null)) {
  // do stuff with gameObject
}
```

This applies to both GameObjects and Components, as well as other Unity objects, which have both native and managed representations. However, some rudimentary testing reveals that either approach still consumes mere nanoseconds on an Intel Core i5 3570K processor. So, unless you are performing massive amounts of `null` reference checks, then the gains might be marginal at best.

However, it is noteworthy in the sense that there can be many other simple alternatives that have yet to be discovered, which can help improve performance by circumventing the native-managed bridge.

Summary

This chapter introduced you to many methods of improving your scripting practices in the Unity Engine, with the aim of improving performance if (and only if) you have already proven them to be the cause of a performance problem. Some of these techniques demand some forethought and profiling investigation before being implemented, since they often come with introducing additional risks or obfuscating our codebase for new developers. Workflow is often just as important as performance and design, so before you make any performance changes to the code, you should consider whether or not you're sacrificing too much on the altar of performance optimization.

We will investigate more advanced scripting improvement techniques later, in *Chapter 7*, *Masterful Memory Management*, but let's take a break from staring at code and explore some ways to improve application performance using built-in Unity features such as Static and Dynamic Batching.

3

The Benefits of Batching

In 3D graphics and games, **batching** is a very general term describing the process of grouping a large number of wayward pieces of data and processing them together as a single, large block of data. The goal of this process is to reduce computation time, often by exploiting parallel processing or reducing overhead costs, if the entire batch is treated as individual elements. In some cases, the act of batching centers around meshes, large sets of vertices, edges, UV coordinates, and so on, which are used to represent a 3D object. However, the term could just as easily refer to the act of batching audio files, sprites, and texture files (also known as Atlasing), and other large datasets.

So, just to clear up any confusion, when the topic of batching is mentioned in Unity, it is usually referring to the two primary mechanisms it offers for batching mesh files: Static and Dynamic Batching. These methods are essentially a form of geometry instancing, where we use the same mesh data in memory to repeatedly render the same object multiple times without needing to prepare the data more than once.

These batching features offer us opportunities to improve the performance of our application, but only as long as they are used wisely. They are fairly nuanced systems, and there has been a lot of confusion surrounding the conditions that they are triggered under, and just as importantly, under what conditions we would even see a performance improvement. In some cases, batching can actually degrade performance if batches are asked to process datasets under conditions that don't fit a very particular mold.

The batching systems in Unity are mostly a black box, in which Unity technologies have not revealed much detailed, technical information about their inner workings. But, based on their behavior, profiler data, and the list of requirements needed to make them work, we can still infer a great deal. This chapter intends to dispel much of the misinformation floating around about batching systems. We will observe, via explanation, exploration, and examples, just how these two batching methods operate. This will enable us to make informed decisions, making the most of them to improve our application's performance.

Draw Calls

Before we discuss Static and Dynamic Batching independently, let's first understand the problems that they are both trying to solve within the graphics pipeline. We will try to keep fairly light on the technicalities. We will explore this topic in greater detail in *Chapter 6, Dynamic Graphics*.

The primary goal of these batching methods is to reduce the number of Draw Calls required to render all objects in the current view. At its most basic form, a **Draw Call** is a request sent from the CPU to the GPU, asking it to draw an object. But, before a Draw Call can be requested, several important criteria need to be met. Firstly, mesh and texture data must be pushed from the CPU memory (RAM) into GPU memory (VRAM), which typically takes place during initialization of the Scene. Next, the CPU must prepare the GPU by configuring the options and rendering features that are needed to process the object that is the target of the Draw Call.

These communication tasks between the CPU and GPU take place through the underlying graphics API, which could be either DirectX or OpenGL depending on the platform we're targeting and certain graphics settings. These APIs feature many complex and interrelated settings, state variables, and datasets that can be configured, and the available features change enormously based on the hardware device we're operating on. The massive array of settings that can be configured before rendering a single object is often condensed into a single term known as the Render State. Until these Render State options are changed, the GPU will maintain the same Render State for all incoming objects and render them in a similar fashion.

Changing the Render State can be a time-consuming process. We won't go too deeply into the particulars of this, but essentially the Render State is a collection of global variables that affect the entire graphics pipeline. Changing a global variable within a parallel system is much easier said than done. A lot of work must happen on the GPU to synchronize the outcome of these state changes, which often involves waiting for the current batch to finish. In a massively parallel system such as a GPU, a lot of valuable time can be lost waiting for one batch to finish before beginning the next. Things that can trigger this synchronization may include pushing a new texture into the GPU, changing a Shader, changing lighting information, shadows, transparency, and changing almost any setting we can think of.

Once the Render State has been configured, the CPU must decide what mesh to draw, what Material it should use, and where to draw the object based on its position, rotation, and scale (all represented within a single transform matrix). In order to keep the communication between CPU and GPU very dynamic, new requests are pushed into a Command Buffer. This is a buffered list, which the CPU sends instructions to, and which the GPU pulls from whenever it finishes the previous command. The Command Buffer behaves like a First In First Out (FIFO) queue, and each time the GPU finishes one command, it pops the oldest command from the front of the queue, processes it, and repeats until the Command Buffer is empty.

Note that a new Draw Call does not necessarily mean that a new Render State must be configured. If two objects share the exact same Render State information, then the GPU can immediately begin rendering the new object since the same Render State is maintained after the last object was finished.

Because the rendering process requires two hardware components to work in tandem, it is very sensitive to bottlenecks, which could originate in one or both components. GPUs can render individual objects incredibly quickly, so if the CPU is spending too much time generating Draw Call commands (or simply generating too many of them), then the GPU will wait for instructions more often than it is working. In this case, our application's graphics would be CPU-bound. We're spending more time waiting on the CPU to decide what to draw, than the GPU spends drawing it. Conversely, being GPU-bound means the Command Buffer fills up with requests as the GPU cannot process requests from the CPU quickly enough.

 You will learn more about what it means to have rendering bottlenecks in either the CPU or GPU, and how to solve both cases, in *Chapter 6, Dynamic Graphics*.

Another component which can impede the speed of graphics activity in this chain of events is within the hardware driver. This component mediates commands coming through the graphics API, which can come from multiple sources such as our application, other applications, and even the Operating System itself (such as rendering the desktop). Because of this, using updated drivers can sometimes result in a fairly significant increase in performance!

Next-generation graphics APIs, such as Microsoft's DirectX 12, Apple's Metal, and the Kronos Group's Vulcan, all aim to reduce the overhead on the driver by simplifying and parallelizing certain tasks; particularly, how instructions are passed into the Command Buffer. Once these APIs become commonplace, we may be able to get away with using significantly more Draw Calls comfortably within our application. But until these APIs mature, we must treat our Draw Call consumption with a good deal of concern, in order to avoid becoming CPU-bound.

Materials and Shaders

Shaders are short programs which define how the GPU should render incoming vertex and pixel data. A Shader on its own does not have the necessary knowledge of state to accomplish anything of value. It requires inputs such as diffuse textures, normal maps, colors, and so on, and must decide what Render State variables are required in order to complete its intended task.

Unity's **Material** system is essential to providing this information to our Shaders. Ultimately, this just means a Shader is dependent upon a Material in order to be used to render an object. Every Shader needs a Material, and every Material must have a Shader. Even newly imported meshes that are introduced into the Scene without any assigned Materials are automatically assigned a default (hidden) Material, which gives them a basic diffuse Shader and a white coloration. So, there is no way of getting around this relationship.

 A single Material can only support a single Shader. The use of multiple Shaders on the same mesh requires separate Materials to be assigned to different parts of the same mesh.

These two systems capture the majority of the Render State variables we discussed in the previous section. As a result, if we can minimize the number of Materials being used to render the Scene, then we minimize the amount of Render State changes required, and hence reduce the amount of time the CPU spends preparing the GPU each frame.

Let's begin with a simple Scene in order to visualize the behavior of Materials and batching. But, before we start, we should disable several global options for rendering features to avoid distracting ourselves with advanced rendering features:

- Navigate to **Edit | Project Settings | Quality** and set **Shadows** to **Disable Shadows** (or select the default **Fastest** quality level)

- Navigate to **Edit | Project Settings | Player**, open the **Other Settings** tab, and disable **Static Batching**, **Dynamic Batching**, and **GPU Skinning** if they are enabled

 The **Static Batching** and **GPU Skinning** options are not available in Unity 4 Free Edition, and require an upgrade to Unity 4 Pro Edition.

Next, we'll create a Scene that contains a single Directional Light and eight meshes; four cubes, and four spheres, where each object has its own unique Material, position, rotation, and scale:

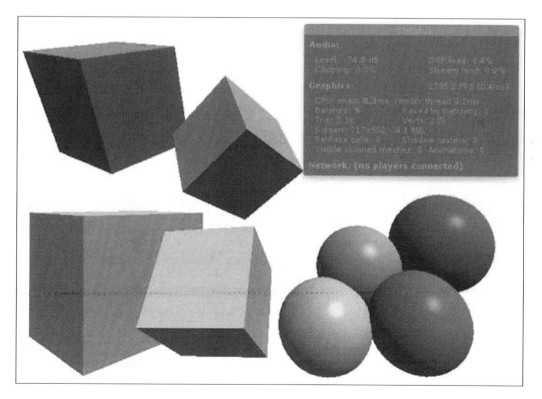

If we observe the **Batching** value in the **GameView's Stats** popup, we see nine total batches (note that this value will be labeled **Draw Calls** in the Unity 4 **Stats** popup). Unless the Camera's **Clear Flags** setting is set to **Don't Clear**, then one batch will be consumed drawing the Camera background. This could be the Scene's Skybox or a single quad that fills the screen with all pixels colored as per the Camera's **Background** color property.

The next eight batches are used to draw our eight objects. In each case, the Draw Call involves preparing the rendering system using the Material's properties and asking the GPU to render the given mesh at its current position, rotation, and scale. The Material also defines which Shader is used, which controls the programmable parts of the graphics pipeline (vertex and fragment steps).

Note that if the Rendering Path setting under the **Player** Settings is set to **Forward**, then we can enable and disable the Directional Light in our Scene and the number of batches remains at nine. The first Directional Light in **Forward** rendering is effectively free at least in terms of Draw Calls. As soon as we add more Lights to our Scene, whether they are Directional, Point, Spot, or Area Lights, we cause all objects to be rendered with an additional "pass" through the Shader for each Light, up to the value of the **Pixel Light Count** value under the **Quality** Settings (lights with high brightness values are prioritized first).

> Lighting options can become a significant source of Draw Calls, and you will learn more about this system in *Chapter 6, Dynamic Graphics*.

As previously mentioned, we can theoretically minimize the number of Draw Calls by reducing how often we cause the system to change Render State information. So, part of the goal therefore is to reduce the amount of Materials we use. But, if we set all objects to use the same Material, we don't see any benefit and the number of batches remains at nine:

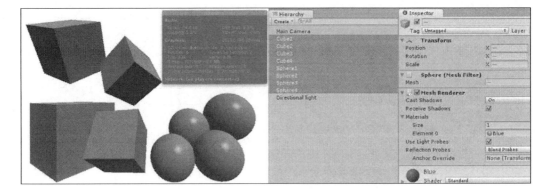

This is because we're not actually reducing the number of Render State changes nor efficiently grouping mesh information. Without any form of batching, the rendering system is not smart enough to realize we're overwriting the exact same Render State values, and then asking it to render the same meshes, over and over again. This presents an opportunity to have the rendering process recognize these situations, render all of these meshes together as one object, and avoid unnecessary Draw Calls. This is basically how Dynamic Batching works to reduce our Draw Calls.

Dynamic Batching

The purpose of Dynamic Batching is to bundle together large groups of simple meshes and push them through the rendering system as if it was a single mesh. Only meshes that are currently visible in the **Camera** view are candidates for Dynamic Batching, which means that most of the batching work is accomplished at runtime, rather than pre-calculated. This means that the objects that are batched together will vary from frame to frame. Hence, the name "Dynamic" Batching.

If we return to the **Player Settings** page and enable **Dynamic Batching**, we should see that the number of batches drops from nine down to six. Dynamic Batching is automatically recognizing that our objects share Material and mesh information and can combine them into a single batch for processing. This is a decent CPU cost-savings technique and reduces the likelihood that our game with be CPU-bound, since it frees up more time for other tasks, such as AI and Physics processing.

At the risk of sounding ungrateful, we should ask ourselves why we only save three Draw Calls, and not six. We would hope that the system is smart enough to group all of the cubes together in one batch and all of the spheres in another, taking only two Draw Calls to render them all (plus one Draw Call for the background).

The complete list of the requirements needed to successfully dynamically batch a mesh can be found in the Unity documentation at `http://docs.unity3d.com/Manual/DrawCallBatching.html`.

- All mesh instances must use the same Material reference

- Only particle systems and mesh renderers are dynamically batched. Skinned mesh renderers (for animated characters) and all other renderable component types cannot be batched

- The total number of vertex attributes used by the Shader must be no greater than 900

- Either all mesh instances should use a uniform scale or all meshes should use a nonuniform scale, but not a mixture of the two

- Mesh instances should refer to the same Lightmap file

- The Material's Shader should not depend on multiple passes
- Mesh instances must not receive real-time Shadows

There are also a couple of undocumented requirements that have been revealed during some Unite Conference panels:

- There is a limit of 300 meshes per batch
- There must be no more than 32,000 mesh indices in the entire batch

However, a couple of these requirements are not completely intuitive or clear from the description, which merits some additional explanation.

Vertex attributes

A vertex attribute is a property contained within a mesh file on a per vertex basis. This includes, but is not limited to, a vertex's position, a normal vector (most often used in lighting calculations), and UV coordinates (used to define how a texture wraps around the mesh). Only meshes with less than 900 total vertex attributes used by the Shader can be included in Dynamic Batching.

 Note that looking into a mesh's raw data file may contain less vertex attribute information than Unity loads into memory because of how the engine converts mesh data from one of several raw data formats into an internal format.

Using more attribute data per vertex within the accompanying Shader will consume more from our 900-attribute budget and hence reduce the number of vertices the mesh is allowed to have before it can no longer be used in Dynamic Batching. For example, a simple Shader which only uses three attributes per vertex, such as some of the legacy diffuse Shaders, can support Dynamic Batching using meshes with up to 300 vertices. But a more complex Shader, requiring five attributes per vertex, can only support Dynamic Batching with meshes up to 180 vertices.

This restriction is why our Scene only saves three Draw Calls with Dynamic Batching enabled, despite having all objects share the same Material reference. The cube that is autogenerated by Unity contains 8 vertices each with position, normal, and UV data, for 24 attributes in total. This is far less than the 900-vertex attribute limit when all of this data is used by the Shader. However, an autogenerated sphere contains 515 vertices, which clearly cannot be dynamically batched if we count a position, normal, and UV coordinate for each vertex. This explains our six Draw Calls: one for the background, one for a batched group of cubes, and four for the spheres that are not being dynamically batched, which must be rendered with separate Draw Calls.

Uniform scaling

The documentation suggests that, generally, objects should either share a uniform scale or each have a unique nonuniform scale in order to be included in dynamic batching. But, in reality, the behavior of this restriction changes slightly depending on which version of Unity we are running due to some changes to the Dynamic Batching system in Unity 5.

 A uniform scale means that all three components of the scale vector (x, y, and z) are identical.

In both versions of Unity, if all instances of a mesh have a uniform scale, then they can be grouped together in the same dynamic batch. In Unity 5, it will dynamically batch all nonuniformly scaled instances of the mesh with the original batch, no matter their scale. However, in Unity 4, nonuniformly scaled objects, using the same mesh and Material, will be grouped together into separate batches.

This assumes we're working with positive scales. The scale restriction gets a little unintuitive when we're dealing with negative scales. In Unity 4, negative scales do not affect Dynamic Batching and all of the same rules apply as before. But, in Unity 5, if the mesh has one or three negative values in its scale vector, then it will not be included in the batch. If it contains two negative values, then it can be batched along with all of the other instances. It does not even matter which of the three values are negative, only that there are zero or two of them.

Presumably, this is a bi-product of the algorithm used to detect valid batchable groups, since mirroring a mesh in two dimensions is mathematically equivalent to rotating the mesh about both of the same axes 180 degrees. Thus, the behavior we observe is just the Dynamic Batching system automatically transforming the object for us.

So, it is worth keeping in mind that Dynamic Batching is a little more efficient in Unity 5, but it has some trade-offs. If we wish to use negative scales as a shortcut to mirror a mesh, then it will be incapable of being Dynamically Batched.

Dynamic Batching summary

There were clearly some significant improvements made to the Dynamic Batching system in Unity 5, allowing it to be more versatile to a variety of situations. However, no matter which version of Unity we are using, Dynamic Batching is very useful when we wish to render very large groups of simple meshes.

The design of the system makes it ideal to use when all of the meshes we're Dynamically Batching are simple and nearly identical in appearance. Possible situations to apply Dynamic Batching could be as follows:

- A large forest filled with rocks, trees, and bushes
- A building, factory, or space station with many common elements (computers, pipes, and so on) throughout the Scene
- A game featuring many dynamic, nonanimated objects with simple geometry and particle effects (a game such as Geometry Wars springs to mind)

The potential benefits of Dynamic Batching are significant enough to set aside some time to investigate if and where we can make use of it in our Scene. There are not too many occasions where Dynamic Batching would actually degrade performance.

The most common mistake with Dynamic Batching is to set up a Scene that generates lots of batches, which each contain only a handful of meshes. In these cases, the overhead cost of detecting and generating the batches might cost more than the time it saves just making a separate Draw Call for each mesh.

In addition, we're far more likely to inflict performance losses on our application by simply assuming Dynamic Batching is taking place, when we've actually forgotten one of the essential requirements. Every situation is unique, so it is worth experimenting with our Materials, meshes, and Shaders to determine what can and cannot be dynamically batched.

Static Batching

Unity offers a second batching mechanism through Static Batching. The purpose of this feature is to grant us a way to batch nonidentical meshes of any size into a single batch with a similar goal and methodology to Dynamic Batching, but solving the problem for a different set of conditions. The essential difference between the two batching methods is that Static Batching occurs during application initialization, whereas Dynamic Batching takes place at runtime. We therefore have a lot more control over when and where Static Batching takes place.

 Static Batching is available in all editions of Unity 5, but only in the Pro Edition of Unity 4. Unity 4 Free users will need to upgrade to the Pro Edition to make use of this feature.

The Static Batching system has its own set of requirements:

- As the name implies, the meshes must be flagged as Static
- Additional memory must be set aside for each mesh being statically batched
- The mesh instances can come from any source mesh, but they must share the same Material

Let's cover each of these requirements in more detail.

The Static flag

Static Batching can only be applied to objects with the Static flag enabled or, more specifically, the **Batching Static** sub flag (also known as StaticEditorFlags). Clicking on the down arrow next to the **Static** option for a GameObject will reveal a dropdown of these StaticEditorFlags, which can alter the object's behavior for various Static processes.

Memory requirements

The additional memory requirement for Static Batching will vary depending on the amount of replication occurring within the batched meshes. Static Batching works by combining all flagged meshes into a single, large mesh, and passing it into the rendering system through a single Draw Call. If all of the meshes being statically batched are *unique*, then this would cost us no additional memory usage compared to rendering the objects normally, as the same amount of memory space is required to store the meshes.

However, statically batched duplicates cost us additional memory equal to the number of meshes multiplied by the size of the original mesh. Ordinarily, rendering one, ten, or a million clones of the same object costs us the same amount of memory, because they're all referencing the same mesh data. The only difference is the transform of each object. But, because Static Batching needs to copy the data into a large buffer, complete with its transform data, this referencing is lost, and a new duplicate of the original mesh is copied into the buffer with a hard-coded transform position, regardless of whether the same mesh has already been copied in.

Therefore, using Static Batching to render 1,000 identical tree objects will cost us 1,000 times more memory than rendering the same objects normally, because each tree must be copied into the Static Batching buffer as a unique set of vertex data. This causes some significant memory consumption and performance issues if Static Batching is not used wisely.

Material references

Finally, we already know about sharing material references as a means of reducing Render State changes, so this requirement is fairly obvious. However, sometimes we're statically batching meshes that require multiple materials. In which case, all meshes using a different material will be grouped together in their own static batch, and again for each unique material being used.

The downside to this design feature is that, at best, Static Batching can only render all of the static meshes using a number of Draw Calls equal to the number of materials they need. But, the benefit is that we can control which meshes get batched together using different materials, effectively forcing it to start a new static batch through some cunning material duplication. This will become clear after we cover some of the Static Batching system's caveats.

Static Batching caveats

The Static Batching system is not without its drawbacks. Because of how it approaches the batching solution, by combining meshes into a single greater mesh, the Static Batching system has a few caveats that we need to be aware of. These concerns range from minor inconveniences to major drawbacks depending on the Scene:

- Draw Call savings are not immediately visible from the **Stats** window until runtime
- Static objects should not be introduced to the Scene at runtime

- Statically batched meshes cannot be moved from their original starting transform
- If any one of the statically batched meshes is visible, then the entire group will be rendered

Edit Mode debugging of Static Batching

Trying to determine the overall effect that Static Batching is having on our Scene can be a little tricky since nothing is being Statically Batched while in Edit Mode. All of the magic happens during Scene initialization, which can make it difficult to determine what benefits Static Batching is actually providing. This is especially true if we leave implementing this feature until late in the project lifecycle, where we can spend a lot of time launching, tweaking, and relaunching our Scene to ensure we're getting the Draw Call savings we're expecting. Consequently, it is best to start working on Static Batching optimization early in the process of building a new Scene.

Avoiding instantiating static meshes at runtime

New static objects introduced into the Scene will not be automatically combined into any existing batch by the Static Batching system. To do so would cause an enormous runtime overhead between recalculating the mesh and synchronizing with the rendering system, so Unity does not even attempt to do it. This restriction means we should not attempt to dynamically instantiate the statically batched content. All meshes we wish to statically batch should be present in the original Scene file.

 Dynamic instantiation of objects can be a costly action in its own right. We will cover solutions to that problem in *Chapter 7, Masterful Memory Management*.

As with the previous caveat, statically batched meshes should not be moved after they have been batched, since doing so would generate a tremendous CPU overhead. The Static Batching system has already taken the original data and combined it into a new mesh object. Moving the original meshes is both impossible while the Static flag is enabled, and not even recognized by the Unity system if the flag is disabled and the object's transform is changed.

Visibility and rendering

The final caveat is perhaps the most important. If even a single vertex of a Statically Batched mesh is visible to the Camera, then the whole mesh will be pushed into the rendering system and processed in its entirely. We need to be smart about how we use Static Batching and optimize its usage to prevent us rendering a gigantic mesh each and every frame!

For example, if we have a Scene with many rooms connected together which all share the same Material, then enabling Static Batching for every room object will cause every single room to be rendered even if only a single room is visible, and even if the player is staring straight into a wall. Such Scenes would fare better using Occlusion Culling (explored in *Chapter 6, Dynamic Graphics*) to prevent nonvisible rooms from being rendered.

Meanwhile, large outdoor scenes will find it useful to duplicate Materials. This is a useful trick to force similar objects to be statically batched into different groups. Assigning identical, but duplicate Materials to different sections of the world will render them the same; however, they will be grouped separately. This would increase the number of Draw Calls, but allow us to reuse the same Texture, Material, and Shader files for the entire Scene.

Duplicating Materials can become a bit of a chore from the maintenance perspective, since any changes made to one Material must also be made to the others. Hypothetically, we might think we can accomplish this through Script by attaching a Component that automatically duplicates a Material and assigns it to the mesh during Scene initialization. Unfortunately, Static Batching happens too early in the initialization process for us to intercept through a custom Component such as this, so the task must be done through the Editor (a good opportunity to make use of Editor scripts).

Static Batching summary

Static Batching is a powerful, but dangerous tool. If we don't use it wisely, we can very easily inflict performance losses via memory consumption and rendering costs on our application. It also takes a good amount of manual tweaking and configuration. However, it does have a significant advantage: it can be used on object sets of any size. There is essentially no limit as far as Static Batching is concerned.

Summary

It is clear that the Static and Dynamic Batching features are no silver bullet. We cannot blindly apply them to any given Scene and expect improvements. If our application and Scene happen to fit a particular set of parameters, then these methods are very effective at reducing CPU load and rendering bottlenecks. But, if not, then some additional work is required to prepare our Scene to match its feature requirements. Ultimately, only a good understanding of the batching systems and how they function can help us determine where and when this feature can be applied.

We will cover more graphics improvement techniques in *Chapter 6, Dynamic Graphics*. Until then, let's move onto a different topic, and look into some of the more subtle performance improvements that we can achieve through managing our art assets in intelligent ways.

4
Kickstart Your Art

Art is a very subjective area, dominated by personal opinion and preference. It can be difficult to say whether one piece of art is "better" than the other, and it's likely that we won't be able to find complete consensus on our opinions. The technical aspects behind art assets that support a game's artistry can also be very subjective. There are multiple workarounds that can be implemented to improve performance, but these tend to result in a loss of quality for the sake of speed. If we're trying to reach peak performance, then it's important that we consult with our team members whenever we decide to make any changes to our art assets as it is primarily a balancing act, which can be an art form in itself.

Whether we're trying to minimize our runtime memory footprint, keeping the smallest possible executable size, maximizing loading speed, or maintaining consistency in frame rate, there are plenty of options to explore. There are some methods that are clearly always ideal, and others which may require a little more care and forethought before being adopted, as they might result in reduced quality or increase the chances of developing bottlenecks in other components.

We will begin examining audio files, followed by Texture files, and finish up with meshes and animations. In each case, we will investigate how Unity loads, stores, and manipulates these assets during runtime, what our options are, and what we can do to avoid behavior that might generate performance bottlenecks.

Audio

Depending on the scope of the project, audio files can range anywhere from the largest disk space consumer, to the smallest. Unity, as a framework, can be used to build small applications that require only a handful of sound effects and a single background track, or to build large expansive role playing games that need millions of lines of spoken dialog, music tracks, and ambient sounds. It will be useful to make sense of how audio files are managed in Unity to better understand what we should do for the sake of optimization in both cases.

Many developers are surprised to find that runtime audio processing can turn into a significant source of CPU and memory consumption. Audio is often neglected on both sides of the gaming industry; developers tend not to commit many resources to it until the last minute, while users will rarely draw attention to it. Nobody notices when the audio is good or passable, but we all know what bad audio sounds like; it's instantly recognizable, jarring, and guaranteed to catch unwanted attention. This makes it crucial not to sacrifice too much audio clarity in the name of performance.

Audio bottlenecks can come from a variety of sources. Excessive compression, too much audio manipulation, too many active audio clips, inefficient memory storage methods, and access speeds are all ways to invite poor memory and CPU performance. But, with a little effort and understanding, all it takes is a few tweaks here and there to save us from a user-experience disaster.

 Several audio options are named slightly differently between Unity 4 and Unity 5, but the features are identical for all intents and purposes. We will proceed using the Unity 5 name for each feature.

Loading audio files

When we select an imported Audio Clip in the Unity Editor, we see that the first option is the file's **Load Type**. There are three possible settings available:

- **Decompress On Load**
- **Compressed In Memory**
- **Streaming**

The actual moment when the file is first loaded will depend on other Audio Clip settings and how they are used during runtime, which we will explore later. This option merely defines the method of loading when it occurs.

Decompress On Load compresses the file on disk to save space, and decompresses it into memory when it is first loaded. This is the standard method of loading an audio file, and should be used in most cases.

Compressed In Memory loads the compressed file straight into memory when it is loaded, and decompresses it during runtime when it is being played. This will sacrifice runtime CPU when the clip is played, but improves loading speed and reduces runtime memory consumption. Hence, this option is best used for very large audio files that are used fairly frequently, or if we're incredibly bottlenecked on memory consumption and are willing to sacrifice some CPU cycles to play the Audio Clip.

Finally, the **Streaming** option will load, decode, and play files on-the-fly at runtime by gradually pushing the file through a small buffer. This method uses the least amount of memory for a particular Audio Clip and the largest amount of runtime CPU. This comes with the unfortunate drawback that they cannot be referenced more than once. Attempting to stream multiple copies of the same Audio Clip will generate a new buffer for each instance, resulting in a significant amount of RAM and runtime CPU cost if used recklessly. Consequently, this option is best reserved for single-instance Audio Clips that play regularly and never need to overlap with other instances. Ergo, this setting is best used with background music and ambient sound effects that need to play during the majority of a Scene's lifetime.

Profiling audio

We can confirm much of this behavior by playing multiple instances of any given Audio Clip via multiple Audio Sources in a Scene, and benchmarking using the Audio View of the Profiler to see how much memory and CPU is consumed using the various **Load Type** options. However, be aware that the Profiler output for audio memory and CPU consumption in Editor Mode can be very misleading, since it performs audio loading differently to how it would occur in a runtime application.

The first time we load the Editor and enter Play Mode, the Editor will decompress audio files, costing a certain amount of memory and CPU cycles during initialization in order to accomplish this. We can observe the memory costs of this process in the Profiler under the Audio Area. However, if we restart the Scene, then we may notice that the memory spent on decompressing audio files suddenly drops to nearly 0 KB, since files have already been decompressed and the Editor has flushed away data it no longer needs. This is not representative of a real situation, as applications would need to perform this decompression.

So, if we want accurate audio profiling in Unity, we should run the Profiler against a standalone, or remote, version of our application on the intended platform/device.

Additional loading options

There is an additional pair of options that affect audio file loading behavior:

* **Load In Background**
* **Preload Audio Data**

In the typical use case, where an Audio Clip is assigned to an Audio Source Component in a Scene, the audio file will be loaded into memory during Scene initialization. But, if the **Load In Background** option is enabled, then loading the Audio Clip will be deferred to a background task that begins once the Scene has finished initializing and gameplay has essentially begun. So, it stands to reason that we can improve the Scene loading speed by enabling this option for Audio Clips that we won't need until later in the Scene's lifetime, such as sound effects used in *mid-level* cut Scenes.

We can use an `AudioClip` object's `loadState` property to verify if the asset is loaded before attempting to use it. But, using the **Load In Background** option risks introducing jarring behavior if we try to access a sound file before it is fully loaded. In these cases, the sound file won't play until the background loading task has completed, in which case the sound will probably play at an inappropriate moment.

The second option, **Preload Audio Data**, is enabled by default, which tells the Unity Engine to automatically begin loading the file during Scene initialization. Disabling this option defers loading to the first instant that the `AudioSource` object's `Play()` or `PlayOneShot()` methods are invoked at runtime. This will cause a spike in the CPU, as the audio data is loaded from the disk, decompressed (or not, depending on the **Load Type** setting), pushed into memory, and eventually played once loaded.

Due to the amount of playback delay, and the performance cost, it is not recommended to rely on loading occurring at the moment that audio playback is needed. We should instead control loading ourselves by calling the `AudioClip` object's `LoadAudioData()` at some convenient moment before the file is needed. Modern games typically implement convenient stopping points in levels to perform tasks such as this, such as an elevator between floors or long corridors, where very little action is taking place. Note that we can also manually control the freeing of audio file memory using the AudioClip object's `UnloadAudioData()` method.

Solutions involving custom loading and unloading of audio data via these methods would need to be tailor-made to the particular game, depending on when Audio Clips are needed, how long they're needed for, how Scenes are put together, and how player(s) traverse them. This can require a significant number of special-case changes, testing, and asset management tweaks to achieve. So, it is recommended to save this approach as a "Nuclear Option" to be used late in production, in the event that all other techniques have not succeeded as well as we hoped.

Encoding formats and quality levels

Unity supports three general-case encoding formats for audio files, with a few specific cases that are platform-dependent (such as HEVAG for the PS Vita and XMA for XBox One). We will focus on the three optional encoding formats:

- **Compressed**
- **PCM**
- **ADPCM**

The compression algorithm used with the **Compressed** format will depend on the platform being targeted. Standalone applications, WebGL, and other non-mobile platforms use Ogg-Vorbis for compression, while mobile platforms use MPEG-3 (MP3).

The audio files we import into the Unity Engine can be one of many popular audio file formats, but the actual encoding that is bundled into the executable will end up in one of the previously mentioned formats. Statistics are provided for the currently selected format in the area following the **Compression Format** option, providing an idea of how much disk space is being saved by the compression, and how much memory the Audio Clip will consume at runtime (note that this also depends on the currently selected **Load Type**).

The encoding/compression format used can have a dramatic effect on the quality, file size, and memory consumption of the audio file during runtime, and only the **Compressed** option gives us the ability to alter the quality without affecting the sampling rate of the file. The **PCM** and **ADPCM** formats do not provide this luxury, and we're stuck with whatever file size those compression formats decide to give us, unless we're willing to reduce audio quality for the sake of file size by reducing the sampling rate.

Each encoding and compression format provides different benefits and pitfalls, and each audio file may be able to sacrifice one metric for another based on its purpose and contents. If we wish to properly optimize our application's audio files, then we need to be willing to use all of the available formats in a single application to make the most of our audio files.

The **PCM** format is a lossless and uncompressed audio format, providing a close approximation of analog audio. It trades large file sizes for higher audio quality, and is best used for very short sound effects that require a lot of clarity where any compression would otherwise distort the experience.

Meanwhile, the **ADPCM** format is far more efficient in both size and CPU consumption than PCM, but compression results in a fair amount of noise. This noise can be hidden if it is reserved for short sound effects with a lot of chaos, such as explosions, collisions, and impact sounds where we might not be aware of any generated artefacts.

Finally, the **Compressed** format will result in small files that have lower quality than **PCM**, but significantly better quality than **ADPCM**, at the expense of additional runtime CPU usage. This format should be used in most cases. This option allows us customize the resultant quality level of the compression algorithm, to tweak quality against file size. Best practices with the **Quality** slider are to search for a quality level that is as small as possible, but unnoticeable to users. Some user testing may be required to find the "sweet spot" for each file.

Do not forget that any additional audio effects applied to the file at runtime will not play through the Editor in Edit Mode, so any changes should be fully tested through the application in Play Mode.

Audio performance enhancements

Now that we have a better understanding of audio file formats, loading methods, and compression modes, let's explore some approaches that we can make to improve performance through tweaking audio behavior.

Minimize active Audio Source count

Since each actively playing Audio Source consumes a particular amount of CPU, then it stands to reason that we can save CPU cycles for each redundant Audio Source that is playing in our Scene. One approach is to control our Audio Sources in such a way that we put a hard cap on how many instances of an Audio Clip can play simultaneously so that we don't attempt to play too many of the same sound effects simultaneously. We can do this by having a management object take control of our Audio Sources. It should accept sound playback requests and plays the file through any Audio Sources that aren't already busy playing an existing sound.

The management object could also throttle the requests such that there is a limit to how many versions of the same sound effect can play, and how many total sound effects are playing at any given time. This would be best used on 2D sound effects or single instances of 3D sound effects (which would require moving the Audio Source to the correct location at the moment of playback).

Almost every Audio Management Asset available in the Unity Asset Store implements an audio-throttling feature of some kind (often known as "audio pooling"), and for good reason; it's the best trade-off in minimizing excessive audio playback with the smallest amount of effort in preparing audio assets to make use of it. For this reason, and because these assets often provide many more subtle performance-enhancing features, it is recommended to use a pre-existing solution, rather than rolling out our own, as the scripting process can be very involved.

Note that ambient 3D sounds still need to be placed at specific locations in the Scene to make use of the logarithmic volume effect, which gives it the pseudo-3D effect, so the audio management system would probably not be an ideal solution. Limiting playback on ambient sound effects is best achieved by reducing the total number of sources. The best approach is to either remove some of them or reduce them down to one larger, louder Audio Source. Naturally, this approach affects the quality of the user experience, since it would appear that the sound is coming from a single source and not multiple sources, and so it should be used with care.

Minimize Audio Clip references

Each Audio Source in the Scene with a reference to an Audio Clip with **Preload Audio Data** enabled will consume a certain amount of memory for the Audio Clip (compressed, decompressed, or buffered, depending on **Load Type**) throughout the entire length of the given Scene. The exception to this rule is if two or more Audio Sources reference the same Audio Clip, in which case no additional memory is consumed as all of the Audio Sources are referencing the same location in memory and reading from it on an as-needed basis.

Audio Clips are unmanaged resources within Unity, which means they will not be released from memory merely by setting all references to `null`. Unity expects us to load and release these resources ourselves, creating and releasing them from memory as-needed. Keeping files in memory for long periods is reasonable for frequently used sound effects, since loading a file into memory every time it is requested would cost us some measure of CPU use.

However, if we find that we are using too much memory from these frequently used sound effects, then we must make the difficult choice of either reducing their quality or removing them entirely, to find memory savings. Removing sound effects completely is not necessarily a bad option. We might be able to achieve a unique sound effect by reusing existing sound effects combined with special effects and filters.

On the other hand, keeping infrequently used sound effects in memory for the length of a Scene can pose a significant problem. We might have many one-time-only sound effects, such as dialog clips, where there is little reason to keep them in memory just for the one unique moment they are needed. Creating Audio Sources with assigned Audio Clips (in their `AudioClip` property) will generate such references, and cause excess memory consumption even if we only use them for a single moment during gameplay.

The solution is to make use of `Resources.Load()` and `Resources.UnloadAsset()` to keep the audio data in memory only for as long as it is being played, and then immediately release it once it is no longer needed. The following code sample will achieve this effect in the simplest manner possible (tracking only a single Audio Source and Audio Clip) using our `SingletonAsComponent` class, just to give us an idea of what such a system might look like:

```
using UnityEngine;
using System.Collections;
using System.Collections.Generic;

public class AudioSystem : SingletonAsComponent<AudioSystem> {

    [SerializeField] AudioSource _source;

    AudioClip _loadedResource;

    public static AudioSystem Instance {
        get { return ((AudioSystem)_Instance); }
        set { _Instance = value; }
    }

    public void PlaySound(string resourceName) {
        _loadedResource = Resources.Load (resourceName) as
        AudioClip;
        _source.PlayOneShot (_loadedResource);
    }

    void Update() {
        if (!_source.isPlaying && _loadedResource != null) {
            Resources.UnloadAsset(_loadedResource);
            _loadedResource = null;
        }
    }
}
```

This class can be tested with the following Component, which loads a sound file when the *A* key is pressed:

```
public class AudioSystemTest : MonoBehaviour {
    void Update() {
        if (Input.GetKeyDown(KeyCode.A)) {
            AudioSystem.Instance.PlaySound("TestSound");
        }
    }
}
```

 Note that, to test this code, an audio file named `TestSound` must be placed within a folder named `Resources` in order for Unity to find it at runtime.

Using this approach to play sound effects, we should note that memory for the sound is only allocated when it is played, and then immediately freed when the sound effect ends. Once again, multiple audio tools in the Unity Asset Store provide this feature, but the `AudioSystem` class can be expanded to handle multiple Audio Sources and Audio Clips fairly easily if we wish to customize the solution.

Enable Force to Mono for 3D sounds

Enabling the **Force to Mono** setting on a stereo Audio File will mix it together with the channels into a single channel, saving 50 percent of the file's total disk and memory space usage. Enabling this option is generally not a good idea for some 2D sound effects where the stereo effect is often used to create a certain audio experience. But we can enable this option for some good space savings on 3D sound effects, where being a stereo source is generally meaningless, and 2D sounds where the stereo effect isn't important.

Resample to lower frequencies

Resampling imported audio files to lower frequencies will reduce the file size and runtime memory footprint. This can be achieved through an Audio Clip's **Sample Rate Setting** and **Sample Rate** properties. Some files require high sample rates to sound reasonable, such as files with high pitches and modern music files. However, lower settings can reduce the file's size without much noticeable quality degradation in most cases. `22050 Hz` is a common value for sources that involve human speech and classical music. Some sound effects may be able to get away with even lower frequency values. But, each sound effect will be affected by this setting in a unique way, so it would be wise to spend some time doing some testing before we finalize our decision on sampling rate.

Consider all encoding formats

If memory and hard disk consumption are not a burden on our application, then the WAV format can be used to reduce CPU costs at runtime, due to having a smaller overhead required to decode the data during each playback. Meanwhile, if we have CPU cycles to spare, we can save space with compressed encoding.

Beware of streaming

Streaming files from disk should be restricted to large, single-instance files only, as it requires runtime hard disk access; one of the slowest forms of data access available to us. Layered or transitioning music clips may run into major hiccups using this method, at which point it would be wise to consider the `Resources.Load()` approach. We should also avoid streaming more than one file at a time as it likely to inflict a lot of cache misses on the disk that interrupt gameplay.

Apply Filter effects through Mixer groups to reduce duplication

Filter effects are additional Components that we can attach to an Audio Source to modify sound playback. Each individual Filter effect will cost some amount of both memory and CPU, and attaching duplicates to many Audio Sources in our Scene can result in dire consequences if they're used too frequently. A better approach is to make use of Unity's Audio Mixer utility to generate common templates that multiple Audio Sources can reference to minimize the amount of memory overhead.

The official tutorial on Audio Mixers covers the topic in excellent detail:

```
https://unity3d.com/learn/tutorials/modules/beginner/5-pre-order-
beta/audiomixer-and-audiomixer-groups
```

Use "WWW.audioClip" responsibly

Unity's `WWW` class can be used to stream game content in via the Web. But, accessing a `WWW` object's `audioClip` property will allocate a whole new Audio Clip resource each time it is invoked, and similarly with other `WWW` resource-acquiring methods. This resource must be freed with the `Resources.UnloadAsset()` method once it is no longer required.

Discarding the reference (setting it to `null`) will not automatically free the resource, so it will continue to consume memory. Ergo, we should only obtain the Audio Clip through the `audioClip` property once to obtain the resource reference, use only that reference from that point forward, and release it when it is no longer required.

Consider Audio Module files for background music

Audio Module files, also known as Tracker Modules, are an excellent means of saving a significant amount of space without any noticeable quality loss. Supported file extensions in Unity are .it, .s3m, .xm, and .mod. Unlike the common PCM audio formats, which are read as bit streams of data that must be decoded at runtime to generate a specific sound, Tracker Modules contain lots of small, high-quality PCM samples and organize the entire track similar to a music sheet; defining when, where, how loud, with what pitch, and with what special effects each sample should be played with. This can provide significant size savings, while maintaining high-quality sampling. So, if the opportunity is available to us to make use of Tracker Module versions of our music files, then it is worth exploring.

Texture files

The terms "Texture" and "Sprite" often get confused in game development, so it's worth making the distinction that in Unity 3D a **Texture** is simply an image file; a big list of *color* data telling the interpreting program what color each pixel of the image should be. Whereas a Sprite is the 2D equivalent of a mesh, which just happens to be a single quad that renders flat against the current camera. There are also things called Sprite Sheets, which are large collections of individual images contained within a larger Texture file, commonly used to contain the animations of a 2D character. These files can be split apart by Unity's Sprite Batch tool, to form individual Textures for the animation frames.

Let's try to ignore all of these confusing naming convention overlaps, and simply talk about Textures: the image files we're importing into our application that were generated in tools such as Adobe Photoshop or Gimp. At runtime, these files are loaded into memory, pushed to the GPU, and rendered by the Shader over the target object during a given Draw Call.

Compression formats

Much like Audio files, Unity provides us with a variety of compression techniques to store our Texture files more efficiently. When a Texture file is imported, there are several settings that we can manipulate. The first is **Texture Type**. This setting does not affect the file itself, but rather how Unity will interpret, manipulate, and compress it within the final executable we build.

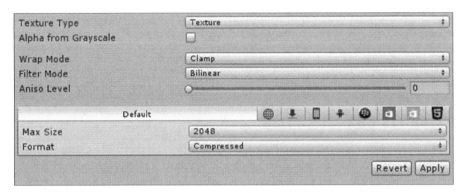

With most of the **Texture Type** options, the only three compression options Unity exposes to us are **Compressed, 16-bit**, and **True Color**. Alternatively, if we set the **Texture Type** to **Advanced**, then we expose a larger number of settings. This gives us far more control over the interpretation of the Texture file.

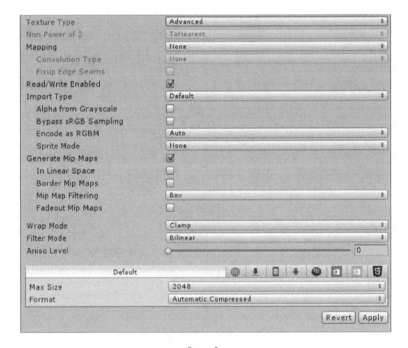

This will be useful information going forward as there are several performance-enhancing opportunities to find through this particular view of a Texture file, which would not be visible ordinarily.

The number of compression formats in **Advanced** mode are significantly more broad and varied, but the options remain identical between Unity 4 and Unity 5. Some formats allow alpha values, whereas some do not, which restricts our choices if we wish to maintain alpha transparency in our Texture (or a fourth float data value from a Texture being used as a Heightmap!).

Some formats also cost different levels of performance during Scene initialization to decompress and push into the GPU, which can vary enormously depending on the platform we're targeting and the chosen format. **Advanced** mode provides the **Automatic Compressed** option, which tries to pick the best option for the given platform and device. We can use this option if we're not completely sure about the best format for our game, or we can spend the time to do some performance-testing with different formats to confirm the best choice(s) for the target device.

Note that the Preview Window at the bottom of the **Inspector** View provides some useful statistics to help us determine how effectively the currently selected compression method is behaving.

Texture performance enhancements

Let's explore some changes we can make to our Texture files, which might help improve performance, depending on the situation and the content of the files we're importing. In each case, we'll explore the changes that need to be made, and the overall effect they have, whether this results in a positive or negative impact on memory or CPU, an increase or decrease in the Texture quality, and under what conditions we can expect to make use of these techniques.

Also, because the Unity 5 Personal Edition has made multiple features available to us that were previously only available in the Pro Edition, some users may not be aware of some additional techniques that we can apply to our Textures to improve application performance. So, we will also cover some of these techniques toward the end of this section.

Reduce Texture file size

The larger a given Texture file, the more GPU memory bandwidth will be consumed pushing the Texture when it is needed. If the total memory pushed per second exceeds the graphics card's total memory bandwidth, then we will have a bottleneck as the GPU waits for all Textures to be loaded before the next rendering pass can begin. Smaller Textures are naturally easier to push through the pipeline than larger Textures, so we need to find a good middle ground between high quality and performance.

A common test to find out if we're bottlenecked in memory bandwidth is to simply reduce the resolution of our game's most abundant and largest Texture files and relaunch the Scene. If the frame rate suddenly improves, then the application was most likely bound by the Texture throughput. If the frame rate does not improve or improves very little, then either we still have some memory bandwidth to make use of, or there are bottlenecks elsewhere in the rendering pipeline preventing us from seeing any further improvement.

Use Mip Maps wisely

There would be no point rendering small, distant objects such as rocks and trees with a high-detail Texture if there's no way the player would ever be able to see that detail, or if the performance loss is too great to warrant a minor detail increase. Mip Maps were invented as a way to solve this problem (as well as helping eliminate aliasing problems that were plaguing video games at around the same time), by pregenerating lower-resolution alternatives of the same Texture and keeping them together in the same memory space. At runtime, the GPU picks the appropriate Mip Map option based on how large the surface appears within the perspective view (essentially based on the texel-to-pixel ratio when the object is rendered), and then picks an appropriately scaled Mip Map of the Texture.

By enabling the **Generate Mip Maps** option, Unity automatically handles the generation of these lower-resolution copies of the Texture. These alternatives are generated using high-quality resampling and filtering methods within the Editor, rather than at runtime.

The following image shows how a 1024x1024 image will be Mip Mapped into multiple lower-resolution duplicates:

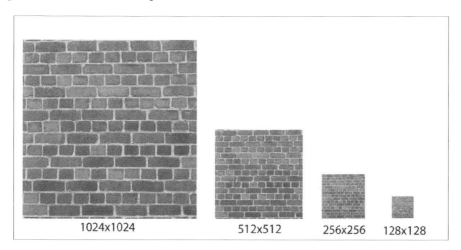

The downside to Mip Mapping is that it has a negative impact on file size and loading time due to the larger combined Texture files that are being automatically generated. The final Texture file will be around 33 percent larger when Mip Mapping is enabled. There are also some situations where the Mip Mapping process is a waste of effort, so we should examine some of our Texture files to see if Mip Maps are being applied wisely.

Mip Mapping is only useful if we have Textures that need to be rendered at varying distances from the camera. If we have Textures that always rendered at a similar distance from the main camera, such that the Mip Mapped alternatives are never used, then enabling Mip Maps is just wasting space. In these cases, we should disable the Mip Mapping feature by disabling the **Generate Mip Maps** option for the Texture.

If only a single Mip Map alternative is used, then we should consider disabling Mip Mapping and downscaling the resolution of the original Texture file.

Additional candidates for disabling the Mip Mapping feature are:

- Almost any Texture file used in a 2D game
- User Interface (GUI) Textures
- Textures for meshes, Sprites, and Particle Effects, which always render near the camera—examples include the player characters themselves, any objects they hold or carry, and any Particle Effects which always center around the player

Manage resolution downscaling externally

Unity puts a lot of effort into making things as easy to use as possible and provides us with the ability to place the project files from external tools to our Project workspace, such as PSD and TIFF files, which are often large and split into multiple layered images. Unity automatically generates a Texture file from the file's contents for the rest of the Engine to make use of, which can be very convenient, as we only need to maintain a single copy of the file through Source Control and the Unity copy is automatically updated when an artist makes changes.

The problem is that the aliasing introduced by Unity's auto-Texture generation and compression techniques from these files may not be as robust and efficient as the tools we use to generate such files, such as Adobe Photoshop or Gimp. Unity may be introducing **artefacts** through aliasing, and we might find ourselves getting into the habit of importing image files with a higher resolution than necessary, just to keep the intended quality level. But, had we downscaled the image through the external application first, we might suffer much less aliasing. In these cases, we may have been able to achieve an acceptable level of quality with a lower resolution, while consuming less overall disk and memory space.

We can either avoid using PSD and TIFF files within our Unity project as a matter of habit (storing them elsewhere and importing the downscaled version into Unity), or just perform some occasional testing to ensure we're not wasting file size, memory, and GPU memory bandwidth using larger resolution files than necessary. This costs us some convenience in project file management, but can provide some significant savings for some Textures, if we're willing to spend the time comparing the different downscaled versions.

Adjust Anisotropic Filtering levels

Anisotropic Filtering is a feature which improves the image quality of Textures when they are viewed at very shallow (oblique) angles. The following screenshot shows the classic example of painted lines on a road with and without Anisotropic Filtering applied. Without Anisotropic Filtering, the painted lines appear blurry and distorted the further they are away from the camera, whereas the view with Anisotropic Filtering applied makes these lines more crisp and clear.

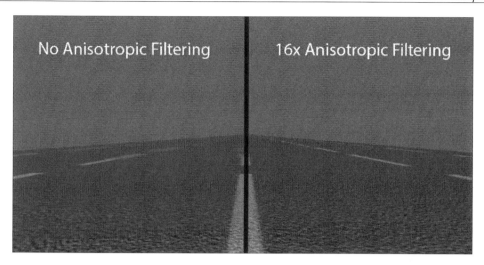

The strength of Anisotropic Filtering applied to the Texture can be hand-modified on a per-Texture basis with the **Aniso Level** setting as well as globally enabled/disabled using the **Anisotropic Textures** option within the **Quality Settings** screen.

Much like Mip Mapping, this effect can be costly and sometimes unnecessary. If there are Textures in our Scene where we are certain will never be viewed at an oblique angle (such as distant background sprites and particle-effect Textures), then we can safely disable Anisotropic Filtering for them to save some runtime overhead. We can also consider adjusting the strength of the Anisotropic Filtering effect on a per-Texture basis to find the magic spot between quality and performance.

Consider Atlasing

Atlasing is the technique of combining lots of smaller, isolated Textures together into a single-large Texture file in order to minimize the number of Materials, and hence Draw Calls, we need to apply by exploiting Dynamic Batching. Conceptually, this technique is very similar to the approaches of minimizing Material usage you learned in *Chapter 3, The Benefits of Batching*.

Each unique Material would require an additional Draw Call, but each Material only supports a single primary Texture (this excludes Normal Maps, Emission Maps, and other secondary Textures). By combining all Textures into a single colossal Texture, we can minimize the number of Draw Calls used to render objects that share this Texture:

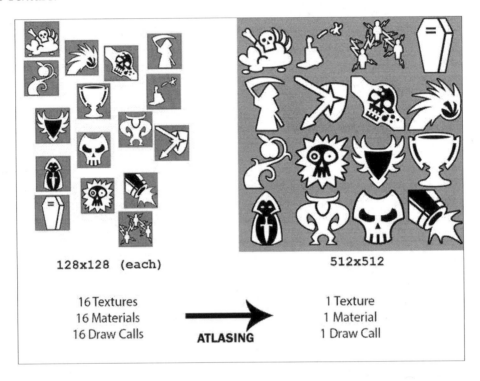

The benefits are clear; reducing Draw Calls results in reducing the CPU workload and improving the frame rate if our application is CPU-bound (or simply frees up cycles for other tasks). There will be no loss of quality, and memory consumption will be essentially identical. All we're doing is exploiting Unity's Dynamic Batching system to reduce Draw Calls. Note that Atlasing does not result in reduced memory bandwidth consumption, since the amount of data being pushed is identical. It just happens to be bundled together in one bigger Texture file.

Atlasing is only an option when all of the given Textures require the same Shader. If some of the Textures need unique graphical effects applied through Shaders, then they must either be isolated into their own Materials or Atlased with other Textures, which use the same Shader.

Atlasing is a common tactic applied to User Interface elements, and in games that feature a lot of 2D graphics. Atlasing becomes practically essential when developing mobile games with Unity, since Draw Calls tend to be the most common bottleneck on those platforms. But, we would not want to generate these atlas files manually. Life would be much simpler if we could continue to edit our Textures individually, and automate the task of combining them into a larger file.

Many GUI-related tools in the Unity Asset Store provide an automated Texture-atlasing feature, there are some standalone programs scattered across the Internet, which can handle this work, and Unity itself provided a built-in Sprite Packer tool with the new UI system in version 4.6, which can be easily customized to pack Textures in different ways.

Check the Unity documentation to discover more about this useful feature, if interested:

```
http://docs.unity3d.com/Manual/SpritePacker.html
```

Either way, it is recommended to make use of an existing solution for atlas generation in order to avoid reinventing the wheel.

 Note that Textures must be defined as the **Sprite** type in order to be recognized and packed by the Sprite Packer tool.

Atlasing does not need to apply to 2D graphics and UI elements either. We can apply this technique to 3D meshes if we happen to be creating a lot of low-resolution Textures. 3D games that feature simple Texture resolutions, or a flat-shaded low-poly art style, are ideal candidates for Atlasing in this way.

However, because Dynamic Batching only affects non-animated meshes (that is, Mesh Renderers, and not Skinned Mesh Renderers), there is no reason to combine Texture files for animated characters into an atlas. Since they are animated, the GPU needs to multiply each object's bones by the transform of the current animation state. This means a unique calculation is needed for each character, and they will result in an extra Draw Call regardless of any attempts we make to have them share Materials.

As a result, combining Textures for animated characters should only be done as a matter of convenience and space-saving; for example, in a flat-shaded low-poly art style game, where everything happens to use a common color palette, we can make some significant space savings by using a single Texture for the entire game world, objects, and characters.

The disadvantages of Atlasing are mostly in terms of development time and workflow costs. It requires a lot of effort to overhaul an existing project to make use of Atlasing, which can be a lot of work just to figure out if it is worth the effort or not. In addition, we need to beware of generating atlas files, which are too large for the target platform.

Some devices (specifically mobile devices) have a relatively low limit on the size of Textures that can be pulled into the lowest memory cache of the GPU. If the atlas is too large, then it must be broken up into smaller Textures, to fit the target memory space. If the renderer happens to need Textures from different pieces of the atlas every other Draw Call, then not only will we inflict a lot of cache misses, but also we might find that we choke the memory bandwidth as Textures are constantly pulled from VRAM and the lower-level cache.

We would probably not have this problem if the atlas was left as individual Textures. The same Texture swapping would occur, but will result in much smaller files being swapped at the cost of additional Draw Calls. Our best options at this stage would be to lower the atlas resolution or generate multiple smaller atlases to have better control over how they will be Dynamically Batched.

So, Atlasing is clearly not a perfect solution. If it is not clear whether it would result in a performance benefit, then we should be careful not to waste too much time on implementation.

In general, we should attempt to apply Atlasing to mid-range/high-quality Mobile games right from the start of the project, keeping within the Texture limit for the target platform, making per-platform and per-device adjustments as necessary. On the other hand, the simplest Mobile games will most likely function without needing any Atlasing.

Meanwhile, we should consider applying Atlasing to high-quality Desktop games, only if our Draw Call count exceeds reasonable hardware expectations, since we will want many of our Textures to maintain high resolutions for maximum quality. Low-quality Desktop games can probably afford to avoid Atlasing, since Draw Calls are unlikely to be the biggest bottleneck.

Of course, no matter what the product is, if we're ever CPU-bound by Draw Calls and we've already exhausted many of the alternative techniques, then Atlasing would be the next best technique to implement, as it can result in some impressive Draw Call savings when used properly.

Adjust compression rates for non-square Textures

It is not recommend to import non-square and/or non-power-of-2 Textures into our application, because GPUs often require the pushed Texture to be square, and a power-of-2 size results in unnecessary workload dealing with malformed Texture sizes. Unity will automatically adjust the Texture and add additional empty space in order to fit the form factor that the GPU expects, which will result in additional memory bandwidth costs, pushing what is essentially useless data to the GPU.

So, the first recommendation is to avoid non-square and/or non-power-of-2 Textures altogether. If the image can be placed within a square, power-of-2 Texture, and does not result in too much quality degradation due to squeezing/stretching, then we should apply those changes just to keep the CPU and GPU happy.

However, if we still want to use non-square Textures, there is a trick we can apply to achieve higher quality without costing any additional space. Since the way non-square Textures are packed by compression algorithms, we can often increase the bit-rate (and hence quality) of the chosen compression format for a non-square Texture and still achieve an identical imported file size and runtime overhead cost. This only costs us the time it takes to find these Textures and test a variety of compression algorithms to find the highest quality version.

Sparse Textures

Sparse Textures, also known as Mega-Textures or Tiled-Textures, provide a way of effectively streaming Texture data from disk at runtime. Relatively speaking, if the CPU performs operations in the order of seconds, then the disk will operate in the order of days. So common advice is that hard disk access during gameplay should be avoided at all costs, since any such technique risks inflicting more disk access than available, causing our application to grind to a halt.

But, Sparse Texturing breaks this rule and offers some interesting performance saving techniques. The aim of Sparse Texturing is to combine many Textures into an enormous Texture file, which would be far too large to load into graphics memory as a single Texture file. This is similar to the concept of Atlasing, except the file containing the Textures is incredibly large (for example, 32,768 x 32,768 resolution) and contains considerable detail (32 bits per pixel). The idea is to save large amounts of runtime memory and memory bandwidth by hand-picking small subsections of the Texture dynamically, and pull them from the disk just before they are needed in the game. The main cost of this technique is the file size requirement (the example resolution file would consume 4 GB of disk space!). Other costs for this technique can be overcome with a great deal of Scene preparation work.

The game world needs to be created in such a way that it minimizes the amount of Texture swapping taking place. In order to avoid jarring, "texture popping" problems, Texture subsections must be pulled from a disk with just enough time to spare that the player does not notice. This takes place in the design of the Texture file itself, by keeping common elements for a given Scene in the same general area of the Texture, and the design of the Scene, by triggering new Texture subsection loading at key moments during gameplay. If it is handled with great care and attention to detail, then Sparse Texturing can result in some impressive Scene quality and equally impressive memory savings.

Sparse Texturing was previously a Pro Edition-only feature in Unity 4, but was made available with the Personal Edition of Unity 5. Sparse Texturing requires specialized hardware and platform support, however, so this option is not available to all games. It is a highly specialized and uncommon technique within the gaming industry, which is reflected in the lack of documentation. The Unity documentation does not provide much information on Sparse Texturing, but it does provide an example Scene showing the effect at work. It can be found at the following URL: `http://docs.unity3d.com/Manual/SparseTextures.html`.

For Unity developers who consider themselves advanced enough to figure it out on their own, it might be worth taking the time to perform some research to see if Sparse Texturing is right for their project and whether they are willing to make the appropriate Scene changes necessary to gain the performance benefits that this feature presents.

Procedural Materials

Also known as Substances, Procedural Materials are a means of procedurally generating Textures at runtime by combining small, high-quality Texture samples with custom mathematical formulas. The goal of Procedural Materials is to greatly minimize the application footprint at the cost of additional runtime memory and CPU processing during initialization. Like Sparse Texturing, this feature was previously only available in the Pro Edition of Unity 4 and is now available in Unity 5.

This gives many users an opportunity to view their Materials from a different perspective, as Procedural Materials are a more modern approach to their games. Texture files are often the biggest disk space consumer of a game project, and it's fairly common knowledge that download times have a tremendous negative impact on the completed download rate and just getting people to try our game (even if it's free!). Procedural Materials offer us the ability to sacrifice some initialization and runtime processing power for much faster downloads. This is very important for an upcoming generation of Mobile games that are trying to compete via graphical fidelity.

The Unity documentation on Procedural Materials is far more extensive than for Sparse Texturing, so it is recommended to work through the documentation for a clearer picture of how Substances work and how they can provide us with performance benefits:

```
http://docs.unity3d.com/Manual/ProceduralMaterials.html
```

Mesh and animation files

Finally, let's cover mesh and animation files. These file types are essentially large arrays of vertex and skinned bone data, and there are a variety of techniques we can apply to minimize file size, while keeping a similar, if not identical, appearance. There are also sometimes ways to lower the cost of rendering large groups of these objects through batching techniques. Let's look into a series of performance-enhancing techniques we can apply to such files.

Reducing polygon count

This is the most obvious way to gain performance, but we should never disregard it. In fact, since we cannot batch objects using Skinned Mesh Renderers, it's one of the only good ways of reducing CPU and GPU runtime overhead for animated objects.

Reducing the polygon count is simple, straightforward, and provides both CPU and memory cost savings for the time required for artists to clean up the mesh. Much of an object's detail is provided almost entirely by detailed Texturing and complex Shading in this day and age, so we can often get away with stripping away a lot of vertices on modern meshes and most users would be unable to tell the difference.

Tweaking Mesh Compression

Unity offers four different **Mesh Compression** settings for imported mesh files: **Off**, **Low**, **Medium**, and **High**. Increasing this setting will strip away more and more parts of the mesh that Unity thinks aren't needed in order to make a good estimate of the same mesh with the aim of reducing overall file size. This is essentially an automated version of having an artist manually reducing the polygon count.

However, automated mesh optimization is a very difficult problem to solve mathematically and even the best algorithms tend to generate a lot of artefacts and irregularities. Different levels of **Mesh Compression** can be attempted as a quick solution to reducing polygon count, but it will probably never compare to having an artist make appropriate polycount reductions by hand.

These 3D tools often provide their own built-in ways of automated mesh optimization, and should be tested as a means of optimizing the mesh before importing them into Unity.

Use Read-Write Enabled appropriately

The **Read-Write Enabled** flag allows changes to be made to the mesh at runtime either via Scripting or automatically by Unity during runtime. Internally, this means it will keep the original mesh data in memory until we want to duplicate it and make changes dynamically. Disabling this option will allow Unity to discard the original mesh data from memory once it has determined the final mesh to use.

If we only ever use a uniformly scaled version of a mesh throughout the entire game, then disabling this option will save runtime memory since we will no longer need the original mesh data to make further rescaled duplicates of the mesh (incidentally, this is how Unity organizes objects by scale factor when it comes to Dynamic Batching). Unity can, therefore, discard this unwanted data early since we will never need it again until the next time the application is launched.

However, if the mesh often reappears at runtime with different scales, then Unity needs to keep this data in memory so that it can recalculate a new mesh more quickly, and so the **Read-Write Enabled** flag should be enabled. Disabling it will require Unity to not only reload the mesh data, but also make the rescaled duplicate at the same time, causing a potential performance hiccup.

Unity tries to detect the correct behavior for this setting at initialization time, but when meshes are instantiated and scaled in a dynamic fashion at runtime, then we must force the issue by enabling this setting. This will improve instantiation speed of the objects, but cost some memory overhead since the original mesh data is kept around until it's needed.

Note that this also applies when using the **Generate Colliders** option.

Import/calculate only what's needed

This appears to be another obvious suggestion, but meshes do not only contain vertex positional data. There could be unnecessary **Normals** and **Tangents** in our mesh that the Shaders won't need, or we could be autogenerating **Normal** and **Tangent** coordinates that we won't use, particularly when the **Smoothing Angle** is very low. In these cases, each vertex requires multiple normal vectors to create the faceted, flat-shading style that results from it.

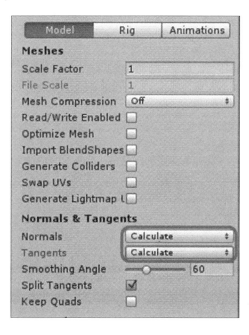

Double-check your mesh import settings and examine the resultant file size and in-game appearance, by tinkering with the import settings to see if you can make any savings by stripping away unwanted and unnecessary data.

Consider baked animations

This will depend on the 3D rigging and animation tool that we are using, and the overall vertex count of our mesh; in some cases baking animations can result in much smaller file sizes and memory overhead than blended/skinned animations. Baked animations work by storing a keyframed position for each vertex for each frame that was sampled, and if the mesh's polygon count is low enough, then we may see some significant savings through this simple change.

In addition, how often the baked sample is taken can usually be customized by the exporting application. Different sample rates should be tested to find a good value where the key moments of the animation still shine-through what is essentially a simplified estimate.

Let Unity optimize meshes

The **Optimize Meshes** option in a mesh's import settings will reorganize the vertex data for quicker readability, and sometimes regenerate the low-level rendering style (down to the level of points versus tris versus strips) to optimize the rendering speed of the mesh. Simply put, this option should be enabled in almost all cases, as there is very little reason to not let Unity make these adjustments for us, unless we've done some profiling and we're positive that it's somehow generating bottlenecks.

If we're generating meshes procedurally, then we can tell Unity to invoke this process using the `Optimize()` method on a Mesh Filter Component. This process can take some time, so it should be used during initialization or other convenient stopping point.

Combine meshes

Combining meshes into a large, single mesh can be convenient to reduce Draw Calls if the meshes are too large for Dynamic Batching and don't play well with other Statically Batched groups. This is essentially the equivalent of Static Batching, but performed manually, so sometimes it's wasted effort if Static Batching could take care of the process for us.

However, if we're using the Unity 4 Free Edition where Static Batching is not available to us or we wish the mesh to move around the Scene, then this is a good option to minimize our Draw Calls. Beware that it comes with the same risk as Static Batching. If any single vertex of the mesh is visible in the Scene, then the entire object will be rendered together as one whole. This can lead to a lot of wasted processing if the mesh is only partially visible most of the time.

This technique also comes with the drawback that it generates a whole new mesh asset file that we must deposit into our Scene, which means any changes we make to the original meshes will not be reflected in the combined one. This results in a lot of tedious workflow effort every time changes need to be made, so if Static Batching is an option, it should be used instead.

There are several tools available online, which can combine mesh files together for us in Unity. They are only an Asset Store search, or Google search away.

Summary

There are many different opportunities that we can explore to achieve performance gains for our application just by tinkering with our imported assets. Or, from another perspective, there are plenty of ways to ruin our application's performance through asset mismanagement.

Almost every single opportunity is a trade-off between one performance metric or workflow task and another. So, we must remain vigilant and only pick the right techniques in the right projects for the right reasons. The worst thing we can do is implement such changes without understanding the impact. It's exciting to stumble on some big performance enhancing suggestion out in the big, wide world, but unless we understand how it works, and the resulting costs, we can invite further performance problems and bottlenecks without realizing it, costing us more time and effort down the road.

This concludes our exploration of improving performance through art asset manipulation. In the next chapter, we will be investigating the Box2D and PhysX physics solutions provided by Unity, the changes we can make to our script code, Scene, and project to make these components process our data faster; and behavior to avoid that might cause them to stumble.

5
Faster Physics

Each of the performance-enhancing suggestions we've explored thus far have been primarily centered on reducing system requirements and avoiding frame rate issues. But at its most fundamental level, seeking peak performance means improving the user experience. This is because every frame rate hiccup, every crash, and every system requirement that is too costly for a given market ultimately detracts from the quality of the product, and leaves us wondering whether we should have tried harder to tweak settings and fix more bugs before release.

There are certainly opportunities to manipulate Physics Engine behavior that improve all of the aforementioned issues, but Physics Engines also fall into a unique category of having a direct impact on gameplay quality. If important gameplay collision events get missed (such as the player falling through the floor), or the game freezes while it calculates a complex situation, then these have a significant impact on gameplay quality. This often results in pulling the player out of the experience, and it's a coin-toss whether the user finds it inconvenient, obnoxious, or hilarious. Unless our game is specifically targeting the Comedy Physics genre (which, incidentally, has grown in popularity in recent years with games like QWOP and Goat Simulator), these are situations we should strive to avoid.

For some games, the Physics Engine is used to handle a significant number of tasks during gameplay, from collision detection with other objects and invisible trigger boxes to raycasting and gathering a list of objects in a given region. For example, it is essential in platformer and action games to tune the physics properly; how the player character reacts to input and how the world reacts to the player character can be two of the most important aspects of what makes the game feel responsive and fun. Other games may only use physics for simple gameplay events, interesting spectacles, and other eye-candy, but the more efficiently the Physics System is used, the more of a spectacle that can be created.

Therefore, in this chapter, we will not only cover ways to reduce CPU spikes, overhead, and memory consumption through Unity's Physics System, but also include ways to alter physics behavior with the aim of improving gameplay quality. In addition, because Unity's Physics Systems are a "black-box", in that we can't do much internal debugging, it can be very tricky to figure out exactly when, where, and why certain physics glitches are plaguing our project, and what we should do to prevent them. As a result, the methods covered in this chapter will include several suggestions on how to reduce instability and problematic physics situations.

Physics Engine internals

Unity technically features two different Physics Engines: Nvidia PhysX for 3D physics and the Open Source project Box2D for 2D physics. However, their implementation is highly abstracted, and from the perspective of the Unity API, both engines operate in a nearly identical fashion.

In either case, the more we understand about Unity's Physics System, the more sense we can make of possible performance enhancements. So, first we'll cover some theory about Unity's Physics Engines.

Physics and time

Physics Engines generally operate under the assumption that time is iterating in fixed values of time, and both of Unity's Physics Engines operate in this manner. The Physics Engine will only calculate using very specific values of time, independent of how much time it took to render the previous frame. This is known as the **Fixed Update Timestep**, and it is set to a value of 20 milliseconds by default, or 50 updates per second.

 It can be very difficult to generate consistent results for collisions and forces between two different computers if a Physics Engine uses a variable timestep. Such engines tend to generate inconsistent results between multiplayer clients, and during recorded replays.

If too much time has passed between frames (a low frame rate), then the Physics System may update multiple times before rendering begins again. Conversely, if not enough time has passed since the previous render (a high frame rate), then the physics update may be skipped until after the next render call.

The `FixedUpdate()` method represents the moment when the Physics System performs simulation timestep updates. It is one of several important Unity callbacks we can define in a MonoBehaviour script and, in general, `FixedUpdate()` is used to define frame-rate-independent behavior. This callback is usually used for calculations such as artificial intelligence (which are also easier to work with if we assume a fixed update frequency), but this is also where we should modify Rigidbody objects during gameplay.

The following diagram shows an important snippet of the Unity Order of Execution diagram:

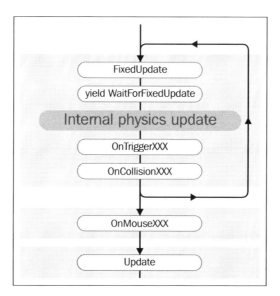

 The full Order of Execution diagram can be found at: `http://docs.unity3d.com/Manual/ExecutionOrder.html`.

The Fixed Update loop

As we can see, `FixedUpdate()` is invoked just prior to the Physics System performing its own update and the two are inextricably linked. The process begins with determining whether enough time has passed to begin the next Fixed Update. The outcome will vary depending on how much time has passed since the last Fixed Update.

If enough time has passed, then the `FixedUpdate()` method is invoked globally, and any Coroutines tied to Fixed Updates (that is, yields to `WaitForFixedUpdate()`) are handled immediately afterward, followed by physics updates and trigger/collider callbacks.

If less than 20 ms has gone by since the last Fixed Update, then the current Fixed Update is skipped. At this point, input, gameplay logic, and rendering must take place and complete before Unity performs the next Fixed Update check, and so on, as this process repeats itself during runtime. This design gives both Fixed Updates and the Physics System a higher priority over rendering, but forces the physics simulation into a fixed frame rate.

> In order to ensure smooth motion during frames where physics updates are skipped, some Physics Engines (including Unity's) interpolate the state between the previous state and the current state based on how much time remains until the next Fixed Update.
>
> This ensures that, graphically, objects appear to move smoothly during high frame rates, even though they are only being updated every 20 ms.

Maximum Allowed Timestep

It is important to note that if a lot of time has passed since the last Fixed Update (for example, the game froze momentarily), then physics and Fixed Updates will continue to be calculated until they have "caught up" with the current time. For example, if the previous frame took 100 ms to render (for example, a sudden performance spike dropping the game to 10 FPS), then the Physics System will need to update five times. The `FixedUpdate()` method will therefore be called five times before `Update()` can be called again due to the default Fixed Update Timestep of 20 ms. If, for whatever reason, the processing of these five updates consumes 20 ms or more, then it will need to invoke a sixth update!

Consequently, it's possible during moments of heavy physics activity that the Physics Engine can take more than 20 ms to complete a physics update, which itself takes another 20 ms, and so on, such that it is never able to escape and allow another frame to render (this is often known as the "spiral of death"). To prevent the Physics Engine from locking up our game during these moments, there is a maximum amount of time that the Physics Engine is allowed to process between each render. This threshold is called the **Maximum Allowed Timestep**, and if the current Fixed Update is taking longer to process than this value, then it will simply stop and forgo further processing until the end of the next render. This design allows the rendering system to at least render the current state, and allow for gameplay logic to make some decisions during rare moments where physics calculation has gone ballistic (pun intended).

Physics updates and runtime changes

When the Physics System processes the next timestep, it must move any active Rigidbody objects, detect any collision, and invoke the collision callbacks on the corresponding objects. It's for exactly this reason that the Unity documentation explicitly warns us to only make changes to Rigidbody objects in `FixedUpdate()` and other physics callbacks. These methods are tightly-coupled with the update frequency of the Physics Engine, as opposed to other parts of the game loop, such as `Update()`.

This means that callbacks such as `OnTriggerEnter()` are safe places to make Rigidbody changes, while methods such as `Update()` and time-based Coroutines are not. Not following this advice could cause unexpected physics behavior as multiple changes are made to the same object before the Physics System is given a chance to catch and process all of them, resulting in some especially confusing gameplay bugs.

It logically follows that the more time we spend in any given Fixed Update iteration, the less time we have for the next gameplay and rendering pass. Most of the time this results in minor, unnoticeable background processing tasks, as the Physics Engine barely has any work to do, and `FixedUpdate()` callbacks have a lot of time to complete their work.

But, in some games, the Physics Engine could be performing a lot of calculations during each and every Fixed Update. This kind of bottlenecking in physics processing time will affect our rendering frame rate, causing it to plummet as the Physics System is tasked with greater and greater workloads. Essentially, the rendering system will proceed as normal, but whenever it's time for a Fixed Update, then it would be given very little time to generate the current display, causing a sudden stutter. This is in addition to the visual effect of the Physics System stopping early because it hit the Maximum Allowed Timestep. All of this together will generate a poor user experience.

Hence, to keep a smooth and consistent frame rate, the goal is to free up as much time as we can for rendering by minimizing the amount of time the Physics System takes to process any given timestep. This applies in both the best-case scenario (nothing moving) and worst-case scenario (everything smashing into everything else at once). There are a number of time-related features and values we can tweak within the Physics System to avoid performance pitfalls such as these.

Static and Dynamic Colliders

There is a rather significant namespace conflict with the term "static" in Unity. We have already covered static GameObjects, the various Static subflags, the Static Batching feature, and then there's the use of static variables and classes in C#. Meanwhile, Unity's original physics implementation for 3D objects has its own concept of Static Colliders. Later, when 2D physics was implemented, it kept the same concept of Static Colliders to keep things consistent between them.

So, with this in mind it is very important to remember that Static Colliders are not objects with the Static flag enabled, since those flags are a Unity Engine concept. Static Colliders are simply colliders that do not have an attached Rigidbody. Meanwhile, colliders with an attached Rigidbody are called Dynamic Colliders.

The Physics System combines Static Colliders into a different, optimized data structure, which helps to simplify future processing tasks. These objects will not react to impulses applied by objects colliding with them, but will prevent other objects from moving through them. This makes Static Colliders ideal for world barriers and other obstacles that must not move.

Collision detection

There are three settings for collision detection in Unity: **Discrete**, **Continuous**, and **ContinuousDynamic**. The **Discrete** setting effectively teleports objects a small distance every timestep based on their velocity and how much time has passed. After all the objects have been moved, it then performs a bounding-volume check for any overlaps, treats them as collisions, and resolves them based on their physical properties and how they overlap. This method risks collisions being missed if small objects are moving too quickly.

Both of the continuous collision detection methods work by interpolating objects from their starting and ending positions for the current timestep and checking for any collisions along the way. This reduces the risk of missed collisions and generates a more accurate simulation, at the expense of significantly greater CPU overhead compared to the **Discrete** setting.

The **Continuous** setting only enables continuous collision detection between the given collider and Static Colliders (recall that Static Colliders are simply colliders without any attached Rigidbody). The same objects will be simultaneously treated as using the **Discrete** setting when it comes to collision detection with other dynamic objects (those with an attached Rigidbody). Meanwhile, the **ContinuousDynamic** setting is slightly different as it enables the same continuous collision detection, but does so between the given collider and all other colliders, both Static and Dynamic.

The following screenshot shows how the discrete and continuous collision detection methods would work for a pair of small, fast-moving objects:

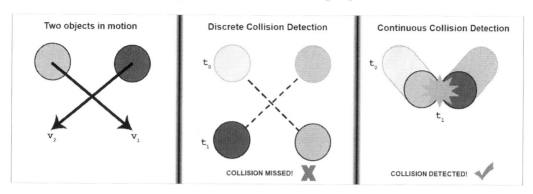

This is an extreme example for the sake of illustration. In the discrete case, we can see that the objects are "teleporting" a distance around four times their own size in a single timestep, which would typically only happen with very small objects with very high velocities, and is hence very rare if our game is running optimally. In most cases, the distances the objects travel in a single 20 ms timestep are much smaller relative to the size of the object, and so the collision is easily detected.

Collider types

There are five different types of 3D Colliders in Unity 5. In order of the lowest performance cost to the greatest, they are: **Sphere**, **Capsule**, **Cylinder**, **Box**, and **Mesh** Colliders. The first four collider types are considered primitives and maintain consistent shapes, although they can generally be scaled in different directions to meet certain needs. Meanwhile Mesh Colliders can be customized to a particular shape depending on the assigned mesh.

There are also three main 2D Colliders: **Circle**, **Box**, and **Polygon**, which are functionally similar to Sphere, Box, and Mesh Colliders in 3D. All of the following information is essentially transferable to the equivalent 2D shape.

In addition, there are two varieties of Mesh Collider: convex and concave. The difference is that a concave shape features at least one *internal* angle (an angle between two edges inside the shape) of greater than 180 degrees. To illustrate this, the following screenshot shows the distinguishing difference between convex and concave shapes:

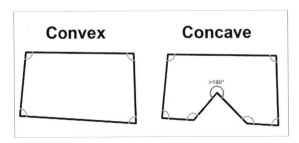

[An easy way to remember the difference between convex and concave shapes is that a concave shape has at least one "cave" within it.]

Both Mesh Collider types use the same Component (a Mesh Collider!), and which type of Mesh Collider gets generated is toggled using the **Convex** checkbox. Enabling this option will allow the object to collide with other Mesh Colliders marked as **Convex**, as well as primitive shapes (Spheres, Boxes, and so on.). In addition, if the **Convex** checkbox is enabled for a Mesh Collider with a concave shape, then the Physics System will automatically simplify the concave shape, generating a collider with the nearest convex shape it can. In the preceding example, if we import the concave mesh on the right, and enable the **Convex** checkbox, it would generate a collider shape closer to the convex mesh on the left.

In either case, the Physics System will attempt to generate a collider that matches the shape of the attached mesh, with an upper limit of 255 vertices. If the target mesh has more vertices than this, then it will throw an error during generation of the mesh. Note that Concave Mesh Colliders with attached Rigidbody objects are not supported in Unity 5. Concave shapes can only be used as Static Colliders (for example, a collidable object in the world that doesn't move), or Trigger Volumes (for example, an oddly-shaped pool of acid).

The Collision Matrix

The Physics System features a Collision Matrix that defines which objects are allowed to collide with which other objects. Objects that do not fit this matrix are automatically ignored by the Physics System when the time comes to resolve bounding volume overlaps and collisions. This saves on physics processing during collision detection stages, and also allows the objects to move through one another without any collisions taking place.

The Collision Matrix system works through Unity's Layer system. The matrix represents every possible layer-to-layer combination that might be possible, and enabling a checkbox means that colliders in both of those layers will be checked during the collision detection phase. Note that there's no way to allow only one of the two objects to respond to the collision. If one layer can collide with another, then they must both respond to the collision (with the exception of Static Colliders, which aren't allowed to respond to collisions).

The Collision Matrix can be accessed through **Edit | Project Settings | Physics** (or **Physics2D**) **| Layer Collision Matrix**.

Note that we are limited to only 32 total layers for our entire project (since the Physics System uses a 32-bit bitmask to determine inter-layer collision opportunities), so we must organize our objects into sensible layers that will extend throughout the entire lifetime of the project. If, for whatever reason, 32 layers are not enough for our project, then we might need to find cunning ways to reuse layers, or remove layers that aren't necessary.

Rigidbody active and sleeping states

Every modern Physics Engine shares a common optimization technique whereby objects that have come to rest have their internal state changed from an active state to a sleeping state. While sleeping, little-to-no processor time will be spent updating the object until it has been awoken by some external force or event.

The value of measurement that is used to determine "rest" tends to vary between engines; it could be calculated using linear and rotational speed, kinetic energy, momentum, or some other physical property of the Rigidbody. In any case, if an object has not exceeded some threshold value in a short time, then the Physics Engine will assume the object will no longer need to move again until it has undergone a new collision, or a new force has been applied to it. Until then, the sleeping object will maintain its current position.

In essence, the Physics Engine is automatically culling some processing tasks for objects that have a small amount of kinetic energy. But this does not remove it entirely from the simulation. If a moving Rigidbody approaches the sleeping object, then it must still perform checks to see whether nearby objects have collided with it, which would reawaken the sleeping object, reintroducing it to the simulation for processing. The threshold value for the sleeping state can be modified under **Edit | Project Settings | Physics | Sleep Threshold**. We can also get a count of the total number of active Rigidbody objects from the Physics area of the Profiler.

Ray and object casting

Another common feature of Physics Engines is the ability to "cast" a ray from one point to another, and gather data about one or more of the objects in its path. It is pretty common to implement important gameplay tasks through casting and bounding-volume checks. Firing guns is typically implemented by performing raycasts from the player to the target location and finding any viable targets in its path (even if it's just a wall).

We can also obtain a list of targets within an explosion radius, such as from a grenade or fireball, using a `Physics.OverlapSphere()` check, and so this is typically how such area-of-effect abilities are implemented.

We can even cast entire objects forward in space, using `Physics.SphereCast()` and `Physics.CapsuleCast()`. These methods are often used if we need rays of larger sizes, or we wish to see what would be in the path of a moving character.

Physics performance optimizations

Now that we have an understanding of the most significant features of the Unity Physics Engine, we can cover some optimization techniques to improve our game's physics performance.

Scene setup

Firstly, there are a number of best practices we can apply to our Scenes to improve consistency of the physics simulation. Note that these techniques will not necessarily improve CPU or memory usage, but they will result in a reduced likelihood of instability from the Physics Engine.

Scaling

We should try to keep all physics object scales in the world as close to 1:1:1 as we possibly can. This means that for the default gravity value of -9.81, the unit scale of the world is implied to be 1 meter per unit, since the force of gravity at the surface of the Earth is 9.81 m/s^2 (most games are trying to simulate this situation). Our object sizes should reflect our implied world scale, since scaling them too large will cause gravity to appear to move the objects much more slowly than we would expect. The converse is also true; scaling objects too small will make them appear to fall too quickly and will not seem realistic.

We can tweak the world's implied scale by modifying the strength of gravity under **Edit** | **Project Settings** | **Physics** (or **Physics2D**) | **Gravity**. However, be aware that any floating-point arithmetic will be more accurate with values closer to 0, so if we have some objects that have scale values far above (1,1,1), even if they match the implied world-scale, then we could still observe erratic physics behavior. So, early in the project we should import and scale our most common physics objects around a scale value of (1,1,1), and then adjust the value of gravity to match. This will give us a reference point to work with as we introduce new objects.

 Be warned that Unity 4 also has a value for **Speed of Sound** in its **Audio** settings, which is used during any Doppler-based audio effects. The default value is 343 to match the speed of sound in air of 343 ms^{-1}. Changing the implied world scale via gravity will require this value to be adjusted to maintain consistency. Unity 5 calculates the Doppler Effect differently and so this variable was removed, no longer making this issue a concern.

Positioning

Similarly, keeping all objects close to (0,0,0) in position will result in better floating-point accuracy, improving the consistency of the simulation. Space Simulator and Free-Running games try to simulate incredibly large spaces, and they typically use this technique as much as possible by secretly teleporting, (or simply keeping) the player character centered in the world. At this point, either everything else is moved to simulate travel, or volumes of space are compartmentalized so that physics calculations are always calculated with values close to zero. This ensures that all objects remain close to (0,0,0) in order to avoid floating-point inaccuracies as the player travels great distances.

Other types of games should not risk introducing floating-point inaccuracy, so unless we're already deep into our project (such that changing and re-testing everything at a late stage would be too much hassle), we should try to keep all of our physics objects close to (0,0,0). Plus, this is simply good practice for our project workflow as it makes it much faster to add and position objects in our game world.

Mass

The Unity documentation recommends that object mass values stay around 0.1, with no values exceeding 10, due to the instability it generates: `http://docs.unity3d.com/ScriptReference/Rigidbody-mass.html`.

This means we should not think of mass in terms of measurements such as pounds or kilograms, but rather a relative value between objects. We should try to maintain consistent and reasonable ratios of mass between colliding objects. Having objects colliding with a mass ratio of greater than 1,000 will most certainly result in erratic behavior due to the large momentum difference and eventual loss of floating point precision. We should try to ensure inter-object collisions occur with objects with similar values of their mass property, and object pairs that have a significant scale difference should be culled with the Collision Matrix (more on this shortly).

 Improper mass ratios are the most common cause for physics instability and erratic behavior.

Note that the force of gravity at the centre of the Earth affects all objects equally, regardless of their mass, so it does not matter if we consider a mass property value of 1 to be the mass of a rubber ball or the mass of a warship. There's no need to adjust the force of gravity to compensate for any assumptions we're making with these relative mass property values. What does matter, however, is the amount of air resistance the given object undergoes while falling (this is why a feather falls slower than a solid object of identical mass). So, to maintain realistic behavior, we may need to customize the drag property for such objects or customize the force of gravity on a per-object basis (such as disabling the **Use Gravity** checkbox and applying a custom gravitational force via Script code).

Use Static Colliders appropriately

As previously mentioned, the Physics System automatically generates a data structure from the data of all Static Colliders (colliders without Rigidbody objects) separately from the structure that manages Dynamic Colliders (colliders with Rigidbody objects). Unfortunately, if new objects are introduced into the data structure at runtime, then it must be regenerated. This is likely to cause a significant CPU spike. This makes it vital that we avoid instantiating new Static Colliders during gameplay.

In addition, merely *moving*, *rotating*, or *scaling* Static Colliders also triggers this regeneration process and should be avoided. If we have colliders that we wish to move around without reacting to other objects colliding with them in a physical way, then we should attach a Rigidbody to make it a Dynamic Collider and set the **Kinematic** flag to `true`. This flag prevents the object from reacting to external impulses from inter-object collisions. This allows it to behave similar to a Static Collider, but it is now in a data structure that properly supports moving objects, so we can move it around from Script code (during Fixed Updates!), and it will apply impulses to other objects.

 It's for this reason that the **Kinematic** flag is often used on objects controlled by players; they can push other objects around but shouldn't be pushed around themselves.

Optimize the Collision Matrix

As we know, the Physics System's Collision Matrix defines which objects assigned to certain layers are allowed to collide with objects assigned to other layers. Or to put it more succinctly, which object pairs are even *considered* by the Physics System. Every other object-layer-pair is simply ignored by the Physics Engine, which makes this an important avenue for minimizing Physics Engine workload since it reduces the number of bounding-volume checks that must be performed at each and every timestep.

 Reminder: the Collision Matrix can be accessed through **Edit | Project Settings | Physics** (or **Physics2D**) | **Layer Collision Matrix**.

The following screenshot shows a common Collision Matrix for an arcade shooter game:

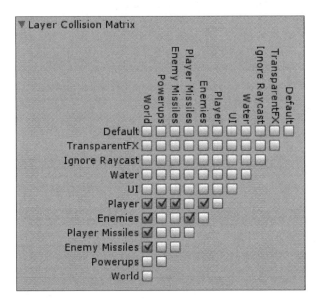

In this example, we have minimized the number of possible inter-object collisions for the Physics System to check. Since powerups can only be picked up by the player, then there is no need to compare collisions between powerups and objects from any other layers. Meanwhile, we don't wish for projectiles to collide with the object that fired it, which excludes Enemy Projectiles from colliding with enemies, and Player Projectiles from colliding with the player. We want everything to collide with the game world (walls and other surfaces), and perhaps we don't want projectiles colliding with other projectiles (although some games might want this!).

We should perform logical sanity checks like this for all of the Layer combinations in the Collision Matrix to see whether we're wasting precious time checking for inter-object collisions between object-pairs that aren't necessary.

Prefer discrete collision detection

We should use the **Discrete** option by default for the majority of objects. Teleporting objects once and performing a single overlap check between nearby object-pairs is a fairly trivial amount of work. However, the amount of calculation it takes to interpolate the objects between their starting and ending positions, and simultaneously verify any slight bounding-volume overlaps between these points over time, is significantly greater.

Consequently, the **Continuous** collision detection option is an order of magnitude more expensive than the **Discrete** detection method, and the **ContinuousDynamic** collision detection setting is an order of magnitude more expensive than **Continuous**! Having too many objects of the continuous types will cause serious performance degradation in complex Scenes. In either case, the costs are multiplied by the number of objects that need to be compared during any given frame and whether or not the comparison collider is Static or Dynamic.

Ergo, the continuous detection settings should only be used in extreme circumstances. The **Continuous** setting should be used when important collisions are frequently missed with the static world, for instance, if we expect certain objects to move quickly, and we wish to be certain they never fall through the game world or teleport through walls. Finally, the **ContinuousDynamic** setting should only be used if the same situation applies but we wish to catch collisions between pairs of very-fast moving Dynamic Colliders. Unless we have good reason to use them, all other situations should favor the **Discrete** setting.

But, perhaps, the **Discrete** setting isn't working well-enough on a large scale. Perhaps our entire game revolves around a lot of small physics objects and discrete collision detection simply isn't catching enough collisions to maintain product quality. Well, we're in luck, because we can customize the physics timestep to give the **Discrete** collision option a better chance of catching such collisions by modifying how frequently the engine checks for Fixed Updates.

Modify the FixedUpdate frequency

As mentioned previously, Fixed Updates and physics timestep processing are strongly-coupled, so by modifying the frequency of Fixed Update checks we not only change the frequency that the Physics System will calculate and resolve the next callback, but we will also change how frequently `FixedUpdate()` callbacks are being invoked. Consequently, changing this value can be risky if we're deep into our project and have a lot of behavior that depends on these callbacks.

Altering the `FixedUpdate` frequency can be accomplished through the **Edit | Project Settings | Time | Fixed Timestep** property in the Editor, or through the `Time.fixedDeltaTime` property in script code.

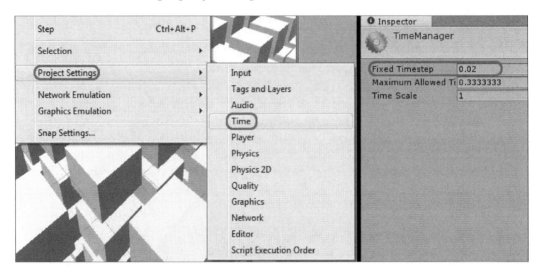

Reducing this value (increasing the frequency) will force the Physics System to process more frequently, giving it a better chance of catching collisions between our Dynamic, Discrete objects. Naturally, this comes with a CPU cost since we're invoking more `FixedUpdate()` callbacks, as well as asking the Physics Engine to update more frequently, having it move objects and verify collisions more often.

Conversely, increasing this value (decreasing the frequency) provides more time for the CPU to complete other tasks before it must handle physics processing again, or looking at it from another perspective, giving the Physics System more time to process the last timestep before it begins processing the next one. But, lowering the `FixedUpdate` frequency would essentially lower the maximum velocity at which objects can be moving before the Physics System can no longer capture collisions between discrete objects (depending on the objects' sizes).

This makes it absolutely vital to perform a significant amount of testing each time the **Fixed Timestep** value is changed. Even with a complete understanding of how this value works, it is difficult to predict what the overall outcome will look like during gameplay, and whether the result is passable for quality purposes. Hence, changes to this value should be made early in the project's lifecycle and then made infrequently in order to get a sufficient amount of testing against as many physics situations as possible.

It might help to create a test Scene that flings some of our high-velocity objects at one another to see if the results are acceptable, and run through this Scene whenever **Fixed Timestep** changes are made. But actual gameplay tends to be rather complex, with many background tasks and unanticipated player behavior that causes additional work for the Physics System, or gives it less time to process the current iteration. Actual gameplay conditions are difficult to duplicate in a vacuum, and there's no substitute for the real thing, so the more testing we can accomplish against the current value of **Fixed Timestep**, the more confident we can be that the changes meet acceptable quality standards.

We always have the continuous collision detection options as a last resort to offset some of the resulting instability we're observing. But unfortunately, even if the changes are targeted, it is more likely that this will cause further performance issues than we started with due to the overhead costs of continuous collision detection. It would be wise to profile our Scene before and after enabling continuous collision detection to verify that the benefits are outweighing the costs.

Adjust the Maximum Allowed Timestep

If the Maximum Allowed Timestep value gets hit regularly, then it will result in some pretty bizarre-looking physics behavior. Rigidbody objects will appear to slow down or freeze in space, since the Physics Engine needs to keep exiting early before it has fully resolved its entire time quota. In this case, it is a clear sign that we need to optimize our physics from other angles. But at the very least we can be confident the threshold will prevent the game from completely locking up during a physics processing spike.

This setting can be accessed through **Edit | Project Settings | Time | Maximum Allowed Timestep**. The default setting is to consume a maximum of **0.333** seconds, which would manifest itself as a very noticeable drop in frame rate (a mere 3 FPS) if it were breached. If we ever feel the need to change this setting, then we obviously have some big problems with our physics workload, so it is recommended to only tweak this value if we have exhausted all other approaches.

Minimize cast and bounding-volume checks

All of the raycasting methods are incredibly useful, but they are relatively expensive (particularly `CapsuleCast()` and `SphereCast()`), requiring us to minimize how often they are called. We should avoid calling these methods regularly within Update callbacks or Coroutines, saving them only for key events in our script code.

If we absolutely must rely on persistent line, ray, or area-of-effect collision areas in our Scene (examples include security lasers, or continuously burning fires), then they would be better simulated using a simple Trigger Collider, rather than performing continuous raycasting or overlap checks.

If such replacements are not possible, and we truly need persistent casting checks using these methods (such as a red-dot laser sight), then we can minimize the amount of processing each call makes by exploiting the LayerMask objects.

For example, a lazy raycast would look like so:

```
[SerializeField] float _maxRaycastDistance;

void PerformRaycast() {
    RaycastHit hitInfo = new RaycastHit();
      if (Physics.Raycast(new Ray(transform.position, transform.
          forward), out hit, _maxRaycastDistance)) {
        // handle raycast result here
      }
}
```

But this overload of Physics.Raycast() will cause the ray to collide with the first object of any layer in its path. The Physics.Raycast method has multiple overloads that accept a LayerMask object for an argument. We can use this to customize which objects should be checked by the raycast, simplifying the workload for the Physics Engine:

```
[SerializeField] float _maxRaycastDistance;
[SerializeField] LayerMask _layerMask;

void PerformRaycast() {
    RaycastHit hitInfo = new RaycastHit();
      if (Physics.Raycast(new Ray(transform.position, transform.
          forward), out hit, _maxRaycastDistance, _layerMask)) {
        // handle raycast result here
      }
}
```

The `LayerMask` object can then be configured through the object's **Inspector** view:

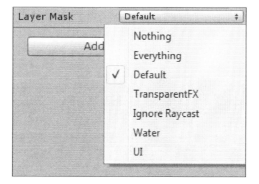

Note that, because the `RaycastHit` and `Ray` classes are managed by the native memory space of the Unity Engine, they don't result in memory allocations that draw the attention of the Garbage Collector. We will learn more about such activity in *Chapter 7, Masterful Memory Management*.

Avoid complex Mesh Colliders

In order of efficiency, the various colliders are: Spheres, Capsules, Cylinders, Boxes, Convex Mesh Colliders, and finally Concave Mesh Colliders. However, the four main primitives are an order of magnitude more efficient than either of the Mesh Colliders, as the mathematical calculations for detecting and resolving collisions between them are fairly succinct and optimized. Performing comparisons between a convex shape and another collider can be a costly process, while comparing between a concave shape and anything else is even more expensive.

Performing runtime bounding-volume checks between pairs of *concave* shapes is perhaps the closest thing to "Mathematical Armageddon" that we might find in a real-time physics simulation (at least for a few more years!). To protect us from our own stupidity, Unity effectively bans us from performing concave-to-concave Mesh Collider bounding volume checks.

A great irony between physics and graphics in 3D applications is how difficult it is to handle spherical and box objects between the two of them. The perfect spherical mesh would require an infinite number of polygons to generate, but how a sphere is represented in a Physics Engine is relatively trivial to resolve for contact points and collisions. Conversely, a simple box takes a miniscule number of polygons and effort to produce graphically, and yet takes significantly more mathematics and processing power to find contact points and resolve collisions for. This implies that getting the most out of both graphics and physics would be to populate our world with low-polygon graphical objects, represented as spheres within the Physics System. However, this would make absolutely no sense to a human observer as they witness sharp, pointy objects rolling around like balls.

It is always important to remember when working with Physics Engines that the physical representation of an object does not necessarily need to match its graphical representation. This is beneficial as a graphical mesh can often be condensed down into a much simpler shape, generating a very similar physics behavior and sparing us the need to use an overly-complex Mesh Collider.

This separation of representations between graphics and physics allows us to optimize the performance of one system without (necessarily) negatively affecting the other. If there would be no noticeable repercussions on gameplay, then we are free to represent complex graphical objects with the simplest physics shapes behind-the-scenes. If the player never notices, then no harm is done!

So, we can solve this problem in one of two ways: either by approximating the physics behavior of the complex shape using one (or more) of the standard primitives, or a using a much simpler Mesh Collider.

Use simpler primitives

Most shapes can be approximated using one of the four primitive colliders (in order of efficiency): Spheres, Capsules, Cylinders, or Boxes. In fact, we do not need to represent the object using only a single collider; we are free to use several colliders if it serves our needs for creating a complex collision shape by attaching additional child GameObjects with their own colliders. This is almost always less costly than using a single Mesh Collider and should be preferred over more complex solutions.

The following image shows a handful of complex graphical objects, represented by one or more simpler primitives in the Physics System:

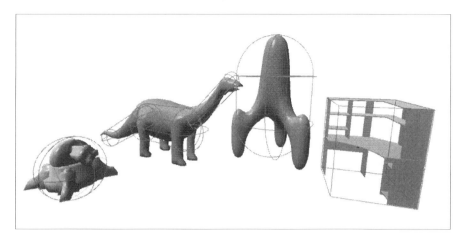

Using a Mesh Collider for any one of these objects would be significantly more costly than the primitive colliders shown here. It is worth exploring any and all opportunities to simplify our objects down using these primitives as much as we can, as they can provide significant performance gains.

For example, concave meshes are unique in that they can feature gaps, or holes, that allow other meshes to "fall" into, or even through them, which introduces opportunities for the objects to fall through the world if concave shapes are used for world collision areas. It is often better to place Box Colliders in strategic locations for this purpose.

Use simpler Mesh Colliders

The mesh assigned to the Mesh Collider does not necessarily need to match the graphical representation of the same object (Unity simply picks it as the default). This gives us an opportunity to replace the Mesh Collider's `mesh` property with a different, simpler mesh for an object's collider from the one we use for its graphical representation.

The following image shows an example of a complex graphical mesh that has been given a simplified mesh for its Mesh Collider:

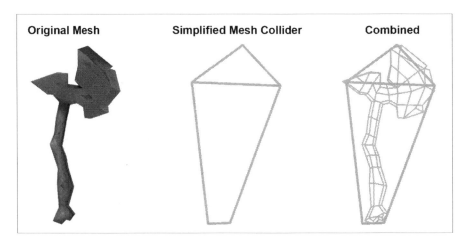

Simplifying the rendered mesh into convex shapes with lower polygon counts in this way will greatly reduce the overhead needed to determine bounding-volume overlaps with other colliders. Depending on how well the original object is estimated, there may be few to no noticeable gameplay differences, especially in the case of this axe, which we expect to be moving quickly as creatures swing it during attacks, making it unlikely that players will notice the difference between the two meshes as colliders.

Avoid complex physics components

Certain special physics Collider Components, such as Terrain, Cloth, and Wheel Colliders, are orders of magnitude more costly than all primitive colliders, and even Mesh Colliders in some cases. We should simply not include such Components in our Scenes unless they are absolutely necessary. For instance, if we have Terrain objects in the distance that the player will never approach, then there's little reason to include an attached Terrain Collider.

Games featuring Cloth Components should consider instantiating different objects without them when running in lower-quality settings, or simply animating cloth behavior (although it is totally understandable if the team has grown attached and fallen in love with how the stuff moves around).

Games using Wheel Colliders should simply try to use fewer wheel colliders! Vehicles with more than four wheels may be able to use only four wheels to generate the correct physics behavior, while faking the graphical representation of additional wheels.

Let physics objects sleep

The Physics Engine's sleep feature can pose several problems for our game.

 Reminder: the sleep threshold can be modified under **Edit** | **Project Settings** | **Physics** | **Sleep Threshold**.

Firstly, some developers don't realize that many of their Rigidbody objects are sleeping during most of the lifetime of their application. This tends to lead developers to assume that they can get away with (for example) doubling the number of Rigidbody objects in their game, and the costs will simply double to match it. This is unlikely. The frequency of collisions and total accumulated time of active objects is more likely to increase in an exponential fashion, rather than a linear one. This leads to unexpected performance costs when new physics objects are introduced into the simulation. We should keep this in mind when we decide to increase the physics complexity of our Scenes.

Secondly, there is the danger of "islands" of sleeping physics objects being generated. Islands are created when a large number of Rigidbody objects are touching one another, and have gradually come to rest—imagine a pile of boxes that have been spawned and formed a large pile. Eventually, all of the Rigidbody objects will fall asleep once enough energy in the system is lost and they all come to rest. However, because they're all still touching one another, as soon as one of these objects is awoken, it will start a chain reaction, awakening all other nearby Rigidbody objects. Suddenly we have a large spike in CPU usage because dozens of objects have now re-entered the simulation, and there are suddenly many more collisions to resolve until the objects fall asleep again.

If we could find a way to detect that islands are forming, we could strategically destroy/despawn some of them to prevent too many large islands from being generated. But workarounds such as these will be dependent upon the game itself, as performing regular, global checks, and distance comparisons between all of our Rigidbody objects is not a cheap task to accomplish. For example, a game that requires the player to move lots of physics objects into an area (for example, a game that involves herding sheep into a pen) could choose to despawn the Dynamic Collider object as soon as the player moves it into position, locking the object to its final destination, and easing the workload on the Physics Engine.

Thirdly, changing any of a Rigidbody's properties at runtime, such as **mass**, **drag**, **Use Gravity**, and so on, will also reawaken the object. If we're regularly changing these values (such as a game where object sizes and masses change over time), then they will remain active for longer periods of time than usual. This is also the case for applying forces, so if we're using a custom gravity solution (such as suggested back in the section entitled *Mass*), we should try to avoid applying the gravitational force every Fixed Update, otherwise the object will be unable to fall asleep.

Sleeping objects can be a blessing and a curse. They can save us a lot of processing power, but if too many of them reawaken at the same time or our simulation is too busy to allow enough of them to fall asleep, then we could be incurring some unfortunate performance costs during gameplay. We should strive to limit these situations as much as possible by letting our objects enter the sleeping state as much as possible, and avoid grouping them together in large clusters.

Modify Solver Iteration Count

Joints, Springs, and other connected Rigidbody objects are not trivial to simulate in the world of Physics Engines. Because of the co-dependent interactivity (internally represented as movement constraints) that occurs with joining two objects together, the system must often make several attempts at solving the necessary mathematical equations. This multi-iteration approach is required to calculate an accurate result whenever there is a change in velocity to any piece of the object-chain.

It therefore becomes a balancing act of limiting the maximum number of attempts the "Solver" makes to resolve a particular situation, versus how accurate a result we can get away with. We don't want the Solver to spend too much time on a single collision, because there is a lot of other work the Physics Engine has to do within the same iteration. But, we also don't want to reduce the maximum number of iterations too far as it will only approximate what the final solution would have been if it had been given more time to calculate the result.

The same Solver also gets involved when resolving inter-object collisions and contacts. It can almost always determine the correct result with a single iteration, with the exception of some very rare and complex collision situations. It is only when third-party objects will be affected through Joints that the Solver requires additional effort to mathematically integrate the final result.

The Solver Iteration Count can be modified under **Edit | Project Settings | Physics | Solver Iteration Count**. In most cases, the default value of six iterations (seven iterations in Unity 4) is perfectly acceptable. But, games that include very complex joint systems may wish to increase this count to suppress any erratic (or downright explosive) Character Joint behaviors, while some projects may be able to get away with reducing this count. Testing must be performed after changing this value to see whether the project still maintains the intended levels of quality.

Incidentally, if we find our game regularly runs into jarring, erratic, and physics-breaking situations with complex Joint-based objects (such as ragdolls), then we should consider gradually increasing the Solver Iteration Count until the problems have been suppressed. These problems typically occur if our ragdolls absorb too much energy from colliding objects and the Solver is unable to iterate the solution down to something reasonable before it is asked to give up. At this point, one of the Joints goes supernova, dragging the rest of them into orbit along with it!

We should also double check that our ragdoll's Rigidbody masses are obeying the rules set forth earlier in this chapter, so that the resultant energy exchange and velocities will be more reasonable.

Optimizing ragdolls

Speaking of Character Joints, ragdolls are incredibly popular features for good reason; they're tons of fun! Ignoring the morbidity of flinging corpses around a game world for the moment, there's something about watching a complex chain of objects flail around and smash into things that hits a lot of psychological "fun buttons".

This makes it very tempting to allow many ragdolls to coexist within our Scene at the same time, but as we quickly discover, this risks an enormous performance hit when too many ragdolls are in motion and/or collide with other objects due to the amount of iterations the Solver would need to resolve them all. So, let's explore some ways to improve the performance of any ragdolls we wish to use.

Reduce Joints and Colliders

Unity provides a simple ragdoll-generation tool under **GameObject | 3D Object | Ragdoll...** in Unity 5, or **GameObject | Create Other | Ragdoll...** in Unity 4. This tool can be used to create ragdolls from a given object by selecting the appropriate child objects to attach colliders to for any given body part or limb. This tool always creates 11 different colliders and associated Joints (pelvis, chest, head, and two colliders per limb), but we might wish to consider using only six colliders (body, head, and one collider per limb) to greatly reduce the overhead cost at the expense of ragdoll realism. This can be achieved by deleting unwanted colliders and reassigning the Character Joint's **Connected Body** properties to the proper parent joints.

Such simplifications could be implemented as a means of reducing overhead for weaker hardware/lower quality settings, as a simple compromise to allow more ragdolls to coexist in our Scene. It could even be used dynamically if a particular number of ragdolls are already present. A god class would need to keep track of how many ragdolls currently exist, but when new ragdolls are introduced, we could instantiate a simpler version in order to keep things running smoothly.

Avoid inter-ragdoll collisions

Unless we really desire inter-ragdoll collisions then we should perhaps disable them using the Collision Matrix. The performance cost of ragdolls grows exponentially when ragdolls collide with one another, since we would be asking the Solver to work extra hard and risking erratic behavior due to the approximations it is forced to make.

Disable or remove inactive ragdolls

Finally, we could consider disallowing ragdolls from re-entering the physics simulation after they have come to rest. In some games, once a ragdoll has reached its final "destination," we no longer need it to remain in the game world as an interactable object.

We can poll any given collider's sleep state with the `IsSleeping` method and, once it has reached this state, we have a number of options we can pursue. We could disable all of the ragdoll's colliders, preventing it from being reintroduced to the simulation, we could remove the ragdoll from the Scene for the sake of cleanup, or we could keep track of this ragdoll and only remove it when a different ragdoll has been introduced to the Scene.

Whatever approach we choose to improve the performance of our ragdolls will no doubt result in limiting ragdolls as a gameplay feature, either by instantiating fewer of them, giving them less complexity, or giving them a shorter lifetime, but these are reasonable compromises to make given the performance-saving opportunities.

Know when to use physics

As always, the best method of improving the performance of a feature is to avoid using it as much as possible. For all moveable objects in our game, we should take a moment to ask ourselves if getting the Physics Engine involved is even necessary. If not, we should look for opportunities to replace them with something simpler and less costly.

Perhaps we're using physics to detect whether the player fell into a kill-zone, but our game is simple enough that we only have kill-zones at a specific height. In this case, we could avoid physics colliders altogether and get away with only checking whether the player's *y* position falls below a particular value.

As another example, maybe we're trying to simulate a meteor shower, and our first instinct was to have many falling objects that move via physics Rigidbody objects, detect collisions with the ground via colliders, and then generate an explosion at the point of impact. But perhaps the ground is consistently flat or we have access to the Terrain's Height Map for some rudimentary collision detection. In this case, object travel could be simplified by tweening the objects' `transform.position` properties over time to simulate the same behavior without requiring any physics components. In both cases, we can reduce the physics overhead by simplifying the situation and pushing the work into Script code.

Tweening is a common short-hand term for in-betweening, which is the act of interpolating properties from one value to another mathematically over time. There are many useful (and free!) tweening libraries, available on the Unity Asset Store, that provide a lot of useful functionality.

The reverse is also possible; there might be occasions where we're performing a great deal of calculation through Script code that could be handled through physics relatively simply. For example, we might have implemented an inventory system with many objects that can be picked up. When the player hits the **Pick up** key, each of these objects might be compared against the player's position to figure out which object is closest. We could consider replacing all of the Script code with a single `Physics.OverlapSphere()` call to get nearby objects when the key is pressed, and then figure out the closest pickup object from the result (or just pick up all of them!). This could greatly reduce the total number of objects that must be compared each time the key is pressed.

The opportunities are as wide and far-reaching as our own ingenuity. The ability to recognize opportunities to remove unnecessary physics grunt-work from our Scenes, and/or use physics to replace behavior that is costly when performed through Script code, is a vital skill that will serve us well when saving performance in current and future game development projects.

Consider upgrading to Unity 5

If we're running Unity 4, an absolute last resort to improve physics performance would be to consider upgrading to Unity 5. There were a multitude of huge performance enhancements with Unity 5's upgrade from PhysX version 2.8.3 to version 3.3. These improvements cannot be overstated as they grant about double the performance of the Physics System as compared to Unity 4. The upgrade includes less overhead in moving Static Colliders, improved performance in continuous collision detection methods, support for more rigid bodies, improved Cloth and Wheel Collider components, as well as multicore physics support. In short, it allows us to reduce the performance cost of the same Scene, or cram more physics activity into our Scenes for the same cost.

However, these changes resulted in some significant API changes for certain tasks, which means Scripting and Components in Unity 4 may not be fully compatible with Unity 5 (and not just for physics-related tasks). Consequently, the upgrade itself is unlikely to be trivial, and we should not forget to make a backup of our project before attempting to do so. The amount of work will ultimately depend on the complexity of our project and how it affects any Asset Store purchases we rely on. Each asset is likely to need updates of its own and any assets that have fallen out of support will need to be replaced.

Summary

We've covered numerous methods to improve our game's physics simulation both in terms of performance, and consistency. The best technique when it comes to costly systems such as Physics Engines is simply avoidance. The less we need to use the system, the less we need to worry about it generating bottlenecks. In the worst case, we may need to reduce the scope of our game to condense physics activity down to only the essentials, but as we've learned, there are plenty of ways to reduce physics complexity without causing any noticeable gameplay effects.

In the next chapter, we will immerse ourselves in Unity's graphics system, discovering how to maximize graphical fidelity using all of the CPU cycles we've freed up using the performance enhancements from earlier chapters.

6

Dynamic Graphics

There is no question that the rendering system of modern graphics devices is complicated. Even rendering a single triangle to the screen engages many of these components, since GPUs are designed for large amounts of parallelism, as opposed to CPUs, which are designed to handle virtually any computational scenario. Modern graphics rendering is a high-speed dance of processing and memory management that spans software, hardware, multiple memory spaces, multiple languages, multiple processors, multiple processor types, and a large number of special-case features that can be thrown into the mix.

To make matters worse, every graphics situation we will come across is different in its own way. Running the same application against a different device, even by the same manufacturer, often results in an apples-versus-oranges comparison due to the different capabilities and functionality they provide. It can be difficult to determine where a bottleneck resides within such a complex chain of devices and systems, and it can take a lifetime of industry work in 3D graphics to have a strong intuition about the source of performance issues in modern graphics systems.

Thankfully, Profiling comes to the rescue once again. If we can gather data about each component, use multiple performance metrics for comparison, and tweak our Scenes to see how different graphics features affect their behavior, then we should have sufficient evidence to find the root cause of the issue and make appropriate changes. So in this chapter, you will learn how to gather the right data, dig just deep enough into the graphics system to find the true source of the problem, and explore various solutions to work around a given problem.

As you learned in earlier chapters, the CPU and GPU work in tandem to determine what textures, meshes, render states, Shaders, and so on, are needed to render our Scenes at any given moment. We've also covered several techniques to reduce some of the rendering workload through Static and Dynamic Batching, and by manipulating our mesh and texture files through compression and encoding, Mip Mapping, Atlasing, and even some procedural alternatives.

However, there are still many more topics to cover when it comes to improving rendering performance, so in this chapter we will begin with some general techniques on how to determine whether our rendering is limited by the CPU or by the GPU, and what we can do about either case. We will discuss optimization techniques such as Occlusion Culling and **Level Of Detail (LOD)** and provide some useful advice on Shader optimization, as well as large-scale rendering features such as lighting and shadows. Finally, since mobile devices are a common target for Unity projects, we will also cover some techniques that may help improve performance on limited hardware.

Profiling rendering issues

Poor rendering performance can manifest itself in a number of ways, depending on whether the device is **CPU-bound**, or **GPU-bound**; in the latter case, the root cause could originate from a number of places within the graphics pipeline. This can make the investigatory stage rather involved, but once the source of the bottleneck is discovered and the problem is resolved, we can expect significant improvements as small fixes tend to reap big rewards when it comes to the rendering subsystem.

We briefly touched upon the subject of being CPU/GPU-bound in *Chapter 3, The Benefits of Batching*. To summarize the earlier discussion, we know that the CPU sends rendering instructions through the graphics API, that funnel through the hardware driver to the GPU device, which results in commands entering the GPU's **Command Buffer**. These commands are processed by the massively parallel GPU system one by one until the buffer is empty. But there are a lot more nuances involved in this process.

The following shows a (greatly simplified) diagram of a typical GPU pipeline (which can vary based on technology and various optimizations), and the broad rendering steps that take place during each stage:

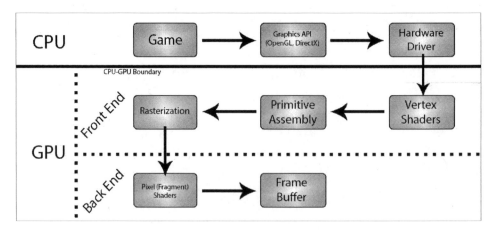

The top row represents the work that takes place on the CPU, the act of calling into the graphics API, through the hardware driver, and pushing commands into the GPU. Ergo, a CPU-bound application will be primarily limited by the complexity, or sheer number, of graphics API calls.

Meanwhile, a GPU-bound application will be limited by the GPU's ability to process those calls, and empty the Command Buffer in a reasonable timeframe to allow for the intended frame rate. This is represented in the next two rows, showing the steps taking place in the GPU. But, because of the device's complexity, they are often simplified into two different sections: the front end and the back end.

The front end refers to the part of the rendering process where the GPU has received mesh data, a draw call has been issued, and all of the information that was fed into the GPU is used to transform vertices and run through Vertex Shaders. Finally, the rasterizer generates a batch of fragments to be processed in the back end. The back end refers to the remainder of the GPU's processing stages, where fragments have been generated, and now they must be tested, manipulated, and drawn via Fragment Shaders onto the frame buffer in the form of pixels.

> Note that "Fragment Shader" is the more technically accurate term for Pixel Shaders. Fragments are generated by the rasterization stage, and only technically become pixels once they've been processed by the Shader and drawn to the Frame Buffer.

There are a number of different approaches we can use to determine where the root cause of a graphics rendering issue lies:

- Profiling the GPU with the Profiler
- Examining individual frames with the Frame Debugger
- Brute Force Culling

GPU profiling

Because graphics rendering involves both the CPU and GPU, we must examine the problem using both the **CPU Usage** and **GPU Usage** areas of the Profiler as this can tell us which component is working hardest.

For example, the following screenshot shows the Profiler data for a CPU-bound application. The test involved creating thousands of simple objects, with no batching techniques taking place. This resulted in an extremely large Draw Call count (around 15,000) for the CPU to process, but giving the GPU relatively little work to do due to the simplicity of the objects being rendered:

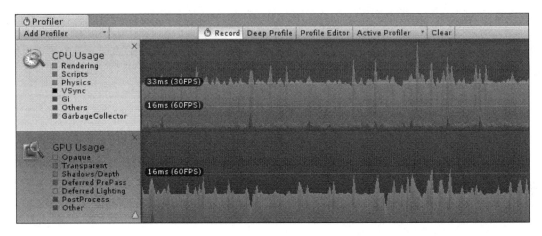

This example shows that the CPU's "rendering" task is consuming a large amount of cycles (around 30 ms per frame), while the GPU is only processing for less than 16 ms, indicating that the bottleneck resides in the CPU.

Meanwhile, Profiling a GPU-bound application via the Profiler is a little trickier. This time, the test involves creating a small number of high polycount objects (for a low Draw Call per vertex ratio), with dozens of real-time point lights and an excessively complex Shader with a texture, normal texture, heightmap, emission map, occlusion map, and so on, (for a high workload per pixel ratio).

The following screenshot shows Profiler data for the example Scene when it is run in a standalone application:

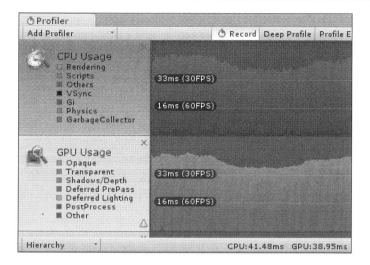

As we can see, the rendering task of the **CPU Usage** area matches closely with the total rendering costs of the **GPU Usage** area. We can also see that the CPU and GPU time costs at the bottom of the image are relatively similar (41.48 ms versus 38.95 ms). This is very unintuitive as we would expect the GPU to be working much harder than the CPU.

> Be aware that the CPU/GPU millisecond cost values are not calculated or revealed unless the appropriate Usage Area has been added to the Profiler window.

However, let's see what happens when we test the same exact Scene through the Editor:

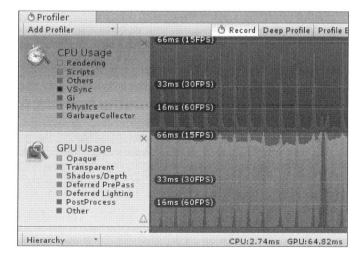

This is a better representation of what we would expect to see in a GPU-bound application. We can see how the CPU and GPU time costs at the bottom are closer to what we would expect to see (2.74 ms vs 64.82 ms).

However, this data is highly polluted. The spikes in the CPU and GPU Usage areas are the result of the Profiler Window UI updating during testing, and the overhead cost of running through the Editor is also artificially increasing the total GPU time cost.

It is unclear what causes the data to be treated this way, and this could certainly change in the future if enhancements are made to the Profiler in future versions of Unity, but it is useful to know this drawback.

 Trying to determine whether our application is truly GPU-bound is perhaps the only good excuse to perform a Profiler test through the Editor.

The Frame Debugger

A new feature in Unity 5 is the Frame Debugger, a debugging tool that can reveal how the Scene is rendered and pieced together, one Draw Call at a time. We can click through the list of Draw Calls and observe how the Scene is rendered up to that point in time. It also provides a lot of useful details for the selected Draw Call, such as the current render target (for example, the shadow map, the camera depth texture, the main camera, or other custom render targets), what the Draw Call did (drawing a mesh, drawing a static batch, drawing depth shadows, and so on), and what settings were used (texture data, vertex colors, baked lightmaps, directional lighting, and so on).

The following screenshot shows a Scene that is only being partially rendered due to the currently selected Draw Call within the Frame Debugger. Note the shadows that are visible from baked lightmaps that were rendered during an earlier pass before the object itself is rendered:

If we are bound by Draw Calls, then this tool can be effective in helping us figure out what the Draw Calls are being spent on, and determine whether there are any unnecessary Draw Calls that are not having an effect on the scene. This can help us come up with ways to reduce them, such as removing unnecessary objects or batching them somehow. We can also use this tool to observe how many additional Draw Calls are consumed by rendering features, such as shadows, transparent objects, and many more. This could help us, when we're creating multiple quality levels for our game, to decide what features to enable/disable under the low, medium, and high quality settings.

Brute force testing

If we're poring over our Profiling data, and we're still not sure we can determine the source of the problem, we can always try the brute force method: cull a specific activity from the Scene and see if it results in greatly increased performance. If a small change results in a big speed improvement, then we have a strong clue about where the bottleneck lies. There's no harm in this approach if we eliminate enough unknown variables to be sure the data is leading us in the right direction.

We will cover different ways to brute force test a particular issue in each of the upcoming sections.

CPU-bound

If our application is CPU-bound, then we will observe a generally poor FPS value within the **CPU Usage** area of the Profiler window due to the rendering task. However, if **VSync** is enabled the data will often get muddied up with large spikes representing pauses as the CPU waits for the screen refresh rate to come around before pushing the current frame buffer. So, we should make sure to disable the **VSync** block in the **CPU Usage** area before deciding the CPU is the problem.

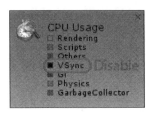

Brute-forcing a test for CPU-bounding can be achieved by reducing Draw Calls. This is a little unintuitive since, presumably, we've already been reducing our Draw Calls to a minimum through techniques such as Static and Dynamic Batching, Atlasing, and so forth. This would mean we have very limited scope for reducing them further.

What we can do, however, is disable the Draw-Call-saving features such as batching and observe if the situation gets significantly worse than it already is. If so, then we have evidence that we're either already, or very close to being, CPU-bound. At this point, we should see whether we can re-enable these features and disable rendering for a few choice objects (preferably those with low complexity to reduce Draw Calls without over-simplifying the rendering of our scene). If this results in a significant performance improvement then, unless we can find further opportunities for batching and mesh combining, we may be faced with the unfortunate option of removing objects from our scene as the only means of becoming performant again.

There are some additional opportunities for Draw Call reduction, including Occlusion Culling, tweaking our Lighting and Shadowing, and modifying our Shaders. These will be explained in the following sections.

However, Unity's rendering system can be multithreaded, depending on the targeted platform, which version of Unity we're running, and various settings, and this can affect how the graphics subsystem is being bottlenecked by the CPU, and slightly changes the definition of what being CPU-bound means.

Multithreaded rendering

Multithreaded rendering was first introduced in Unity v3.5 in February 2012, and enabled by default on multicore systems that could handle the workload; at the time, this was only PC, Mac, and Xbox 360. Gradually, more devices were added to this list, and since Unity v5.0, all major platforms now enable multithreaded rendering by default (and possibly some builds of Unity 4).

Mobile devices were also starting to feature more powerful CPUs that could support this feature. Android multithreaded rendering (introduced in Unity v4.3) can be enabled through a checkbox under **Platform Settings | Other Settings | Multithreaded Rendering**. Multithreaded rendering on iOS can be enabled by configuring the application to make use of the Apple Metal API (introduced in Unity v4.6.3), under **Player Settings | Other Settings | Graphics API**.

When multithreaded rendering is enabled, tasks that must go through the rendering API (OpenGL, DirectX, or Metal), are handed over from the main thread to a "worker thread". The worker thread's purpose is to undertake the heavy workload that it takes to push rendering commands through the graphics API and driver, to get the rendering instructions into the GPU's Command Buffer. This can save an enormous number of CPU cycles for the main thread, where the overwhelming majority of other CPU tasks take place. This means that we free up extra cycles for the majority of the engine to process physics, script code, and so on.

Incidentally, the mechanism by which the main thread notifies the worker thread of tasks operates in a very similar way to the Command Buffer that exists on the GPU, except that the commands are much more high-level, with instructions like "render this object, with this Material, using this Shader", or "draw *N* instances of this piece of procedural geometry", and so on. This feature has been exposed in Unity 5 to allow developers to take direct control of the rendering subsystem from C# code. This customization is not as powerful as having direct API access, but it is a step in the right direction for Unity developers to implement unique graphical effects.

 Confusingly, the Unity API name for this feature is called "CommandBuffer", so be sure not to confuse it with the GPU's Command Buffer.

Check the Unity documentation on CommandBuffer to make use of this feature: `http://docs.unity3d.com/ScriptReference/Rendering.CommandBuffer.html`.

Getting back to the task at hand, when we discuss the topic of being CPU-bound in graphics rendering, we need to keep in mind whether or not the multithreaded renderer is being used, since the actual root cause of the problem will be slightly different depending on whether this feature is enabled or not.

In single-threaded rendering, where all graphics API calls are handled by the main thread, and in an ideal world where both components are running at maximum capacity, our application would become bottlenecked on the CPU when 50 percent or more of the time per frame is spent handling graphics API calls. However, resolving these bottlenecks can be accomplished by freeing up work from the main thread. For example, we might find that greatly reducing the amount of work taking place in our AI subsystem will improve our rendering significantly because we've freed up more CPU cycles to handle the graphics API calls.

But, when multithreaded rendering is taking place, this task is pushed onto the worker thread, which means the same thread isn't being asked to manage both engine work and graphics API calls at the same time. These processes are mostly independent, and even though additional work must still take place in the main thread to send instructions to the worker thread in the first place (via the internal CommandBuffer system), it is mostly negligible. This means that reducing the workload in the main thread will have little-to-no effect on rendering performance.

 Note that being GPU-bound is the same regardless of whether multithreaded rendering is taking place.

GPU Skinning

While we're on the subject of CPU-bounding, one task that can help reduce CPU workload, at the expense of additional GPU workload, is GPU Skinning. **Skinning** is the process where mesh vertices are transformed based on the current location of their animated bones. The animation system, working on the CPU, only transforms the bones, but another step in the rendering process must take care of the vertex transformations to place the vertices around those bones, performing a weighted average over the bones connected to those vertices.

This vertex processing task can either take place on the CPU or within the front end of the GPU, depending on whether the **GPU Skinning** option is enabled. This feature can be toggled under **Edit | Project Settings | Player Settings | Other Settings | GPU Skinning**.

Front end bottlenecks

We have already covered some techniques on mesh optimization in *Chapter 4, Kickstart Your Art*, which can help reduce our mesh's vertex attributes. As a quick reminder, it is not uncommon to use a mesh that contains a lot of unnecessary UV and Normal vector data, so our meshes should be double-checked for this kind of superfluous fluff. We should also let Unity optimize the structure for us, which minimizes cache misses as vertex data is read within the front end.

We will also learn some useful Shader optimization techniques shortly, when we begin to discuss back end optimizations, since many optimization techniques apply to both Fragment and Vertex Shaders.

The only attack vector left to cover is finding ways to reduce actual vertex counts. The obvious solutions are simplification and culling; either have the art team replace problematic meshes with lower polycount versions, and/or remove some objects from the scene to reduce the overall polygon count. If these approaches have already been explored, then the last approach we can take is to find some kind of middle ground between the two.

Level Of Detail

Since it can be difficult to tell the difference between a high quality distance object and a low quality one, there is very little reason to render the high quality version. So, why not dynamically replace distant objects with something more simplified?

Level Of Detail (LOD), is a broad term referring to the dynamic replacement of features based on their distance or form factor relative to the camera. The most common implementation is mesh-based LOD: dynamically replacing a mesh with lower and lower detailed versions as the camera gets farther and farther away. Another example might be replacing animated characters with versions featuring fewer bones, or less sampling for distant objects, in order to reduce animation workload.

> The built-in LOD feature is available in the Unity 4 Pro Edition and all editions of Unity 5. However, it is entirely possible to implement it via Script code in Unity 4 Free Edition if desired.

Making use of LOD can be achieved by placing multiple objects in the Scene and making them children of a GameObject with an attached LODGroup component. The LODGroup's purpose is to generate a bounding box from these objects, and decide which object should be rendered based on the size of the bounding box within the camera's field of view. If the object's bounding box consumes a large area of the current view, then it will enable the mesh(es) assigned to lower LOD groups, and if the bounding box is very small, it will replace the mesh(es) with those from higher LOD groups. If the mesh is too far away, it can be configured to hide all child objects. So, with the proper setup, we can have Unity replace meshes with simpler alternatives, or cull them entirely, which eases the burden on the rendering process.

Check the Unity documentation for more detailed information on the LOD feature: `http://docs.unity3d.com/Manual/LevelOfDetail.html`.

This feature can cost us a large amount of development time to fully implement; artists must generate lower polygon count versions of the same object, and level designers must generate LOD groups, configure them, and test them to ensure they don't cause jarring transitions as the camera moves closer or farther away. It also costs us in memory and runtime CPU; the alternative meshes need to be kept in memory, and the LODGroup component must routinely test whether the camera has moved to a new position that warrants a change in LOD level.

In this era of graphics card capabilities, vertex processing is often the least of our concerns. Combined with the additional sacrifices needed for LOD to function, developers should avoid preoptimizing by automatically assuming LOD will help them. Excessive use of the feature will lead to burdening other parts of our application's performance, and chew up precious development time, all for the sake of paranoia. If it hasn't been proven to be a problem, then it's probably not a problem!

Scenes that feature large, expansive views of the world, and lots of camera movement, should consider implementing this technique very early, as the added distance and massive number of visible objects will exacerbate the vertex count enormously. Scenes that are always indoors, or feature a camera with a viewpoint looking down at the world (real-time strategy and MOBA games, for example) should probably steer clear of implementing LOD from the beginning. Games somewhere between the two should avoid it until necessary. It all depends on how many vertices are expected to be visible at any given time and how much variability in camera distance there will be.

Note that some game development middleware companies offer third-party tools for automated LOD mesh generation. These might be worth investigating to compare their ease of use versus quality loss versus cost effectiveness.

Disable GPU Skinning

As previously mentioned, we could enable GPU Skinning to reduce the burden on a CPU-bound application, but enabling this feature will push the same workload into the front end of the GPU. Since Skinning is one of those "embarrassingly parallel" processes that fits well with the GPU's parallel architecture, it is often a good idea to perform the task on the GPU. But this task can chew up precious time in the front end preparing the vertices for fragment generation, so disabling it is another option we can explore if we're bottlenecked in this area. Again, this feature can be toggled under **Edit | Project Settings | Player Settings | Other Settings | GPU Skinning**.

GPU Skinning is available in Unity 4 Pro Edition, and all editions of Unity 5.

Reduce tessellation

There is one last task that takes place in the front end process and that we need to consider: tessellation. Tessellation through Geometry Shaders can be a lot of fun, as it is a relatively underused technique that can really make our graphical effects stand out from the crowd of games that only use the most common effects. But, it can contribute enormously to the amount of processing work taking place in the front end.

There are no simple tricks we can exploit to improve tessellation, besides improving our tessellation algorithms, or easing the burden caused by other front end tasks to give our tessellation tasks more room to breathe. Either way, if we have a bottleneck in the front end and are making use of tessellation techniques, we should double-check that they are not consuming the lion's share of the front end's budget.

Back end bottlenecks

The back end is the more interesting part of the GPU pipeline, as many more graphical effects take place during this stage. Consequently, it is the stage that is significantly more likely to suffer from bottlenecks.

There are two brute force tests we can attempt:

- Reduce resolution
- Reduce texture quality

These changes will ease the workload during two important stages at the back end of the pipeline: fill rate and memory bandwidth, respectively. Fill rate tends to be the most common source of bottlenecks in the modern era of graphics rendering, so we will cover it first.

Fill rate

By reducing screen resolution, we have asked the rasterization system to generate significantly fewer fragments and transpose them over a smaller canvas of pixels. This will reduce the fill rate consumption of the application, giving a key part of the rendering pipeline some additional breathing room. Ergo, if performance suddenly improves with a screen resolution reduction, then fill rate should be our primary concern.

Fill rate is a very broad term referring to the speed at which the GPU can draw fragments. But, this only includes fragments that have survived all of the various conditional tests we might have enabled within the given Shader. A fragment is merely a "potential pixel," and if it fails any of the enabled tests, then it is immediately discarded. This can be an enormous performance-saver as the pipeline can skip the costly drawing step and begin work on the next fragment instead.

One such example is Z-testing, which checks whether the fragment from a closer object has already been drawn to the same pixel already. If so, then the current fragment is discarded. If not, then the fragment is pushed through the Fragment Shader and drawn over the target pixel, which consumes exactly one draw from our fill rate. Now imagine multiplying this process by thousands of overlapping objects, each generating hundreds or thousands of possible fragments, for high screen resolutions causing millions, or billions, of fragments to be generated each and every frame. It should be fairly obvious that skipping as many of these draws as we can will result in big rendering cost savings.

Graphics card manufacturers typically advertise a particular fill rate as a feature of the card, usually in the form of gigapixels per second, but this is a bit of a misnomer, as it would be more accurate to call it gigafragments per second; however this argument is mostly academic. Either way, larger values tell us that the device can potentially push more fragments through the pipeline, so with a budget of 30 GPix/s and a target frame rate of 60 Hz, we can afford to process *30,000,000,000/60 = 500* million fragments per frame before being bottlenecked on fill rate. With a resolution of 2560x1440, and a best-case scenario where each pixel is only drawn over once, then we could theoretically draw the entire scene about 125 times without any noticeable problems.

Sadly, this is not a perfect world, and unless we take significant steps to avoid it, we will always end up with some amount of redraw over the same pixels due to the order in which objects are rendered. This is known as **overdraw**, and it can be very costly if we're not careful.

The reason that resolution is a good attack vector to check for fill rate bounding is that it is a multiplier. A reduction from a resolution of 2560x1440 to 800x600 is an improvement factor of about eight, which could reduce fill rate costs enough to make the application perform well again.

Overdraw

Determining how much overdraw we have can be represented visually by rendering all objects with additive alpha blending and a very transparent flat color. Areas of high overdraw will show up more brightly as the same pixel is drawn over with additive blending multiple times. This is precisely how the **Scene** view's **Overdraw** shading mode reveals how much overdraw our scene is suffering.

The following screenshot shows a scene with several thousand boxes drawn normally, and drawn using the **Scene** view's **Overdraw** shading mode:

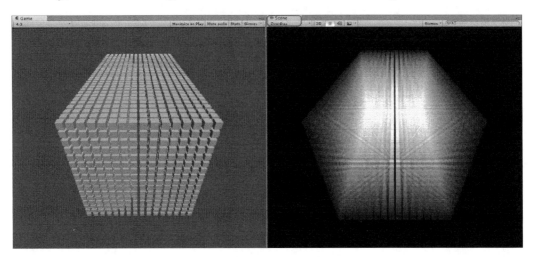

At the end of the day, fill rate is provided as a means of gauging the best-case behavior. In other words, it's primarily a marketing term and mostly theoretical. But, the technical side of the industry has adopted the term as a way of describing the back end of the pipeline: the stage where fragment data is funneled through our Shaders and drawn to the screen.

If every fragment required an absolute minimum level of processing (such as a Shader that returned a constant color), then we might get close to that theoretical maximum. The GPU is a complex beast, however, and things are never so simple. The nature of the device means it works best when given many small tasks to perform. But, if the tasks get too large, then fill rate is lost due to the back end not being able to push through enough fragments in time and the rest of the pipeline is left waiting for tasks to do.

There are several more features that can potentially consume our theoretical fill rate maximum, including but not limited to alpha testing, alpha blending, texture sampling, the amount of fragment data being pulled through our Shaders, and even the color format of the target render texture (the final Frame Buffer in most cases). The bad news is that this gives us a lot of subsections to cover, and a lot of ways to break the process, but the good news is it gives us a lot of avenues to explore to improve our fill rate usage.

Occlusion Culling

One of the best ways to reduce overdraw is to make use of Unity's Occlusion Culling system. The system works by partitioning Scene space into a series of cells and flying through the world with a virtual camera making note of which cells are invisible from other cells (are occluded) based on the size and position of the objects present.

Note that this is different to the technique of Frustum Culling, which culls objects not visible from the current camera view. This feature is always active in all versions, and objects culled by this process are automatically ignored by the Occlusion Culling system.

 Occlusion Culling is available in the Unity 4 Pro Edition and all editions of Unity 5.

Occlusion Culling data can only be generated for objects properly labeled **Occluder Static** and **Occludee Static** under the **StaticFlags** dropdown. **Occluder Static** is the general setting for static objects where we want it to hide other objects, and be hidden by large objects in its way. **Occludee Static** is a special case for transparent objects that allows objects behind them to be rendered, but we want them to be hidden if something large blocks their visibility.

Naturally, because one of the static flags must be enabled for Occlusion Culling, this feature will not work for dynamic objects.

The following screenshot shows how effective Occlusion Culling can be at reducing the number of visible objects in our Scene:

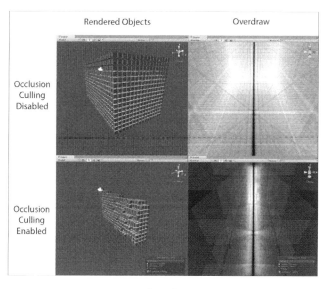

This feature will cost us in both application footprint and incur some runtime costs. It will cost RAM to keep the Occlusion Culling data structure in memory, and there will be a CPU processing cost to determine which objects are being occluded in each frame.

The Occlusion Culling data structure must be properly configured to create cells of the appropriate size for our Scene, and the smaller the cells, the longer it takes to generate the data structure. But, if it is configured correctly for the Scene, Occlusion Culling can provide both fill rate savings through reduced overdraw, and Draw Call savings by culling non-visible objects.

Shader optimization

Shaders can be a significant fill rate consumer, depending on their complexity, how much texture sampling takes place, how many mathematical functions are used, and so on. Shaders do not directly consume fill rate, but do so indirectly because the GPU must calculate or fetch data from memory during Shader processing. The GPU's parallel nature means any bottleneck in a thread will limit how many fragments can be pushed into the thread at a later date, but parallelizing the task (sharing small pieces of the job between several agents) provides a net gain over serial processing (one agent handling each task one after another).

The classic example is a vehicle assembly line. A complete vehicle requires multiple stages of manufacture to complete. The critical path to completion might involve five steps: stamping, welding, painting, assembly, and inspection, and each step is completed by a single team. For any given vehicle, no stage can begin before the previous one is finished, but whatever team handled the stamping for the last vehicle can begin stamping for the next vehicle as soon as it has finished. This organization allows each team to become masters of their particular domain, rather than trying to spread their knowledge too thin, which would likely result in less consistent quality in the batch of vehicles.

We can double the overall output by doubling the number of teams, but if any team gets blocked, then precious time is lost for any given vehicle, as well as all future vehicles that would pass through the same team. If these delays are rare, then they can be negligible in the grand scheme, but if not, and one stage takes several minutes longer than normal each and every time it must complete the task, then it can become a bottleneck that threatens the release of the entire batch.

The GPU parallel processors work in a similar way: each processor thread is an assembly line, each processing stage is a team, and each fragment is a vehicle. If the thread spends a long time processing a single stage, then time is lost on each fragment. This delay will multiply such that all future fragments coming through the same thread will be delayed. This is a bit of an oversimplification, but it often helps to paint a picture of how poorly optimized Shader code can chew up our fill rate, and how small improvements in Shader optimization provide big benefits in back end performance.

Shader programming and optimization have become a very niche area of game development. Their abstract and highly-specialized nature requires a very different kind of thinking to generate Shader code compared to gameplay and engine code. They often feature mathematical tricks and back-door mechanisms for pulling data into the Shader, such as precomputing values in texture files. Because of this, and the importance of optimization, Shaders tend to be very difficult to read and reverse-engineer.

Consequently, many developers rely on prewritten Shaders, or visual Shader creation tools from the Asset Store such as Shader Forge or Shader Sandwich. This simplifies the act of initial Shader code generation, but might not result in the most efficient form of Shaders. If we're relying on pre-written Shaders or tools, we might find it worthwhile to perform some optimization passes over them using some tried-and-true techniques. So, let's focus on some easily reachable ways of optimizing our Shaders.

Consider using Shaders intended for mobile platforms

The built-in mobile Shaders in Unity do not have any specific restrictions that force them to only be used on mobile devices. They are simply optimized for minimum resource usage (and tend to feature some of the other optimizations listed in this section).

Desktop applications are perfectly capable of using these Shaders, but they tend to feature a loss of graphical quality. It only becomes a question of whether the loss of graphical quality is acceptable. So, consider doing some testing with the mobile equivalents of common Shaders to see whether they are a good fit for your game.

Use small data types

GPUs can calculate with smaller data types more quickly than larger types (particularly on mobile platforms!), so the first tweak we can attempt is replacing our float data types (32-bit, floating point) with smaller versions such as half (16-bit, floating point), or even fixed (12-bit, fixed point).

 The size of the data types listed above will vary depending on what floating point formats the target platform prefers. The sizes listed are the most common. The importance for optimization is in the relative size between formats.

Color values are good candidates for precision reduction, as we can often get away with less precise color values without any noticeable loss in coloration. However, the effects of reducing precision can be very unpredictable for graphical calculations. So, changes such as these can require some testing to verify whether the reduced precision is costing too much graphical fidelity.

Note that the effects of these tweaks can vary enormously between one GPU architecture and another (for example, AMD versus Nvidia versus Intel), and even GPU brands from the same manufacturer. In some cases, we can make some decent performance gains for a trivial amount of effort. In other cases, we might see no benefit at all.

Avoid changing precision while swizzling

Swizzling is the Shader programming technique of creating a new vector (an array of values) from an existing vector by listing the components in the order in which we wish to copy them into the new structure. Here are some examples of swizzling:

```
float4 input = float4(1.0, 2.0, 3.0, 4.0);  // initial test value

float2 val1 = input.yz;  // swizzle two components

float3 val2 = input.zyx;  // swizzle three components in a
different order

float4 val3 = input.yyy;  // swizzle the same component multiple
times

float sclr = input.w;
float3 val4 = sclr.xxx  // swizzle a scalar multiple times
```

We can use both the `xyzw` and `rgba` representations to refer to the same components, sequentially. It does not matter whether it is a color or vector; they just make the Shader code easier to read. We can also list components in any order we like to fill in the desired data, repeating them if necessary.

Converting from one precision type to another in a Shader can be a costly operation, but converting the precision type while simultaneously swizzling can be particularly painful. If we have mathematical operations that rely on being swizzled into different precision types, it would be wiser if we simply absorbed the high-precision cost from the very beginning, or reduced precision across the board to avoid the need for changes in precision.

Use GPU-optimized helper functions

The Shader compiler often performs a good job of reducing mathematical calculations down to an optimized version for the GPU, but compiled custom code is unlikely to be as effective as both the Cg library's built-in helper functions and the additional helpers provided by the Unity Cg included files. If we are using Shaders that include custom function code, perhaps we can find an equivalent helper function within the Cg or Unity libraries that can do a better job than our custom code can.

These extra `include` files can be added to our Shader within the `CGPROGRAM` block like so:

```
CGPROGRAM
// other includes
#include "UnityCG.cginc"
// Shader code here
ENDCG
```

Example Cg library functions to use are `abs()` for absolute values, `lerp()` for linear interpolation, `mul()` for multiplying matrices, and `step()` for step functionality. Useful `UnityCG.cginc` functions include `WorldSpaceViewDir()` for calculating the direction towards the camera, and `Luminance()` for converting a color to grayscale.

Check the following URL for a full list of Cg standard library functions: `http://http.developer.nvidia.com/CgTutorial/cg_tutorial_appendix_e.html`.

Check the Unity documentation for a complete and up-to-date list of possible include files and their accompanying helper functions: `http://docs.unity3d.com/Manual/SL-BuiltinIncludes.html`.

Disable unnecessary features

Perhaps we can make savings by simply disabling Shader features that aren't vital. Does the Shader really need multiple passes, transparency, Z-writing, alpha-testing, and/or alpha blending? Will tweaking these settings or removing these features give us a good approximation of our desired effect without losing too much graphical fidelity? Making such changes is a good way of making fill rate cost savings.

Remove unnecessary input data

Sometimes the process of writing a Shader involves a lot of back and forth experimentation in editing code and viewing it in the Scene. The typical result of this is that input data that was needed when the Shader was going through early development is now surplus fluff once the desired effect has been obtained, and it's easy to forget what changes were made when/if the process drags on for a long time. But, these redundant data values can cost the GPU valuable time as they must be fetched from memory even if they are not explicitly used by the Shader. So, we should double check our Shaders to ensure all of their input geometry, vertex, and fragment data is actually being used.

Only expose necessary variables

Exposing unnecessary variables from our Shader to the accompanying Material(s) can be costly as the GPU can't assume these values are constant. This means the Shader code cannot be compiled into a more optimized form. This data must be pushed from the CPU with every pass since they can be modified at any time through the Material's methods such as `SetColor()`, `SetFloat()`, and so on. If we find that, towards the end of the project, we always use the same value for these variables, then they can be replaced with a constant in the Shader to remove such excess runtime workload. The only cost is obfuscating what could be critical graphical effect parameters, so this should be done very late in the process.

Reduce mathematical complexity

Complicated mathematics can severely bottleneck the rendering process, so we should do whatever we can to limit the damage. Complex mathematical functions could be replaced with a texture that is fed into the Shader and provides a pre-generated table for runtime lookup. We may not see any improvement with functions such as `sin` and `cos`, since they've been heavily optimized to make use of GPU architecture, but complex methods such as `pow`, `exp`, `log`, and other custom mathematical processes can only be optimized so much, and would be good candidates for simplification. This is assuming we only need one or two input values, which are represented through the X and Y coordinates of the texture, and mathematical accuracy isn't of paramount importance.

This will cost us additional graphics memory to store the texture at runtime (more on this later), but if the Shader is already receiving a texture (which they are in most cases) and the alpha channel is not being used, then we could sneak the data in through the texture's alpha channel, costing us literally no performance, and the rest of the Shader code and graphics system would be none-the-wiser. This will involve the customization of art assets to include such data in any unused color channel(s), requiring coordination between programmers and artists, but is a very good way of saving Shader processing costs with no runtime sacrifices.

In fact, Material properties and textures are both excellent entry points for pushing work from the Shader (the GPU) onto the CPU. If a complex calculation does not need to vary on a per pixel basis, then we could expose the value as a property in the Material, and modify it as needed (accepting the overhead cost of doing so from the previous section *Only expose necessary variables*). Alternatively, if the result varies per pixel, and does not need to change often, then we could generate a texture file from script code, containing the results of the calculations in the RGBA values, and pulling the texture into the Shader. Lots of opportunities arise when we ignore the conventional application of such systems, and remember to think of them as just raw data being transferred around.

Reduce texture lookups

While we're on the subject of texture lookups, they are not trivial tasks for the GPU to process and they have their own overhead costs. They are the most common cause of memory access problems within the GPU, especially if a Shader is performing samples across multiple textures, or even multiple samples across a single texture, as they will likely inflict cache misses in memory. Such situations should be simplified as much as possible to avoid severe GPU memory bottlenecking.

Even worse, sampling a texture in a random order would likely result in some very costly cache misses for the GPU to suffer through, so if this is being done, then the texture should be reordered so that it can be sampled in a more sequential order.

Avoid conditional statements

In modern day CPU architecture, conditional statements undergo a lot of clever predictive techniques to make use of instruction-level parallelism. This is a feature where the CPU attempts to predict which direction a conditional statement will go in before it has actually been resolved, and speculatively begins processing the most likely result of the conditional using any free components that aren't being used to resolve the conditional (fetching some data from memory, copying some floats into unused registers, and so on). If it turns out that the decision is wrong, then the current result is discarded and the proper path is taken instead.

So long as the cost of speculative processing and discarding false results is less than the time spent waiting to decide the correct path, and it is right more often than it is wrong, then this is a net gain for the CPU's speed.

However, this feature is not possible on GPU architecture because of its parallel nature. The GPU's cores are typically managed by some higher-level construct that instructs all cores under its command to perform the same machine-code-level instruction simultaneously. So, if the Fragment Shader requires a float to be multiplied by 2, then the process will begin by having all cores copy data into the appropriate registers in one coordinated step. Only when all cores have finished copying to the registers will the cores be instructed to begin the second step: multiplying all registers by 2.

Thus, when this system stumbles into a conditional statement, it cannot resolve the two statements independently. It must determine how many of its child cores will go down each path of the conditional, grab the list of required machine code instructions for one path, resolve them for all cores taking that path, and repeat for each path until all possible paths have been processed. So, for an if-else statement (two possibilities), it will tell one group of cores to process the "true" path, then ask the remaining cores to process the "false" path. Unless every core takes the same path, it must process both paths every time.

So, we should avoid branching and conditional statements in our Shader code. Of course, this depends on how essential the conditional is to achieving the graphical effect we desire. But, if the conditional is not dependent on per pixel behavior, then we would often be better off absorbing the cost of unnecessary mathematics than inflicting a branching cost on the GPU. For example, we might be checking whether a value is non-zero before using it in a calculation, or comparing against some global flag in the Material before taking one action or another. Both of these cases would be good candidates for optimization by removing the conditional check.

Reduce data dependencies

The compiler will try its best to optimize our Shader code into the more GPU-friendly low-level language so that it is not waiting on data to be fetched when it could be processing some other task. For example, the following poorly-optimized code, could be written in our Shader:

```
float sum = input.color1.r;
sum = sum + input.color2.g;
sum = sum + input.color3.b;
sum = sum + input.color4.a;
float result = calculateSomething(sum);
```

If we were able to force the Shader compiler to compile this code into machine code instructions as it is written, then this code has a data dependency such that each calculation cannot begin until the last finishes due to the dependency on the sum variable. But, such situations are often detected by the Shader compiler and optimized into a version that uses instruction-level parallelism (the code shown next is the high-level code equivalent of the resulting machine code):

```
float sum1, sum2, sum3, sum4;
sum1 = input.color1.r;
sum2 = input.color2.g;
sum3 = input.color3.b
sum4 = input.color4.a;
float sum = sum1 + sum2 + sum3 + sum4;
float result = CalculateSomething(sum);
```

In this case, the compiler would recognize that it can fetch the four values from memory in parallel and complete the summation once all four have been fetched independently via thread-level parallelism. This can save a lot of time, relative to performing the four fetches one after another.

However, long chains of data dependency can absolutely murder Shader performance. If we create a strong data dependency in our Shader's source code, then it has been given no freedom to make such optimizations. For example, the following data dependency would be painful on performance, as one step cannot be completed without waiting on another to fetch data and performing the appropriate calculation.

```
float4 val1 = tex2D(_tex1, input.texcoord.xy);
float4 val2 = tex2D(_tex2, val1.yz);
float4 val3 = tex2D(_tex3, val2.zw);
```

Strong data dependencies such as these should be avoided whenever possible.

Surface Shaders

If we're using Unity's Surface Shaders, which are a way for Unity developers to get to grips with Shader programming in a more simplified fashion, then the Unity Engine takes care of converting our Surface Shader code for us, abstracting away some of the optimization opportunities we have just covered. However, it does provide some miscellaneous values that can be used as replacements, which reduce accuracy but simplify the mathematics in the resulting code. Surface Shaders are designed to handle the general case fairly efficiently, but optimization is best achieved with a personal touch.

The `approxview` attribute will approximate the view direction, saving costly operations. `halfasview` will reduce the precision of the view vector, but beware of its effect on mathematical operations involving multiple precision types. `noforwardadd` will limit the Shader to only considering a single directional light, reducing Draw Calls since the Shader will render in only a single pass, but reducing lighting complexity. Finally, `noambient` will disable ambient lighting in the Shader, removing some extra mathematical operations that we may not need.

Use Shader-based LOD

We can force Unity to render distant objects using simpler Shaders, which can be an effective way of saving fill rate, particularly if we're deploying our game onto multiple platforms or supporting a wide range of hardware capability. The LOD keyword can be used in the Shader to set the onscreen size factor that the Shader supports. If the current LOD level does not match this value, it will drop to the next fallback Shader and so on until it finds the Shader that supports the given size factor. We can also change a given Shader object's LOD value at runtime using the `maximumLOD` property.

This feature is similar to the mesh-based LOD covered earlier, and uses the same LOD values for determining object form factor, so it should be configured as such.

Memory bandwidth

Another major component of back end processing and a potential source of bottlenecks is **memory bandwidth**. Memory bandwidth is consumed whenever a texture must be pulled from a section of the GPU's main video memory (also known as VRAM). The GPU contains multiple cores that each have access to the same area of VRAM, but they also each contain a much smaller, local Texture Cache that stores the current texture(s) the GPU has been most recently working with. This is similar in design to the multitude of CPU cache levels that allow memory transfer up and down the chain, as a workaround for the fact that faster memory will, invariably, be more expensive to produce, and hence smaller in capacity compared to slower memory.

Whenever a Fragment Shader requests a sample from a texture that is already within the core's local Texture Cache, then it is lightning fast and barely perceivable. But, if a texture sample request is made, that does not yet exist within the Texture Cache, then it must be pulled in from VRAM before it can be sampled. This fetch request risks cache misses within VRAM as it tries to find the relevant texture. The transfer itself consumes a certain amount of memory bandwidth, specifically an amount equal to the total size of the texture file stored within VRAM (which may not be the exact size of the original file, nor the size in RAM, due to GPU-level compression).

It's for this reason that, if we're bottlenecked on memory bandwidth, then performing a brute force test by reducing texture quality would suddenly result in a performance improvement. We've shrunk the size of our textures, easing the burden on the GPU's memory bandwidth, allowing it to fetch the necessary textures much quicker. Globally reducing texture quality can be achieved by going to **Edit | Project Settings | Quality | Texture Quality** and setting the value to **Half Res**, **Quarter Res**, or **Eighth Res**.

In the event that memory bandwidth is bottlenecked, then the GPU will keep fetching the necessary texture files, but the entire process will be throttled as the Texture Cache waits for the data to appear before processing the fragment. The GPU won't be able to push data back to the Frame Buffer in time to be rendered onto the screen, blocking the whole process and culminating in a poor frame rate.

Ultimately, proper usage of memory bandwidth is a budgeting concern. For example, with a memory bandwidth of 96 GB/sec per core and a target frame rate of 60 frames per second, then the GPU can afford to pull 96/60 = 1.6 GB worth of texture data every frame before being bottlenecked on memory bandwidth.

> Memory bandwidth is often listed on a per core basis, but some GPU manufacturers may try to mislead you by multiplying memory bandwidth by the number of cores in order to list a bigger, but less practical number. Because of this, research may be necessary to confirm the memory bandwidth limit we have for the target GPU hardware is given on a per core basis.

Note that this value is not the maximum limit on the texture data that our game can contain in the project, nor in CPU RAM, not even in VRAM. It is a metric that limits how much texture swapping can occur during one frame. The same texture could be pulled back and forth multiple times in a single frame depending on how many Shaders need to use them, the order that the objects are rendered, and how often texture sampling must occur, so rendering just a few objects could consume whole gigabytes of memory bandwidth if they all require the same high quality, massive textures, require multiple secondary texture maps (normal maps, emission maps, and so on), and are not batched together, because there simply isn't enough Texture Cache space available to keep a single texture file long enough to exploit it during the next rendering pass.

There are several approaches we can take to solve bottlenecks in memory bandwidth.

Use less texture data

This approach is simple, straightforward, and always a good idea to consider. Reducing texture quality, either through resolution or bit rate, is not ideal for graphical quality, but we can sometimes get away with using 16-bit textures without any noticeable degradation.

Mip Maps (*Chapter 4*, *Kickstart Your Art*) are another excellent way of reducing the amount of texture data being pushed back and forth between VRAM and the Texture Cache. Note that the Scene View has a **Mipmaps** Shading Mode, which will highlight textures in our scene blue or red depending on whether the current texture scale is appropriate for the current Scene View's camera position and orientation. This will help identify what textures are good candidates for further optimization.

 Mip Maps should almost always be used in 3D Scenes, unless the camera moves very little.

Test different GPU Texture Compression formats

The Texture Compression techniques you learned back in *Chapter 4*, *Kickstart Your Art*, were described in such a way that helped reduce our application's footprint (executable file size), and runtime CPU memory usage, that is, the storage area where all texture resource data is kept until it is needed by the GPU. However, once the data reaches the GPU, it uses a different form of compression to keep texture data small. The common formats are DXT, PVRTC, ETC, and ASTC.

To make matters more confusing, each platform and GPU hardware supports different compression formats, and if the device does not support the given compression format, then it will be handled at the software level. In other words, the CPU will need to stop and recompress the texture to the desired format the GPU wants, as opposed to the GPU taking care of it with a specialized hardware chip.

The compression options are only available if a texture resource has its **Texture Type** field set to **Advanced**. Using any of the other texture type settings will simplify the choices, and Unity will make a best guess when deciding which format to use for the target platform, which may not be ideal for a given piece of hardware and thus will consume more memory bandwidth than necessary.

The best approach to determining the correct format is to simply test a bunch of different devices and Texture Compression techniques and find one that fits. For example, common wisdom says that ETC is the best choice for Android since more devices support it, but some developers have found their game works better with the DXT and PVRTC formats on certain devices.

Beware that, if we're at the point where individually tweaking Texture Compression techniques is necessary, then hopefully we have exhausted all other options for reducing memory bandwidth. By going down this road, we could be committing to supporting many different devices each in their own specific way. Many of us would prefer to keep things simple with a general solution instead of personal customization and time-consuming handiwork to work around problems like this.

Minimize texture sampling

Can we modify our Shaders to remove some texture sampling overhead? Did we add some extra texture lookup files to give ourselves some fill rate savings on mathematical functions? If so, we might want to consider lowering the resolution of such textures or reverting the changes and solving our fill rate problems in other ways. Essentially, the less texture sampling we do, the less often we need to use memory bandwidth and the closer we get to resolving the bottleneck.

Organize assets to reduce texture swaps

This approach basically comes back to Batching and Atlasing again. Are there opportunities to batch some of our biggest texture files together? If so, then we could save the GPU from having to pull in the same texture files over and over again during the same frame. As a last resort, we could look for ways to remove some textures from the entire project and reuse similar files. For instance, if we have fill rate budget to spare, then we may be able to use some Fragment Shaders to make a handful of textures files appear in our game with different color variations.

VRAM limits

One last consideration related to textures is how much VRAM we have available. Most texture transfer from CPU to GPU occurs during initialization, but can also occur when a non-existent texture is first required by the current view. This process is asynchronous and will result in a blank texture being used until the full texture is ready for rendering. As such, we should avoid too much texture variation across our Scenes.

Texture preloading

Even though it doesn't strictly relate to graphics performance, it is worth mentioning that the blank texture that is used during asynchronous texture loading can be jarring when it comes to game quality. We would like a way to control and force the texture to be loaded from disk to the main memory and then to VRAM before it is actually needed.

A common workaround is to create a hidden GameObject that features the texture and place it somewhere in the Scene on the route that the player will take towards the area where it is actually needed. As soon as the textured object becomes a candidate for the rendering system (even if it's technically hidden), it will begin the process of copying the data towards VRAM. This is a little clunky, but is easy to implement and works sufficiently well in most cases.

We can also control such behavior via Script code by changing a hidden Material's texture:

```
GetComponent<Renderer>().material.texture = textureToPreload;
```

Texture thrashing

In the rare event that too much texture data is loaded into VRAM, and the required texture is not present, the GPU will need to request it from the main memory and overwrite the existing texture data to make room. This is likely to worsen over time as the memory becomes fragmented, and it introduces a risk that the texture just flushed from VRAM needs to be pulled again within the same frame. This will result in a serious case of memory "thrashing", and should be avoided at all costs.

This is less of a concern on modern consoles such as the PS4, Xbox One, and WiiU, since they share a common memory space for both CPU and GPU. This design is a hardware-level optimization given the fact that the device is always running a single application, and almost always rendering 3D graphics. But, all other platforms must share time and space with multiple applications and be capable of running without a GPU. They therefore feature separate CPU and GPU memory, and we must ensure that the total texture usage at any given moment remains below the available VRAM of the target hardware.

Note that this "thrashing" is not precisely the same as hard disk thrashing, where memory is copied back and forth between main memory and virtual memory (the swap file), but it is analogous. In either case, data is being unnecessarily copied back and forth between two regions of memory because too much data is being requested in too short a time period for the smaller of the two memory regions to hold it all.

Thrashing such as this can be a common cause of dreadful graphics performance when games are ported from modern consoles to the desktop and should be treated with care.

Avoiding this behavior may require customizing texture quality and file sizes on a per-platform and per-device basis. Be warned that some players are likely to notice these inconsistencies if we're dealing with hardware from the same console or desktop GPU generation. As many of us will know, even small differences in hardware can lead to a lot of apples-versus-oranges comparisons, but hardcore gamers will expect a similar level of quality across the board.

Lighting and Shadowing

Lighting and Shadowing can affect all parts of the graphics pipeline, and so they will be treated separately. This is perhaps one of the most important parts of game art and design to get right. Good Lighting and Shadowing can turn a mundane scene into something spectacular as there is something magical about professional coloring that makes it visually appealing. Even the low-poly art style (think Monument Valley) relies heavily on a good lighting and shadowing profile in order to allow the player to distinguish one object from another. But, this isn't an art book, so we will focus on the performance characteristics of various Lighting and Shadowing features.

Unity offers two styles of dynamic light rendering, as well as baked lighting effects through lightmaps. It also provides multiple ways of generating shadows with varying levels of complexity and runtime processing cost. Between the two, there are a lot of options to explore, and a lot of things that can trip us up if we're not careful.

The Unity documentation covers all of these features in an excellent amount of detail (start with this page and work through them: `http://docs.unity3d.com/Manual/Lighting.html`), so we'll examine these features from a performance standpoint.

Let's tackle the two main light rendering modes first. This setting can be found under **Edit** | **Project Settings** | **Player** | **Other Settings** | **Rendering**, and can be configured on a per-platform basis.

Forward Rendering

Forward Rendering is the classical form of rendering lights in our scene. Each object is likely to be rendered in multiple passes through the same Shader. How many passes are required will be based on the number, distance, and brightness of light sources. Unity will try to prioritize which directional light is affecting the object the most and render the object in a "base pass" as a starting point. It will then take up to four of the most powerful point lights nearby and re-render the same object multiple times through the same Fragment Shader. The next four point lights will then be processed on a per-vertex basis. All remaining lights are treated as a giant blob by means of a technique called **spherical harmonics**.

Some of this behavior can be simplified by setting a light's Render Mode to values such as **Not Important**, and changing the value of **Edit | Project Settings | Quality | Pixel Light Count**. This value limits how many lights will be treated on a per pixel basis, but is overridden by any lights with a **Render Mode** set to **Important**. It is therefore up to us to use this combination of settings responsibly.

As you can imagine, the design of Forward Rendering can utterly explode our Draw Call count very quickly in scenes with a lot of point lights present, due to the number of render states being configured and Shader passes being reprocessed. CPU-bound applications should avoid this rendering mode if possible.

> More information on Forward Rendering can be found in the Unity documentation: http://docs.unity3d.com/Manual/RenderTech-ForwardRendering.html.

Deferred Shading

Deferred Shading or Deferred Rendering as it is sometimes known, is only available on GPUs running at least Shader Model 3.0. In other words, any desktop graphics card made after around 2004. The technique has been around for a while, but it has not resulted in a complete replacement of the Forward Rendering method due to the caveats involved and limited support on mobile devices. Anti-aliasing, transparency, and animated characters receiving shadows are all features that cannot be managed through Deferred Shading alone and we must use the Forward Rendering technique as a fallback.

Deferred Shading is so named because actual shading does not occur until much later in the process; that is, it is deferred until later. From a performance perspective, the results are quite impressive as it can generate very good per pixel lighting with surprisingly little Draw Call effort. The advantage is that a huge amount of lighting can be accomplished using only a single pass through the lighting Shader. The main disadvantages include the additional costs if we wish to pile on advanced lighting features such as Shadowing and any steps that must pass through Forward Rendering in order to complete, such as transparency.

> The Unity documentation contains an excellent source of information on the Deferred Shading technique, its advantages, and its pitfalls: http://docs.unity3d.com/Manual/RenderTech-DeferredShading.html.

Vertex Lit Shading (legacy)

Technically, there are more than two lighting methods. Unity allows us to use a couple of legacy lighting systems, only one of which may see actual use in the field: Vertex Lit Shading. This is a massive simplification of lighting, as lighting is only considered per vertex, and not per pixel. In other words, entire faces are colored based on the incoming light color, and not individual pixels.

It is not expected that many, or really any, 3D games will make use of this legacy technique, as a lack of shadows and proper lighting make visualizations of depth very difficult. It is mostly relegated to 2D games that don't intend to make use of shadows, normal maps, and various other lighting features, but it is there if we need it.

Real-time Shadows

Soft Shadows are expensive, Hard Shadows are cheap, and No Shadows are free. **Shadow Resolution**, **Shadow Projection**, **Shadow Distance**, and **Shadow Cascades** are all settings we can find under **Edit | Project Settings | Quality | Shadows** that we can use to modify the behavior and complexity of our shadowing passes. That summarizes almost everything we need to know about Unity's real-time shadowing techniques from a high-level performance standpoint. We will cover shadows more in the following section on optimizing our lighting effects.

Lighting optimization

With a cursory glance at all of the relevant lighting techniques, let's run through some techniques we can use to improve lighting costs.

Use the appropriate Shading Mode

It is worth testing both of the main rendering modes to see which one best suits our game. Deferred Shading is often used as a backup in the event that Forward Rendering is becoming a burden on performance, but it really depends on where else we're finding bottlenecks as it is sometimes difficult to tell the difference between them.

Use Culling Masks

A Light Component's **Culling Mask** property is a layer-based mask that can be used to limit which objects will be affected by the given Light. This is an effective way of reducing lighting overhead, assuming that the layer interactions also make sense with how we are using layers for physics optimization. Objects can only be a part of a single layer, and reducing physics overhead probably trumps lighting overhead in most cases; thus, if there is a conflict, then this may not be the ideal approach.

Note that there is limited support for Culling Masks when using Deferred Shading. Because of the way it treats lighting in a very global fashion, only four layers can be disabled from the mask, limiting our ability to optimize its behavior through this method.

Use Baked Lightmaps

Baking Lighting and Shadowing into a Scene is significantly less processor-intensive than generating them at runtime. The downside is the added application footprint, memory consumption, and potential for memory bandwidth abuse. Ultimately, unless a game's lighting effects are being handled exclusively through Legacy Vertex Lighting or a single Directional Light, then it should probably include Lightmapping to make some huge budget savings on lighting calculations. Relying entirely on real-time lighting and shadows is a recipe for disaster unless the game is trying to win an award for the smallest application file size of all time.

Optimize Shadows

Shadowing passes mostly consume our Draw Calls and fill rate, but the amount of vertex position data we feed into the process and our selection for the **Shadow Projection** setting will affect the front end's ability to generate the required shadow casters and shadow receivers. We should already be attempting to reduce vertex counts to solve front end bottlenecking in the first place, and making this change will be an added multiplier towards that effort.

Draw Calls are consumed during shadowing by rendering visible objects into a separate buffer (known as the shadow map) as either a shadow caster, a shadow receiver, or both. Each object that is rendered into this map will consume another Draw Call, which makes shadows a huge performance cost multiplier, so it is often a setting that games will expose to users via quality settings, allowing users with weaker hardware to reduce the effect or even disable it entirely.

Shadow Distance is a global multiplier for runtime shadow rendering. The fewer shadows we need to draw, the happier the entire rendering process will be. There is little point in rendering shadows at a great distance from the camera, so this setting should be configured specific to our game and how much shadowing we expect to witness during gameplay. It is also a common setting that is exposed to the user to reduce the burden of rendering shadows.

Higher values of **Shadow Resolution** and **Shadow Cascades** will increase our memory bandwidth and fill rate consumption. Both of these settings can help curb the effects of artefacts in shadow rendering, but at the cost of a much larger shadow map size that must be moved around and of the canvas size to draw to.

> The Unity documentation contains an excellent summary on the topic of the aliasing effect of shadow maps and how the **Shadow Cascades** feature helps to solve the problem: `http://docs.unity3d.com/Manual/DirLightShadows.html`.

It's worth noting that Soft Shadows do not consume any more memory or CPU overhead relative to Hard Shadows, as the only difference is a more complex Shader. This means that applications with enough fill rate to spare can enjoy the improved graphical fidelity of Soft Shadows.

Optimizing graphics for mobile

Unity's ability to deploy to mobile devices has contributed greatly to its popularity among hobbyist, small, and mid-size development teams. As such, it would be prudent to cover some approaches that are more beneficial for mobile platforms than for desktop and other devices.

Note that any, and all, of the following approaches may become obsolete soon, if they aren't already. The mobile device market is moving blazingly fast, and the following techniques as they apply to mobile devices merely reflect conventional wisdom from the last half decade. We should occasionally test the assumptions behind these approaches from time-to-time to see whether the limitations of mobile devices still fit the mobile marketplace.

Minimize Draw Calls

Mobile applications are more often bottlenecked on Draw Calls than on fill rate. Not that fill rate concerns should be ignored (nothing should, ever!), but this makes it almost necessary for any mobile application of reasonable quality to implement Mesh Combining, Batching, and Atlasing techniques from the very beginning. Deferred Rendering is also the preferred technique as it fits well with other mobile-specific concerns, such as avoiding transparency and having too many animated characters.

Minimize the Material count

This concern goes hand in hand with the concepts of Batching and Atlasing. The fewer Materials we use, the fewer Draw Calls will be necessary. This strategy will also help with concerns relating to VRAM and memory bandwidth, which tend to be very limited on mobile devices.

Minimize texture size and Material count

Most mobile devices feature a very small Texture Cache relative to desktop GPUs. For instance, the iPhone 3G can only support a total texture size of 1024x1024 due to running OpenGLES1.1 with simple vertex rendering techniques. Meanwhile the iPhone 3GS, iPhone 4, and iPad generation run OpenGLES 2.0, which only supports textures up to 2048x2048. Later generations can support textures up to 4096x4096. Double check the device hardware we are targeting to be sure it supports the texture file sizes we wish to use (there are too many Android devices to list here). However, later-generation devices are never the most common devices in the mobile marketplace. If we wish our game to reach a wide audience (increasing its chances of success), then we must be willing to support weaker hardware.

Note that textures that are too large for the GPU will be downscaled by the CPU during initialization, wasting valuable loading time, and leaving us with unintended graphical fidelity. This makes texture reuse of paramount importance for mobile devices due to the limited VRAM and Texture Cache sizes available.

Make textures square and power of 2

We have already covered this topic in *Chapter 4, Kickstart Your Art*, but it is worth revisiting the subject of GPU-level Texture Compression. The GPU will find it difficult, or simply be unable to compress the texture if it is not in a square format, so make sure you stick to the common development convention and keep things square and sized to a power of 2.

Use the lowest possible precision formats in Shaders

Mobile GPUs are particularly sensitive to precision formats in its Shaders, so the smallest formats should be used. On a related note, format conversion should be avoided for the same reason.

Avoid Alpha Testing

Mobile GPUs haven't quite reached the same levels of chip optimization as desktop GPUs, and Alpha Testing remains a particularly costly task on mobile devices. In most cases it should simply be avoided in favor of Alpha Blending.

Summary

If you've made it this far without skipping ahead, then congratulations are in order. That was a lot of information to absorb for just one component of the Unity Engine, but then it is clearly the most complicated of them all, requiring a matching depth of explanation. Hopefully, you've learned a lot of approaches to help you improve your rendering performance and enough about the rendering pipeline to know how to use them responsibly!

By now we should be used to the idea that, with the exception of algorithm improvements, every performance enhancement we implement will come with some related cost that we must be willing to bear for the sake of removing one bottleneck. We should also be ready to implement multiple techniques until we've squashed them all.

We've just covered a very abstract system in great detail, so let's move things along with an exploration of a more concrete system: Unity's underlying Engine and the C# language. In the next chapter, we will take a look at our Script code in a more advanced light and investigate some methods to improve our CPU and memory management.

7
Masterful Memory Management

Using memory properly within the Unity Engine requires a good amount of understanding of the underlying Unity Engine and Mono Framework. This can be a bit of an intimidating place for some developers, since many picked Unity as their solution primarily to avoid the kind of low-level grunt work that comes from engine development and memory management. They would prefer instead to focus on higher-level concerns related to gameplay implementation, level design, and art asset management.

Many games of limited scope can get away with focusing on such higher-level concerns, at the cost of wasted resources, and may never run into any problems related to memory. This is all well and good until the day it becomes a problem. At this point, their neglect in understanding the important components of the engine leads to a scramble to find solutions that can be difficult to understand and implement without proper knowledge to back it up.

Therefore, understanding what is happening with memory allocations and C# language features, how they interact with the Mono Platform, how Mono interacts with the underlying engine, and the various libraries we have available are absolutely paramount to making high-quality, efficient script code. So, in this chapter, you will learn about all of the nuts and bolts of the underlying Unity Engine, Mono Platform, C# language, and .NET Framework.

Let's start by exploring the familiar part of the engine, which handles most of the work for our game's scripting code—the Mono platform.

The Mono platform

Mono is a magical sauce, mixed into the Unity recipe, which gives it a lot of its cross-platform capability. Mono is an open source project that built its own framework and libraries based on the API, specifications, and tools from Microsoft's .NET Framework and common libraries. Essentially, it is a recreation of the .NET Framework, as it was accomplished with little to no access to the source code. Note that, despite Mono's libraries being an open source recreation of Microsoft's base .NET class library, it is fully compatible with the original library from Microsoft.

The goal of the Mono project is to provide a framework to allow cross-platform compatibility using the .NET Framework as a common layer. It allows applications to be written in a common programming language and run against many different hardware platforms, including Linux, OS X, Windows, ARM, PowerPC, and more. Mono also supports many languages, not just the C#, Boo, and UnityScript we may be familiar with. Any language that can be compiled into .NET's pure **Common Intermediate Language** (CIL – more on this later) is sufficient to integrate with the Mono platform. This includes C#, but even includes languages such as F#, Java, Visual Basic .NET, PythonNet, and IronPython.

A common misconception about the Unity Engine is that it is built on top of the Mono platform. This is untrue, as the Mono side does not handle many important game tasks such as audio, rendering, physics, and so on. Unity Technologies built a native C++ backend for the sake of speed, and allows its users control of the engine through Mono as a scripting interface. As such, Mono is merely a component of the underlying Unity Engine. This is equivalent to many other game engines, which run C++ under the hood, handling important tasks such as rendering, animation, resource management, and so on, while simultaneously providing a scripting language for gameplay logic to be implemented. The Mono platform was chosen by Unity Technologies for this task.

 Native code simply means code that is compiled directly to the target OS, and executes without additional layers of complexity in the runtime environment. This keeps overhead costs low, but at the expense of needing to manage memory and other tasks within the code in a more direct fashion.

Scripting languages typically abstract away complex memory management through automatic garbage collection, and provide various safety features, which simplify the act of programming at the expense of runtime overhead. Some scripting languages can also be interpreted at runtime, meaning that they don't need to be compiled before execution. The raw instructions are converted dynamically into machine code and executed the moment they are read during runtime. The last feature, and probably the most important one, is that they allow simpler syntax of programming commands. This usually improves the development workflow immensely, as team members without much experience using languages such as C++ can contribute to the codebase. This enables them to implement things such as gameplay logic in a simpler format, at the expense of a certain amount of control and runtime execution speed.

Note that such languages are often called "managed" languages, which feature *managed code*. Technically, this was a term coined by Microsoft to refer to any source code that must run inside their **Common Language Runtime (CLR)** environment (more later), as opposed to code that is compiled and run natively through the target **Operating System (OS)**. But, because of the prevalence and common features that exist between the CLR and other languages that feature their own similarly designed runtime environments (such as Java), the term "managed" has since become a little vague. It tends to be used to refer to any language or code that depends on its own runtime environment and that may, or may not, include automatic garbage collection. For the rest of this chapter, we will use the term "managed" to refer to code that both depends on a separate runtime environment and has undergone automatic garbage collection.

The runtime performance cost of managed languages is becoming less and less significant every year. This is partly due to gradual optimizations in tools and runtime environments, and partly due to the computing power of the average device gradually becoming greater. But the main point of controversy in managed languages still remains their automatic memory management. Managing memory manually can be a complex task that can take many years of difficult debugging to be proficient at, but many developers feel that managed languages solve this problem in ways that are too unpredictable, risking too much product quality. Such developers might cite that managed code will never reach the same level of performance as native code, and it is foolhardy to build high-performance applications with them.

This is true to an extent, as managed languages invariably inflict runtime overheads, and we lose partial control over runtime memory allocations. But, as with all things, it becomes a balancing act, since not all resource usage will necessarily result in a bottleneck, and the best games aren't necessarily the ones that use every single byte to their fullest. For example, imagine a user interface that refreshes in 30 microseconds via native code versus 60 microseconds in managed code due to an extra 100 percent overhead (extreme example). The managed code version is still fast enough such that the user will never be able to notice the difference, so is there really any harm in using managed code for such a task?

In reality, working with managed languages often just means that developers have a unique set of concerns to worry about compared to native code developers. As such, choosing to use a managed language is partly a matter of preference, and partly a compromise of control over development speed.

The compilation process

When we make changes to our C# code, it is typically compiled immediately after we switch back from our favorite IDE (which is typically either MonoDevelop or, the much more feature-rich Visual Studio) to the Unity Editor. However, the C# code is not converted directly into machine code, as we would expect to happen with static compilers in the land of C++. Instead, the code is converted into an intermediate language called Common Intermediate Language (CIL), which is an abstraction above native code. CIL is similar to Java bytecode, upon which it is based, but CIL code is entirely useless on its own, as CPUs have no idea how to run the instructions defined in this language.

At runtime, this intermediate code is run through the Mono Virtual Machine (VM), which is an infrastructure component that allows the same code to run against multiple platforms without needing to change the code itself. This is an implementation of the .NET Common Language Runtime or CLR. If we're running on iOS, we run on the iOS-based Virtual Machine infrastructure, and if we're running on Linux, then we simply use a different one that is better suited for Linux.

Within the CLR, the intermediate CIL code will actually be compiled into native code on demand. This on-demand native compilation can be accomplished either by an **Ahead-Of-Time (AOT)** or **Just-In-Time (JIT)** compiler, depending on which platform is being targeted. These compilers allow code segments to be compiled into native code (that is, machine code specific to the OS it is running against), and the main difference between the two types is *when* the code is compiled.

AOT compilation happens early (ahead of time), either during the build process or during initialization. In either case, the code has been precompiled and no further runtime costs are inflicted due to dynamic compilation. In the current version of Unity (Version 5.2.2), the only platforms that support AOT compilation are WebGL (and only when UnityScript is being used) and iOS.

JIT compilation happens dynamically at runtime in a separate thread and begins just prior to execution ("just in time" for execution). Often, this dynamic compilation causes the first invocation of a piece of code to run a little (or a lot!) more slowly, because the code must finish compiling before it can be executed. But, from that point forward, whenever the same code block is executed, there is no need for recompilation, and the instructions run through the previously compiled native code.

It is common in software that 90 percent of the work is being done by only 10 percent of the code. This generally means that JIT compilation turns out to be a net positive on performance than if we simply tried to interpret the CIL code directly. However, because the JIT compiler must compile code quickly, it is not able to make use of many optimization techniques that static compilers are able to exploit.

Manual JIT compilation

In the event that JIT compilation is causing a runtime performance loss, be aware that it is actually possible to force JIT compilation of a method at any time via reflection. **Reflection** is a useful feature of the C# language, that allows our codebase to explore itself introspectively for type information, methods, values, and metadata. Using reflection is often a *very* costly process. It should be avoided at runtime or, at the very least, only used during initialization or other loading times. Not doing so can easily cause significant CPU spikes and gameplay freezing.

We can manually force JIT compilation of a method using reflection to obtain a function pointer to it:

```
var method = typeof(MyComponent).GetMethod("MethodName");
if (method != null) {
    method.MethodHandle.GetFunctionPointer();
    Debug.Log("JIT compilation complete!");
}
```

This code only works on public methods. Obtaining non-public methods can be accomplished through the use of `BindingFlags`:

```
using System.Reflection;
// ...
var method = typeof(MyComponent).GetMethod("MethodName",
BindingFlags.NonPublic | BindingFlags.Instance);
```

This kind of code should only be run for *very* targeted methods where we are certain that JIT compilation is causing CPU spikes. This can be verified by restarting the application and profiling a method's first invocation versus all subsequent invocations. The difference will tell us the JIT compilation overhead.

> Note that the official method for forcing JIT compilation in the .NET library is `RuntimeHelpers.PrepareMethod()`, but this is not properly implemented in the current version of Mono that comes with Unity (Mono Version 2.6.5). The aforementioned workaround should be used until Unity has pulled in a more recent version of the Mono project.

Memory usage optimization

In most game engines, we would have the luxury of being able to port inefficient script code into the faster C++ area if we were hitting performance issues. This is not an option unless we invest serious cash in obtaining the Unity source code, which is offered as a license separate from the Free/Personal/Pro licensing system, and on a per case, per title basis. This forces the overwhelming majority of us into a position of needing to make our C# script-level code as performant as possible. So, what does all of this backstory we've been covering mean for us when it comes to the task of performance optimization?

Firstly, we won't be covering anything that is specific to the UnityScript and Boo languages (although much of the knowledge translates to those languages).

Secondly, even though all of our script code might be in C#, we need to be aware that the overall Unity Engine is built from multiple components that each maintains its own memory domains.

Thirdly, only some tasks we perform will awaken the dreaded garbage collector. There are quite a few memory allocation approaches that we can use to avoid it entirely.

Finally, things can change quite a bit depending on the target platform we're running against and every assumption should be tested for validity if we're stumbling into unexpected memory bottlenecks.

Unity memory domains

The memory space within the Unity Engine can be essentially split into three different memory domains. Each domain stores different types of data and takes care of a very different set of tasks.

The first domain is the **Native Domain**. This is the underlying foundation of the Unity Engine, which is written in C++ and compiled to native code depending on which platform is being targeted. This area takes care of allocating memory space for things such as Asset data, for example Textures and Meshes, memory space for various subsystems, such as the Rendering system, Physics, Input, and so on. Finally, it includes native representations of important gameplay objects such as `GameObject` and `Component`. This is where a lot of the base `Component` classes keep their data, such as the Transform and Rigidbody Components.

The second memory domain, the **Managed Domain**, is where the Mono platform does its work, and is the area of memory that is maintained by the Garbage Collector. Any scripting objects and custom classes are stored within this memory domain. It also includes wrappers for the very same object representations that are stored within the Native Domain. This is where the bridge between Mono code and Native code derives from; each domain has its own representation for the same entity, and crossing the bridge between them too much can inflict some fairly significant performance hits on our game, as we learned in the previous chapters.

When a new GameObject or Component is instantiated, it involves allocating memory in both the Managed and Native Domains. This allows subsystems such as Physics and Rendering systems to control and render an object through its transform data on the Native Domain, while the Transform Component from our script code is merely a way to reference through the bridge into the Native memory space and change the object's transform data. Crossing back and forth across this bridge should be minimized as much as possible, due to the overhead involved, as we've learned through techniques such as caching position/rotation changes before applying them, back in *Chapter 2, Scripting Strategies*.

The third and final memory domain(s) are those of Native and External DLLs, such as DirectX, OpenGL, and any custom DLLs, we attach to our project. Referencing from Mono C# code into such DLLs will cause a similar memory space transition as that between Mono code and Native code.

Native memory

We have no direct control over what is going on in the Native Domain without the Unity Engine source code, but we do have a lot of indirect control by means of various script-level functions. There are technically a variety of memory allocators available, which are used internally for things such as GameObjects, Graphics objects, and the Profiler, but these are hidden behind the Native code wall.

However, we can observe how much memory has been allocated and reserved in this memory domain via the Memory Area of the Profiler. Native memory allocations show up under the values labeled "Unity", and we can even get more information using the **Detailed** view and sampling the current frame.

Simple ▼
Used Total: 140.6 MB   Unity: 34.7 MB   Mono: 14.3 MB   GfxDriver: 8.6 MB   FMOD: 2.1 MB   Profiler: 83.1 MB
Reserved Total: 286.8 MB   Unity: 175.4 MB   Mono: 14.7 MB   GfxDriver: 8.6 MB   FMOD: 2.1 MB   Profiler: 88.0 MB
Total System Memory Usage: 440.0 MB
(WP8) Commited Limit: 0 B   Commited Total: 0 B

Under the Scene Memory section of the **Detailed** view, we can observe that MonoBehaviour objects always consume a constant amount of memory, regardless of their member data. This is the memory consumed by the Native representation of the object. Note that 376 bytes of memory is consumed by a MonoBehaviour in Editor Mode, while only 156 bytes is consumed when profiling through a standalone application.

 Memory consumption in Editor Mode is always wildly different to that of a standalone version, due to various debugging and editor hook data being applied. This adds a further incentive to avoid using Editor Mode for profiling and benchmarking purposes (although it can still be useful at times).

We can also use the `Profiler.GetRuntimeMemorySize()` method to get the Native memory allocation size of a particular object.

Managed object representations are intrinsically linked to their Native representations. The best way to minimize our Native memory allocations is to simply optimize our Managed memory usage.

Managed memory

Memory in most modern operating systems splits dynamic memory into two categories: the stack and the heap. The **stack** is a special reserved space in memory, dedicated to small, short-lived data values, which are automatically deallocated the moment they go out of scope. The stack contains local variables, as well as handles the loading and unloading of functions as they're called, and expands and contracts along with the call stack. Deallocations in the stack are basically free because the data is essentially instantly forgotten about and no longer referenceable. New data simply overwrites the old data, since the start of the next memory allocation is always known, and there's no reason to perform any clean-up operations.

Because data in the stack is very short-lived, the total stack size is usually very small; in the order of Megabytes. It's possible to cause a stack overflow by allocating more space than the stack can support. This can occur during exceptionally large call stacks (for example, infinite loops), or having a large number of local variables, but in most cases causing a stack overflow should not be a concern despite its relatively small size.

The heap represents all remaining memory space, and it is used for the overwhelming majority of dynamic memory allocation. Whenever a data type is too big to fit in the stack or must exist outside the function it was declared in, then it must be allocated on the heap. Mono's **heap** is special in that it is managed by a Garbage Collector (it is sometimes referred to as a **Managed Heap**). During application initialization, Mono will request a given chunk of memory from the OS and use it to generate the heap. The heap starts off fairly small, less than one Megabyte, but will grow as new blocks of memory are needed by our script code.

We can verify how much memory has been allocated and reserved for the heap using the Memory Area of the Profiler, but under the values labeled "Mono".

```
Simple

Used Total 75.6 MB   Unity: 10.3 MB   Mono: 280.0 KB   GfxDriver: 4.8 MB   FMOD: 0.8 MB   Profiler: 60.2 MB
Reserved Total 123.4 MB   Unity: 50.1 MB   Mono: 0.5 MB   GfxDriver: 4.8 MB   FMOD: 0.8 MB   Profiler: 68.0 MB
Total System Memory Usage: 181.0 MB
(WP8) Commited Limit: 0 B   Commited Total: 0 B
```

We can also determine the current used and reserved heap space at runtime using the `Profiler.GetMonoUsedSize()` and `Profiler.GetMonoHeapSize()` methods, respectively.

Garbage collection

When a memory request is made, and there is enough empty space in the reserved heap block to satisfy the request, then Mono allocates the space and hands it over to whoever requested it. But, if the heap does *not* have room for it, then the Garbage Collector will awaken and scan all the existing memory allocations for anything which is no longer being used and cleans them up first, before attempting to expand the current heap space.

The Garbage Collector in the version of Mono that Unity uses is a type of Tracing Garbage Collector, which uses a Mark-and-Sweep strategy. This algorithm works in two phases: each allocated object is tracked with an additional bit. This flags whether the object has been marked or not. These flags start off set to 0 (or `false`).

When the collection process begins, it marks (sets the flag to 1 or `true`) all objects that are still reachable to the program. Either the reachable object is a direct reference, such as static or local variables on the stack, or it is an indirect reference through the fields (member data) of other directly or indirectly accessible objects. In this way, it is gathering a set of objects that are still referenceable.

The second phase involves iterating through every object reference in the heap (which Mono will have been tracking throughout the lifetime of the application) and verifying whether or not they are marked. If so, then the object is ignored. But, if it is not marked, then it is a candidate for deallocation. During this phase, all marked objects are skipped over, but not before setting their flag back to `false` for the first phase of the next garbage collection.

Once the second phase ends, all unmarked objects are deallocated to free space, and then the initial request to create the object is revisited. If there is enough space for the object, then it is allocated in that space and the process ends. But, if not, then it must allocate a new block for the heap by requesting it from the Operating System, at which point the memory allocation request can finally be completed.

In an ideal world, where we only keep allocating and deallocating objects but only a finite number of them exist at once, the heap would maintain a constant size because there's always enough space to fit the object. However, all objects in an application are rarely deallocated in the same order they were allocated, and even more rarely do they all have the same size in memory. This leads to memory fragmentation.

Memory fragmentation

Fragmentation occurs when objects are allocated and deallocated in different orders. This is best explained through an example. The following shows four stages of memory allocation within a typical heap memory space:

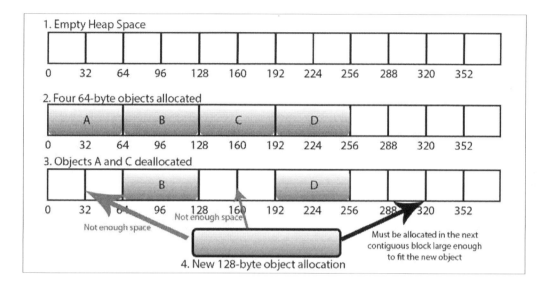

Here is how the memory allocation takes place:

1. We start with an empty heap space (1).

2. We then allocate four objects on the heap, *A*, *B*, *C* and *D*, each sized at 64 bytes (2).

3. At some later time, we deallocate two of the objects *A* and *C* (3).

4. This technically frees 128 bytes worth of space, but since the objects were not contiguous (adjoining neighbors) in memory, we have really only deallocated two separate 64-byte regions of memory. If, at some point later, we wish to allocate a new object that is larger than 64 bytes (4), then we cannot use the space that was previously freed by objects *A* and *C*, since neither is individually large enough to fit the new object (objects must always consume contiguous memory spaces). Therefore, the new object must be allocated in the next available 128 contiguous bytes in the heap space.

Over time, our heap memory will become riddled with more and more, smaller and smaller empty spaces such as these, as objects of different sizes are deallocated, and then the system later tries to allocate new objects within the smallest available space that it can fit within. The smaller these regions become, the less usable they are for new memory allocations. To use an analogy, the memory space begins to resemble Swiss cheese with many small holes that become unusable to us. In the absence of background techniques that automatically clean up this fragmentation, this effect would occur in literally any memory space—RAM, heap space, and even hard drives—which are just larger, slower, and more permanent memory storage areas (this is why it's a good idea to defragment our hard drives from time-to-time!).

Memory fragmentation causes two problems. Firstly, it effectively reduces the total usable memory space for new objects over long periods of time, depending on the frequency of allocations and deallocations. Secondly, it makes new allocations take longer to resolve, due to the extra time it takes to find a new memory space large enough to fit the object.

This becomes important when new memory allocations are made in a heap, since *where* the free spaces are located becomes just as important as *how much* free space is available. Even if we technically have 128 bytes of free space to fit a new object, if it is not contiguous space, then the heap must either continue searching until it finds a large enough space or the entire heap size must be increased to fit the new object, by requesting a new memory allocation from the OS in order to expand the heap space.

Garbage collection at runtime

So, in a worst case scenario, when a new memory allocation is being requested by our game, the CPU would have to spend cycles completing the following tasks before the allocation is finally completed:

1. Verify if there is enough contiguous space for the new object.
2. If not, iterate through all known direct and indirect references, marking them as reachable.
3. Iterate through the entire heap, flagging unmarked objects for deallocation.
4. Verify a second time if there is enough contiguous space for the new object.
5. If not, request a new memory block from the OS, in order to expand the heap.
6. Allocate the new object at the front of the newly allocated block.

This can be a lot of work for the CPU to handle, particularly if this new memory allocation is an important game object such as a particle effect, a new character entering the scene, a cutscene transition, and so on. Users are likely to note moments where the Garbage Collector is freezing gameplay to handle these tasks. To make matters worse, the garbage collection workload scales as the allocated heap space grows, since sweeping through a few megabytes of space will be significantly faster than scanning several gigabytes of space.

All of this makes it absolutely critical to control our heap space intelligently. The lazier our memory usage tactics are, the worse the Garbage Collector will behave in an almost exponential fashion. So, it's a little ironic that, despite the efforts of managed languages to solve the memory management problem, managed language developers can still find themselves being just as, if not *more*, concerned with memory consumption than developers of native applications!

Threaded garbage collection

The Garbage Collector runs on two separate threads: the **Main thread** and the **Finalizer thread**. When the Garbage Collector is invoked, it will run on the Main thread and flag heap memory blocks for future deallocation. This does not happen immediately. The Finalizer thread, controlled by Mono, can have a delay of several seconds before the memory is finally freed and available for reallocation.

We can observe this behavior in the **Total Allocated block** (the green line with apologies to that 5 percent of the population with deuteranopia/deuteranomaly) of the Memory Area within the Profiler. It can take several seconds for the total allocated value to drop after a garbage collection has occurred. Because of the delay, we should not rely on memory being available the moment it has been deallocated, and as such, we should never waste time trying to eke out every last byte of memory that we believe should be available. We must ensure that there is always some kind of buffer zone available for future allocations.

Blocks that have been freed by the Garbage Collector may sometimes be given back to the Operating System after some time, which would reduce the reserved space consumed by the heap and allow the memory to be allocated for something else, such as another application. But, this is very unpredictable and depends on the platform being targeted, so we shouldn't rely on it. The only safe assumption to make is that, as soon as the memory has been allocated to Mono, it's then reserved and is no longer available to either the Native Domain or any other application running on the same system.

Garbage collection tactics

One strategy to minimize garbage collection problems is concealment; manually invoke the Garbage Collector at opportune moments, when the player may not notice. A collection can be invoked by simply calling the following method:

```
System.GC.Collect();
```

Good opportunities to invoke a collection may be during level loading, when gameplay is paused, shortly after a menu interface has been opened, in the middle of cutscene transitions, or really any break in gameplay that the player would not witness, or care about a sudden performance drop. We could even use the `Profiler.GetMonoUsedSize()` and `Profiler.GetMonoHeapSize()` methods at runtime to determine if a garbage collection needs to be invoked in the near future.

We can also cause the deallocation of a handful of specific objects. If the object in question is one of the Unity object wrappers, such as a GameObject or MonoBehaviour component, then the Finalizer will first invoke the `Dispose()` method within the Native Domain. At this point, the memory consumed by both the Native and Managed Domains will then be freed. In some rare instances, if the Mono wrapper implements the `IDisposable` interface (that is, it has a `Dispose()` method available from script code), then we can actually control this behavior and force the memory to be freed instantly.

The only known and useful case of this (that this author is currently aware of) is the WWW class. This class is most often used to connect to a web server and download Asset data during runtime. This class needs to allocate several buffers in the Native Domain in order to accomplish this task. It needs to make room for the compressed file, a decompression buffer, and the final decompressed file. If we kept all of this memory for a long time, it would be a colossal waste of precious space. So, by calling its `Dispose()` method from script code, we can ensure that the memory buffers are freed promptly and precisely when they need to be.

All other Asset objects offer some kind of unloading method to clean up any unused asset data, such as `Resources.UnloadUnusedAssets()`. Actual asset data is stored within the Native Domain, so the Garbage Collector technically isn't involved here, but the idea is basically the same. It will iterate through all Assets of a particular type, check if they're no longer being referenced, and, if so, deallocate them. But, again, this is an asynchronous process and we cannot guarantee when deallocation will occur. This method is automatically called internally after a Scene is loaded, but this still doesn't guarantee instant deallocation.

At the very least, `Resources.UnloadAsset()` (that is, unloading one specific Asset at a time) is the preferred way to clean up Asset data, since time will not be spent iterating through the entire collection. However, it's worth noting that these unloading methods were upgraded to be multithreaded in Unity 5, which improves the performance cost of cleaning up Asset data rather significantly on most platforms.

However, the best strategy for garbage collection will always be avoidance; if we allocate as little heap memory and control its usage as much as possible, then we won't have to worry about the Garbage Collector inflicting performance costs as frequently or as hard. You will learn many tactics for this during the remainder of the chapter, but you should first cover some theory on how and where memory is allocated.

Value types and Reference types

Not all memory allocations we make within Mono will go through the heap. The .NET Framework (and by extension the C# language, which merely implements the .NET specification) has the concept of Value types and Reference types, and only the latter of which needs to be marked by the Garbage Collector while it is performing its Mark-and-Sweep algorithm. Reference types are expected to (or need to) last a long time in memory either due to their complexity, their size, or how they're used. Large datasets, and any kind of object instantiated from a class, is a Reference type. This also includes arrays (whether it is of Value types or Reference types), delegates, all classes, such as MonoBehaviour, GameObject, and any custom classes we define.

Value types are normally allocated on the stack. Primitive data types such as bools, ints, and floats are examples of Value types, but only if they're standalone and not a member of a Reference type. As soon as a primitive data types is contained within a Reference type, such as a class or an array, then it is implied that it is either too large for the stack or will need to survive longer than the current scope and must be allocated on the heap instead.

All of this can be best explained through examples. The following code will create an integer as a Value type that exists on the stack only temporarily:

```
public class TestComponent : MonoBehaviour {
    void Start() {
        int data = 5; // allocated on the stack
        DoSomething(data);
    } // integer is deallocated from the stack here
}
```

As soon as the Start() method ends, then the integer is deallocated from the stack. This is essentially a free operation since, as mentioned previously, it doesn't bother doing any cleanup; it just moves the stack pointer back to the previous memory location in the call stack. Any future stack allocations simply overwrite the old data. Most importantly, no heap allocation took place to create the data, and so, the Garbage Collector would be completely unaware of its existence.

But, if we created an integer as a member variable of the MonoBehaviour class definition, then it is now contained within a Reference type (a class) and must be allocated on the heap along with its container:

```
public class TestComponent : MonoBehaviour {

    private int _data = 5;

    void Start() {
        DoSomething(_data);
    }
}
```

Similarly, if we put the integer into an independent class, then the rules for Reference types still apply, and the object is allocated on the heap:

```
public class TestData {
    public int data = 5;
}

public class TestComponent : MonoBehaviour {
    void Start() {
        TestData dataObj = new TestData(); // allocated on the
                                                      heap
        DoSomething(dataObj.data);
    } // 'dataObj' is not deallocated here, but it will become a
        candidate during the next garbage collection
}
```

So, there is a big difference between temporarily allocating memory within a class method and storing long-term data in a class' member data. In both cases, we're using a Reference type (a class) to store the data, which means it can be referenced elsewhere. For example, imagine DoSomething() stored the reference to dataObj within a member variable:

```
private TestData _testDataObj;

void DoSomething (TestData dataObj) {
```

```
    _testDataObj = dataObj; // a new reference created! The
                             referenced object will now be marked
                             during mark-and-sweep
}
```

In this case, we would not be able to deallocate the object pointed to `dataObj` as soon as the `Start()` method ended because the total number of things referencing the object would go from 2 to 1. This is not 0, and hence the Garbage Collector would still mark it during mark-and-sweep. We will also need to set `_testDataObj` to `null`, or make it reference something else, before the object was no longer reachable.

Note that a Value type must have a value, and can never be `null`. If a stack-allocated Value type is assigned to a Reference type, then the data is simply copied. This is true even for arrays of the Value types:

```
public class TestClass {
    private int[] _intArray = new int[1000]; // Reference type
                                              full of Value types
    void StoreANumber(int num) {
        _intArray[0] = num; // store a Value within the array
    }
}
```

When the initial array is created (during object initialization), 1,000 integers will be allocated on the heap set to a value of `0`. When the `StoreANumber()` method is called, the value of `num` is merely copied into the zeroth element of the array, rather than storing a reference to it.

The subtle change in the referencing capability is what ultimately decides whether something is a Reference type or a Value type, and we should try to use standalone Value types whenever we have the opportunity, so that they generate stack allocations instead of heap allocations. Any situation where we're just sending around a piece of data that doesn't need to live longer than the current scope is a good opportunity to use a Value type instead of a Reference type. Ostensibly, it does not matter if we pass the data into another method of the same class or a method of another class; it still remains a Value type that will exist on the stack until the method that created it goes out of the scope.

Pass by value and pass by reference

Technically, something is duplicated every time a data value is passed as an argument from one method to another, and this is true whether it is a Value type or a Reference type. This is known as **passing by value**. The main difference is that a Reference type is merely a pointer which consumes only 4 or 8 bytes in memory (32-bit or 64-bit, depending on the architecture) regardless of what it is actually pointing to. When a Reference type is passed as an argument it is actually the value of this pointer that gets copied, which is very quick since the data is very small.

Meanwhile, a Value type contains the full and complete bits of data stored within the object. Hence, all of the data of a Value type gets copied whenever they are passed between methods, or stored in other Value types. In some cases, it can mean that passing a large Value type as arguments around too much can be more costly than just using a Reference type. For most Value types, this is not a problem, since they are comparable in size to a pointer. But this becomes important when we begin to talk about structs, in the next section.

Data can be passed around by reference as well, by using the `ref` keyword, but this is very different from the concept of Value and Reference types, and it is very important to keep them distinct in our mind when we try to understand what is going on under the hood. We can pass a Value type by value, or by reference, and we can pass a Reference type by value, or by reference. This means that there are four distinct data passing situations that can occur depending on which type is being passed and whether the **ref** keyword is being used or not.

When data is passed by reference (even if it is a Value type!) then making any changes to the data will change the original. For example, the following code would print the value 10:

```
void Start() {
    int myInt = 5;
    DoSomething(ref myInt);
    Debug.Log(String.Format("Value = {0}", myInt));
}

void DoSomething(ref int val) {
    val = 10;
}
```

Removing the `ref` keyword from both places would make it print the value 5 instead. This understanding will come in handy when we start to think about some of the more interesting data types we have access to. Namely, structs, arrays, and strings.

Structs are Value types

Structs are an interesting special case in C#. If we come from a C++ background to C#, then we would probably assume that the only difference between a struct and a class is that a struct has a default access specifier, `public`, while a class defaults to `private`. However, in C#, structs are similar to classes in that they can contain other private/protected/public data, have methods, can be instantiated at runtime, and so on. The core difference between the two is that structs are Value types and classes are Reference types.

There are some other important differences between how structs and classes are treated in C#; structs don't support inheritance, their properties cannot be given custom default values (member data always defaults to values such as `0` or `null`, since it is a Value type), and their default constructors cannot be overridden. This greatly restricts their usage compared to classes, so simply replacing all classes with structs (under the assumption that it will just allocate everything on the stack) is not a wise course of action.

However, if we're using a class in a situation whose only purpose is to send a blob of data to somewhere else in our application, and it does not need to last beyond the current scope, then we should use a struct instead, since a class would result in a heap allocation for no particularly good reason:

```
public class DamageResult {
    public Character attacker;
    public Character defender;
    public int totalDamageDealt;
    public DamageType damageType;
    public int damageBlocked;
    // etc
}

public void DealDamage(Character _target) {
    DamageResult result =
    CombatSystem.Instance.CalculateDamage(this, _target);
    CreateFloatingDamageText(result);
}
```

In this example, we're using a class to pass a bunch of data from one subsystem (the combat system) to another (the UI system). The only purpose of this data is to be calculated and read by various subsystems, so this is a good candidate to convert into a struct.

Merely changing the `DamageResult` definition from a class to a struct could save us quite a few unnecessary garbage collections, since it would be allocated on the stack.

```
public struct DamageResult {
    // ...
}
```

This is not a catch-all solution. Since structs are Value types, this means something rather unique when it is passed as an argument between methods. As we previously learned, every time a Value type is passed as an argument between one function and another, it will be duplicated since it is passed by value. This creates a duplicate Value type for the next method to use, which will be deallocated as soon as that method goes out of scope, and so on each time it is passed around. So, if a struct is passed by value between five different methods in a long chain, then five different stack copies will occur at the same time. Recall that stack deallocations are free, but data copying is not.

The copying is pretty much negligible for small values, such as a single integer or float, but passing around ridiculously large datasets through structs over and over again is obviously not a trivial task and should be avoided. In such cases, it would be wiser to pass the struct by reference using the `ref` keyword to minimize the amount of data being copied each time (just a 32-bit or 64-bit integer for the memory reference). However, this can be dangerous since passing by reference allows any subsequent methods to make changes to the struct, in which case it would be prudent to make its data values `readonly` (it can only be initialized in the constructor, and never again, even by its own member functions) to prevent later changes.

All of the above is also true when structs are contained within Reference types:

```
public struct DataStruct {
    public int val;
}
public class StructHolder {
    public DataStruct _memberStruct;
    public void StoreStruct(DataStruct ds) {
        _memberStruct = ds;
    }
}
```

To the untrained eye, the preceding code appears to be attempting to store a stack-allocated struct within a Reference type. Does this mean that a `StructHolder` object on the heap can now reference an object on the stack? What will happen when the `StoreStruct()` method goes out of scope and the struct is erased? It turns out that these are the wrong questions.

What's actually happening is that, while a `DataStruct` object (`_memberStruct`) has been allocated on the heap within the `StructHolder` object, it is still a Value type and does not magically transform into a Reference type. So, all of the usual rules for Value types apply. The `_memberStruct` variable cannot have a value of `null` and all of its fields will be initialized to `0` or `null` values. When `StoreStruct()` is called, the data from `ds` will be copied into `_memberStruct`. There are no references to stack objects taking place, and there is no concern about lost data.

Arrays are Reference types

Arrays can potentially contain a huge amount of data within them, which make them difficult to treat as a Value type since there's probably not enough room on the stack to support them. Therefore, they are treated as a Reference type so that the entire dataset can be passed around via a single reference, instead of duplicating the entire array every time it is passed around. This is true irrespective of whether the array contains Value types or Reference types.

This means that the following code will result in a heap allocation:

```
TestStruct[] dataObj = new TestStruct[1000];
for(int i = 0; i < 1000; ++i) {
    dataObj[i].data = i;
    DoSomething(dataObj[i]);
}
```

The following, functionally equivalent code, would not result in any heap allocations, since the structs are Value types, and hence would be created on the stack:

```
for(int i = 0; i < 1000; ++i) {
    TestStruct dataObj = new TestStruct();
    dataObj.data = i;
    DoSomething(dataObj);
}
```

The subtle difference in the second code-block is that only one `TestStruct` exists on the stack at a time (at least for this function `DoSomething()` can potentially create more), whereas the first block needs to allocate 1,000 of them via an array. Obviously, these methods are kind of ridiculous as they're written, but they illustrate an important point to consider. The compiler isn't smart enough to automatically find these situations for us and make the appropriate changes. Opportunities to optimize our memory usage through Value type replacements will be entirely down to our ability to detect them, and understand why a change will result in stack allocations, rather than heap allocations.

Note that, when we allocate an array of Reference types, we're creating an array of references, which can each reference other locations on the heap. However, when we allocate an array of Value types, we're creating a packed list of Value types on the heap. Each of these Value types will be initialized with a value of 0 (or equivalent), since they cannot be null, while each reference within an array of Reference types will always initialize to null, since no references have been assigned, yet.

Strings are immutable Reference types

We briefly touched upon the subject of strings back in *Chapter 2, Scripting Strategies*, but now it's time to go into more detail about why proper string usage is extremely important.

Because strings are essentially arrays of characters (chars), they are Reference types, and follow all of the same rules as other Reference types; the value that is actually copied and passed between functions is merely a pointer, and they will be allocated on the heap.

The confusing part really begins when we discover that strings are **immutable**, meaning they cannot be changed after they've been allocated. Being an array implies that the entire list of characters must be contiguous in memory, which cannot be true if we allowed strings to expand or contract at-will within a dynamic memory space (how could we quickly and safely expand the string if we've allocated something else immediately after it?).

This means that, if a string is modified, then a new string must be allocated to replace it, where the contents of the original will be copied and modified as-needed into a whole new character array. In which case, the old version will no longer be referenced anywhere, will not be marked during mark-and-sweep and will therefore eventually be garbage-collected. As a result, lazy string programming can result in a lot of unnecessary heap allocations and garbage collection.

For example, if we believed that strings worked just like other Reference types, we might be forgiven for assuming the log output of the following to be World!:

```
void Start() {
    string testString = "Hello";
    DoSomething(testString);
    Debug.Log(testString);
}

void DoSomething(string localString) {
    localString = "World!";
}
```

However, this is not the case, and it will still print out `Hello`. What is actually happening is that the `localString` variable, within the scope of `DoSomething()`, starts off referencing the same place in memory as `testString`, due to the reference being passed by value. This gives us two references pointing to the same location in memory as we would expect if we were dealing with any other Reference type. So far, so good.

But, as soon as we change the value of `localString`, we run into a little bit of a conflict. Strings are immutable, and we cannot change them, so therefore we must allocate a new string containing the value `World!` and assign its reference to the value of `localString`; now the number of references to the `Hello` string returns back to one. The original string (`Hello`) will remain in memory because the value of `testString` has not been changed, and that is still the value which will be printed by `Debug.Log()`. All we've succeeded in doing by calling `DoSomething()` is creating a new string on the heap which gets garbage-collected, and doesn't change anything. This is the textbook definition of wasteful.

If we change the method definition of `DoSomething()` to pass the string by reference, via the `ref` keyword, the output would indeed change to `World!`. This is what we would expect to happen with a Value type, which leads a lot of developers to incorrectly assume that strings are Value types. But, this is an example of the fourth and final data-passing case where a Reference type is being passed by reference, which allows us to change what the original reference is *referencing*!

So, to recap; if we pass a Value type by value, we can only change the value of the *copy*. If we pass a Value type by reference, we can change the actual value attributed to the original version. If we pass a Reference type by value, we can make changes to the object that the original reference is referencing. And finally, if we pass a Reference type by reference, we can change which object the original reference is referencing.

String concatenation

Concatenation is the act of appending strings to one another to form a larger string. As we've learned, any such cases are likely to result in excess heap allocations. The biggest offender in string-based memory waste is concatenating strings using the `+` and `+=` operators, because of the allocation chaining effect they cause.

For example, the following code tries to combine a group of strings together to print some information about a combat result:

```
void CreateFloatingDamageText(DamageResult result) {
    string outputText = result.attacker.GetCharacterName() + "
    dealt " + result.totalDamageDealt.ToString() + " " +
    result.damageType.ToString() + " damage to " +
    result.defender.GetCharacterName() + " (" +
    result.damageBlocked.ToString() + " blocked)";
    // ...
}
```

An example output of this function might be a string that reads:

```
Dwarf dealt 15 Slashing damage to Orc (3 blocked)
```

This function features a handful of string literals (hard-coded strings that are allocated during application initialization) such as `dealt`, `damage to`, and `blocked`. But, because of the usage of variables within this combined string, it cannot be compiled away at build time, and therefore must be generated dynamically at runtime.

A new heap allocation will be generated each time a +, or +=, operator is executed; only a single pair of strings will be merged at a time, and it allocates a new string each time. Then, the result of one merger will be fed into the next, and merged with another string, and so on until the entire string has been built.

So, the previous example will result in 9 different strings being allocated all in one go. All of the following strings would be allocated to satisfy this instruction, and all would eventually need to be garbage collected (note that the operators are resolved from right-to-left):

```
"3 blocked)"
" (3 blocked)"
"Orc (3 blocked)"
" damage to Orc (3 blocked)"
"Slashing damage to Orc (3 blocked)"
" Slashing damage to Orc (3 blocked)"
"15 Slashing damage to Orc (3 blocked)"
" dealt 15 Slashing damage to Orc (3 blocked)"
"Dwarf dealt 15 Slashing damage to Orc (3 blocked)"
```

That's 262 characters being used, instead of 49; or because a char is a 2-byte data type, that's 524 bytes of data being allocated when we only need 98 bytes. Chances are that, if this code exists in the codebase once, then it exists all over the place, so for an application that's doing a lot of lazy string concatenation like this, that is a ton of memory being wasted on generating unnecessary strings.

Note that big, constant string literals can be safely combined using the + and += operators to make them more readable within the codebase, but only if they will result in a constant string. If so, the compiler will take care of merging all of the string literals together at compile time.

Better approaches for generating strings are to use either the `StringBuilder` class, or one of several string class methods.

The `StringBuilder` class is effectively a mutable (changeable) string class. It works by allocating a buffer to copy the target strings into and allocates additional space whenever it is needed. We can retrieve the string using the `ToString()` method which, naturally, results in a memory allocation for the resultant string, but at least we avoided all of the unnecessary string allocations we would have generated using the + or += operators.

Conventional wisdom says that if we roughly know the final size of the resultant string, then we can allocate an appropriate buffer ahead of time and save ourselves undue allocations. For our example above, we might allocate a buffer of 100 characters to make room for long character names and damage values:

```
using System.Text;
// ...
StringBuilder sb = new StringBuilder(100);
sb.Append(result.attacker.GetCharacterName());
sb.Append(" dealt " );
sb.Append(result.totalDamageDealt.ToString());
// etc ...
string result = sb.ToString();
```

If we don't know the final size, then using a `StringBuilder` class is likely to generate a buffer that doesn't fit the size exactly, or closely. We will either end up with a buffer that's too large (wasted allocation time and space), or, worse, a buffer that's too small, which must keep expanding as we generate the complete string. If we're unsure about the total size of the string, then it might be best to use one of the various `string` class methods.

There are three `string` class methods available for generating strings; `Format()`, `Join()`, and `Concat()`. Each operates slightly differently, but the overall output is the same; a new string is allocated containing the contents of the string(s) we pass into them, and it is all done in a single action which reduces excess string allocations.

It is surprisingly hard to say which one of the two approaches would be more beneficial in a given situation as there are a lot of really deep nuances involved. There's a lot of discussion surrounding the topic (just do a Google search for `"c sharp string concatenation performance"` and you'll see what I mean), so the best approach is to implement one or the other using the conventional wisdom described previously. Whenever we run into bad performance with one method, we should try the other, profile them both, and pick the best option of the two.

Boxing

Technically, everything in C# is an object (caveats apply). Even primitive data types such as ints, floats, and bools are derived from `System.Object` at their lowest level (a Reference Type!), which allows them access to helper methods such as `ToString()`, so that they can customize their string representation.

But these primitive types are treated as special cases via being treated as Value types. Whenever a Value type is implicitly treated in such a way that it must act like an object, the CLR automatically creates a temporary object to store, or "box", the value inside so that it can be treated as a typical Reference type object. As we should expect, this results in a heap allocation to create the containing vessel.

 Note that boxing is not the same thing as using Value types as member variables of Reference types. It only takes place when Value types are treated like objects themselves.

For example, the following code would cause the variable `i` to be boxed inside object `obj`:

```
int i = 128;
object obj = i;
```

The following would use the object representation `obj` to replace the value stored within the integer, and "unbox" it back into an integer, storing it in `i`. The final value of `i` would be 256:

```
obj = 256;
i = (int)obj;
```

These types can technically be changed dynamically. The following is perfectly legal C# code, which uses the same object `obj` as above, which was originally boxed from an `int`:

```
obj = 512f;
float f = (float)obj;
```

The following is also legal:

```
obj = false;
bool b = (bool)obj;
```

Note that attempting to unbox `obj` into a type that isn't the most recently assigned type would result in an `InvalidCastException`. All of this can be a little tricky to wrap our head around until we remember that, at the end of the day, everything is just bits in memory. What's important is knowing that we can treat our primitive types as objects by boxing them, converting their types, and then unboxing them into a different type at a later time.

 Note that it's possible to convert a boxed object's type using one of the many `System.Convert.To...()` methods.

Boxing can be either implicit, as per the examples above, or explicit, by typecasting to `System.Object`. Unboxing must always be explicit by typecasting back to its original type. Whenever we pass a Value type into a method which uses `System.Object` as arguments, boxing will be applied implicitly.

Methods such as `String.Format()`, which take `System.Objects` as arguments, are one such example. We typically use them by passing in Value types such as ints, floats, bools and so on, to generate a string with. Boxing is automatically taking place in these situations, causing additional heap allocations which we should be aware of. `Collections.Generic.ArrayList` is another such example, since `ArrayLists` always contain `System.Object` references.

Any time we use a function definition that takes `System.Object` as arguments, and we're passing in Value types, we should be aware that we're implicitly causing heap allocations due to boxing.

The importance of data layout

The importance of how our data is organized in memory can be surprisingly easy to forget about, but can result in a fairly big performance boost if it is handled properly. Cache misses should be avoided whenever possible, which means that in most cases, arrays of data that are contiguous in memory should be iterated over sequentially, as opposed to any other iteration style.

This means that data layout is also important for garbage collection, since it is done in an iterative fashion, and if we can find ways to have the Garbage Collector skip over problematic areas, then we can potentially save a lot of iteration time.

In essence, we want to keep large groups of Reference types separated from large groups of Value types. If there is even just one Reference type within a Value type, such as a struct, then the Garbage Collector considers the entire object, and all of its data members, indirectly referenceable objects. When it comes time to mark-and-sweep, it must verify all fields of the object before moving on. But, if we separate the various types into different arrays, then we can make the Garbage Collector skip the majority of the data.

For instance, if we have an array of structs containing data like so, then the Garbage Collector will need to iterate over every member of every struct, which could be fairly time consuming:

```
public struct MyStruct {
    int myInt;
    float myFloat;
    bool myBool;
    string myString;
}
MyStruct[] arrayOfStructs = new MyStruct[1000];
```

But, if we replace all of this data with simple arrays, then the Garbage Collector will ignore all of the primitive data types, and only check the strings. This would result in much a faster garbage collection sweep:

```
int[] myInts = new int[1000];
float[] myFloats = new float[1000];
bool[] myBools = new bool[1000];
string[] myStrings = new string[1000];
```

The reason this works is because we're giving the Garbage Collector fewer indirect references to check. When the data is split into separate arrays (Reference types), it finds three arrays of Value types, marks the arrays, and then immediately moves on because there's no reason to mark Value types. It must still iterate through all of the strings within the string array, since each is a Reference type and it needs to verify that there are no indirect references within it. Technically, strings cannot contain indirect references, but the Garbage Collector works at a level where it only knows if the object is a Reference type or Value type. However, we have still spared the Garbage Collector from needing to iterate over an extra 3,000 pieces of data (all 1,000 ints, floats, and bools).

The Unity API

There are several instructions within the Unity API which result in heap memory allocations, which we should be aware of. This essentially includes everything that returns an array of data. For example, the following methods allocate memory on the heap:

```
GetComponents<T>(); // (T[])
Mesh.vertices; // (Vector3[])
Camera.allCameras; // (Camera[])
```

Such methods should be avoided whenever possible, or at the very least called once and cached so that we don't cause memory allocations more often than necessary.

Note that Unity Technologies has hinted it might come out with allocation-less versions of these methods sometime in the lifecycle of Unity 5. Presumably, it might look something like the way `ParticleSystems` allows access to `Particle` data, which involves providing a `Particle[]` array reference to point to the required data. This avoids allocation since we reuse the same buffer between calls.

The foreach loops

The `foreach` loop keyword is a bit of a controversial issue in Unity development circles. It turns out that a lot of `foreach` loops implemented in Unity C# code will incur unnecessary heap memory allocations during these calls, as they allocate an `Enumerator` object as a class on the heap, instead of a struct on the stack. It all depends on the given collection's implementation of the `GetEnumerator()` method.

It turns out that every single collection that has been implemented in the version of Mono that comes with Unity (Mono version 2.6.5) will create classes instead of structs, which results in heap allocations. This includes, but is not limited to, `List<T>`, `LinkedList<T>`, `Dictionary<K,V>`, `ArrayList`, and so on. But, note that it is actually safe to use `foreach` loops on typical arrays! The Mono compiler secretly converts `foreach` over arrays into simple `for` loops.

The cost is fairly negligible as the heap allocation cost does not scale with the number of iterations. Only one `Enumerator` object is allocated, and reused over and over again, which only costs a handful of bytes of memory overall. So unless our `foreach` loops are being invoked every update (which is typically dangerous in and of itself) then the costs will be mostly negligible on small projects. The time taken to convert everything to a `for` loop may not be worth the time. But it's definitely something to keep in mind for the next project we begin to write.

If we're particularly savvy with C#, Visual Studio, and manual compilation of the Mono assembly, then we can have Visual Studio perform code compilation for us, and copy the resulting assembly DLL into the `Assets` folder, which will fix this mistake for the generic collections.

Note that performing foreach over a Transform Component is a typical shortcut to iterating over a Transform's children. For example:

```
foreach (Transform child in transform) {
    // do stuff with 'child'
}
```

However, this results in the same heap allocations mentioned above. As a result, that coding style should be avoided in favor of the following:

```
for (int i = 0; i < transform.childCount; ++i) {
    Transform child = transform.GetChild(i);
    // do stuff with 'child'
}
```

Coroutines

Starting a Coroutine costs a small amount of memory to begin with, but note that no further costs are incurred when the method *yields*. If memory consumption and garbage collection are significant concerns, we should try to avoid having too many short-lived Coroutines, and avoid calling `StartCoroutine()` too much during runtime.

Closures

Closures are useful, but dangerous tools. Anonymous methods and lambda expressions are not always Closures, but they can be. It all depends on whether the method uses data outside of its own scope and parameter list, or not.

For example, the following anonymous function would not be a Closure, since it is self-contained and functionally equivalent to any other locally defined function:

```
System.Func<int,int> anon = (x) => { return x; };
int result = anon(5);
```

But, if the anonymous function pulled in data from outside itself, then it becomes a Closure, as it "closes the environment" around the required data. The following would result in a Closure:

```
int i = 1024;
System.Func<int,int> anon = (x) => { return x + i; };
int result = anon(5);
```

In order to complete this transaction, the compiler must define a new class that can reference the environment where the data value `i` would be accessible. At runtime it creates the corresponding object on the heap and provides it to the anonymous function. Note that this includes Value types (as per the above example), which were originally on the stack, possibly defeating the purpose of them being allocated on the stack in the first place. So, we should expect each invocation of the second method to result in heap allocations and inevitable garbage collection.

.NET library functions

The .NET library offers a huge amount of common functionality that helps solve numerous problems that programmers may come across during day-to-day implementation. Most of these classes and functions are optimized for general use cases, which may not be optimal for a specific situation. It may be possible to replace a particular .NET library class with a custom implementation that is more suited to our specific use case.

There are also two big features in the .NET library that often become big performance hogs whenever they're used. This tends to be because they are only included as a quick-and-hacky solution to a given problem without much effort put into optimization. These features are LINQ and Regular Expressions.

LINQ provides a way to treat arrays of data as miniature databases and perform queries against them using SQL-like syntax. The simplicity of its coding style, and complexity of the underlying system (through its usage of Closures), implies that it has a fairly large overhead cost. LINQ is a handy tool, but is not really intended for high-performance, real-time applications such as games, and does not even function on platforms that do not support JIT compilation, such as iOS.

Meanwhile, Regular Expressions, using the `Regex` class, allow us to perform complex string parsing to find substrings that match a particular format, replace pieces of a string, or construct strings from various inputs. Regular Expression is another very useful tool, but tends to be overused in places where it is largely unnecessary, or in seemingly "clever" ways to implement a feature such as text localization, when straightforward string replacement would be far more efficient.

Specific optimizations for both of these features go far beyond the scope of this book, as they could fill entire volumes by themselves. We should either try to minimize their usage as much as possible, replace their usage with something less costly, bring in a LINQ or Regex expert to solve the problem for us, or do some Googling on the subject to optimize how we're using them.

One of the best ways to find the correct answer online is to simply post the wrong answer! People will either help us out of kindness, or take such great offense to our implementation that they consider it their civic duty to correct us! Just be sure to do some kind of research on the subject first. Even the busiest of people are generally happy to help if they can see that we've put in our fair share of effort beforehand.

Temporary work buffers

If we get into the habit of using large, temporary work buffers for one task or another, then it just makes sense that we should look for opportunities to reuse them, instead of reallocating them over and over again, as this lowers the overhead involved in allocation, as well as garbage collection (so-called "memory pressure"). It might be worthwhile to extract such functionality from case-specific classes into a generic god class that contains a big work area for multiple classes to reuse.

Object pooling

Speaking of temporary work buffers, object pooling is an excellent way of both minimizing and establishing control over our memory usage by avoiding deallocation and reallocation. The idea is to formulate our own system for object creation, which hides away whether the object we're getting has been freshly allocated or has been recycled from an earlier allocation. The typical terms to describe this process are to "spawn" and "despawn" the object, rather than creating and deleting them, since any time an object is despawned we're simply hiding it from view until we need it again, at which point it is respawned and reused.

Let's cover a quick implementation of an object pooling system.

The first requirement is to allow the pooled object to decide how to recycle itself when the time comes. The following interface will satisfy the requirements nicely:

```
public interface IPoolableObject{
    void New();
    void Respawn();
}
```

This interface defines two methods; `New()` and `Respawn()`. These should be called when the object is first created, and when it has been respawned, respectively.

The second requirement is to provide a base implementation of this interface that allows objects of any type to handle any bookkeeping required to take care of the initial creation and respawning of objects.

The following ObjectPool class definition is a fairly simple implementation of the object pooling concept. It uses generics to support any object type so long as it fits two criteria; it must implement the IPoolableObject interface, and must allow for a parameter-less constructor (the new() keyword in the class declaration).

```
public class ObjectPool<T> where T : IPoolableObject, new() {
    private Stack<T> _pool;
    private int _currentIndex = 0;
    public ObjectPool(int initialCapacity) {
        _pool = new Stack<T>(initialCapacity);
        for(int i = 0; i < initialCapacity; ++i) {
            Spawn (); // instantiate a pool of N objects
        }
        Reset ();
    }

    public int Count {
        get { return _pool.Count; }
    }
    public void Reset() {
        _currentIndex = 0;
    }
    public T Spawn() {
        if (_currentIndex < Count) {
            T obj = _pool.Pop ();
            _currentIndex++;

            IPoolableObject ip = obj as IPoolableObject;
            ip.Respawn();

            return obj;
        } else {
            T obj = new T();
            _pool.Push(obj);
            _currentIndex++;

            IPoolableObject ip = obj as IPoolableObject;
            ip.New();
```

```
                    return obj;
            }
        }
    }
```

An example Poolable object would look like so. It must implement two public methods, `New()` and `Respawn()`, which are invoked by the `ObjectPool` class at the appropriate times:

```
public class TestObject : IPoolableObject {
    public void New() {
        // very first initialization here
    }
    public void Respawn() {
        // reset data which allows the object to be recycled here
    }
}
```

And finally, an example usage to create a pool of 100 `TestObject` objects:

```
private ObjectPool<TestObject> _objectPool = new
ObjectPool<TestObject>(100);
```

The first 100 calls to `Spawn()` on the `_objectPool` object will cause the objects to be respawned and provided to the caller. If the stack runs out of space, then it will add even more `TestObject` objects to the stack. Finally, if `Reset()` is called on `_objectPool`, then it will begin again from the start, recycling objects and providing them to the caller.

Note that this pooling solution will not work for classes we haven't defined, and cannot derive from, such as Vector3, and Quaternion. In these cases, we would need to define a containing class:

```
public class PoolableVector3 : IPoolableObject {
    public Vector3 vector = new Vector3();

    public void New() {
        Reset();
    }

    public void Respawn() {
        Reset();
    }
```

```
    public void Reset() {
        vector.x = vector.y = vector.z = 0f;
    }
}
```

We could extend this system in a number of ways, such as defining a `Despawn()` method to handle destruction of the object, making use of the `IDisposable` interface and `using` blocks when we wish to automatically spawn and despawn objects within a small scope, and/or allowing objects instantiated outside the pool to be added to it.

Prefab pooling

The previous pooling solution is useful for typical classes, but it won't work for special Unity objects, such as GameObject and MonoBehaviour. These objects tend to consume a large chunk of our runtime memory, can cost us a great deal of CPU usage when they're created and destroyed, and tend to risk a large amount of garbage collection at runtime. In other words, the main goal of Prefab pooling is to push the overwhelming majority of object instantiation to Scene initialization, rather than letting them get created at runtime. This can provide some big runtime CPU savings, and avoids a lot of spikes caused by object creation/destruction and garbage collection, at the expense of Scene loading times, and runtime memory consumption. As a result, there are quite a few pooling solutions available on the Asset Store for handling this task, with varying degrees of simplicity, quality, and feature sets.

 It is often recommended that pooling should be implemented in any game that intends to deploy on mobile devices, due to the greater overhead costs involved in the allocation and deallocation of memory compared to desktop applications.

However, creating a pooling solution is an interesting topic, and building one from scratch is a great way of getting to grips with a lot of important internal Unity Engine behavior. Also, knowing how such a system is built makes it easier to extend if we wish it to meet the needs of our particular game, rather than relying on a prebuilt solution.

The general idea of Prefab pooling is to create a system that contains lists of active and inactive GameObjects that were all instantiated from the same Prefab reference. The following diagram shows how the system might look after several spawns, despawns, and respawns of various objects derived from four different Prefabs (Orc, Troll, Ogre, and Dragon):

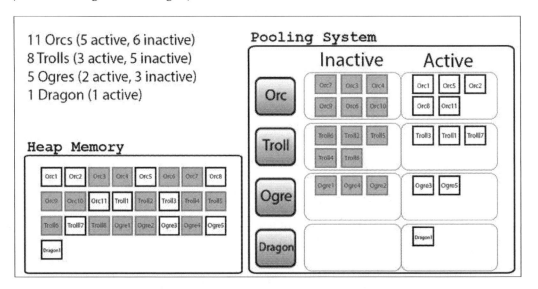

 Note that the **Heap Memory** area represents the objects as they exist in memory, while the **Pooling System** area represents references to those objects.

In this example, several instances of each Prefab were instantiated (11 Orcs, 8 Trolls, 5 Ogres, and 1 Dragon). Currently only eleven of these objects are active, while the other fourteen have previously been despawned, and are inactive. Note that the despawned objects still exist in memory, although they are not visible and cannot interact with the game world until they have been respawned. Naturally, this costs us a constant amount of heap memory at runtime in order to maintain the inactive objects, but when a new object is instantiated, we can reuse one of the existing inactive objects, rather than allocating *more* memory in order to satisfy the request. This saves significant runtime CPU costs during object creation and destruction, and avoids garbage collection.

The following diagram shows the chain of events that needs to occur when a new Orc is spawned:

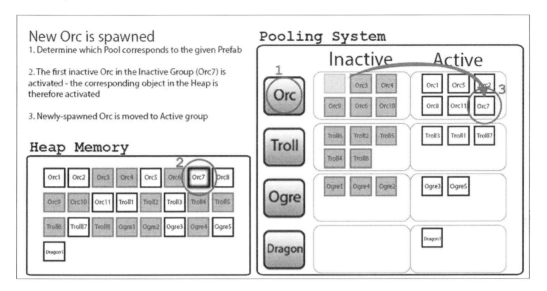

The first object in the Inactive Orc pool (Orc7) is reactivated and moved into the Active pool. We now have 6 active Orcs, and 5 inactive Orcs.

The following figure shows the order of events when an `Ogre` object is despawned:

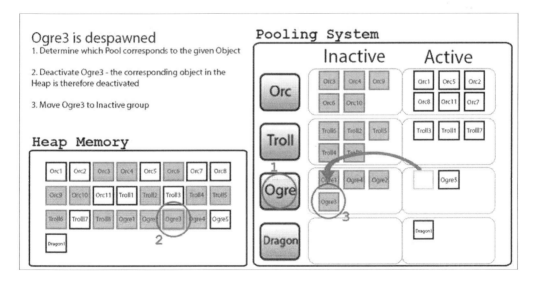

This time the object is deactivated and moved from the Active pool into the Inactive pool, leaving us with 1 active Ogre and 4 inactive Ogres.

Finally, the following diagram shows what happens when a new object is spawned, but there are no inactive objects to satisfy the request:

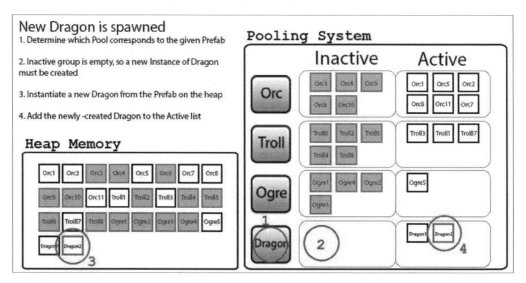

In this scenario, more memory must be allocated to instantiate the new Dragon object, since there are no Dragon objects in its Inactive pool to reuse. Therefore, in order to avoid runtime memory allocations for our GameObjects, it is critical that we know beforehand how many we will need. This will vary depending on the type of object in question, and requires occasional testing and debugging to ensure we have a sensible number of each Prefab instantiated at runtime.

With all of this in mind, let's create a pooling system for Prefabs!

Poolable Components

Let's first define an interface for a Poolable Component:

```
public interface IPoolableComponent {
    void Spawned();
    void Despawned();
}
```

The approach for `IPoolableComponent` will be very different from the approach taken for `IPoolableObject`. The objects being created this time are GameObjects, which are a lot trickier to work with than standard objects because of how much of their runtime behavior is already handled through the Unity Engine, and how little access we have to it.

GameObjects do not give us access to an equivalent `New()` method that we can invoke any time the object is created, and we cannot derive from the `GameObject` class in order to implement one. GameObjects are created either by placing them in a Scene, or by instantiating them at runtime through `GameObject.Instantiate()`, and the only inputs we can apply are an initial position and rotation. Of course, their Components have an `Awake()` method we can define, which is invoked the first time the Component is brought to life, but this is merely a compositional object—it's not the actual parent object we're spawning and despawning.

So, because we only have control over a GameObject class's Components, it is assumed that the `IPoolableComponent` interface is implemented by *at least one* of the Components that is attached to the GameObject we wish to pool.

The `Spawned()` method should be invoked on every implementing Component each time the pooled GameObject is respawned, while the `Despawned()` method gets invoked whenever it is despawned. This gives us entry points to control the data variables and behavior during the creation and destruction of the parent GameObject.

The act of despawning a GameObject is trivial; turn its active flag to `false` (through `SetActive()`). This disables the Collider and Rigidbody for physics calculations, removes it from the list of renderable objects, and essentially takes care of disabling interactions with all built-in Unity Engine subsystems in a single stroke. The only exception is any Coroutines that are currently invoking on the object, since as we learned earlier in *Chapter 2*, *Scripting Strategies*, Coroutines are invoked independently of `Update()` and GameObject activity. We will therefore need to call `StopCoroutine()`, or `StopAllCoroutines()` during the despawning of such objects.

In addition, Components typically hook into our own custom gameplay subsystems as well, and so the `Despawn()` method gives our Components the opportunity to take care of any custom cleanup before shutting down. For example, we would probably want to use `Despawn()` to deregister the Component from the Messaging System we defined back in *Chapter 2*, *Scripting Strategies*.

Unfortunately, successfully respawning the GameObject is a lot more complicated. When we respawn an object, there will be many settings that were left behind when the object was previously active, and these must be reset in order to avoid conflicting behaviors. A common problem with this is Rigidbody velocity. If this value is not explicitly reset before the object is reactivated, then the newly respawned object will continue moving with the same velocity the old version had when it was despawned.

This problem becomes further complicated by the fact that built-in Components are `sealed`, and therefore cannot be derived from. So, to avoid these issues, we can create a custom Component that resets the attached Rigidbody whenever the object is despawned:

```
public class ResetPooledRigidbodyComponent : MonoBehaviour,
IPoolableComponent {
    Rigidbody _body;
    public void Spawned() {  }
    public void Despawned() {
        if (_body == null) {
            _body = GetComponent<Rigidbody>();
            if (_body == null) {
                // no Rigidbody!
                return;
            }
        }
        _body.velocity = Vector3.zero;
        _body.angularVelocity = Vector3.zero;
    }
}
```

Note that the best place to perform this task is during despawning, because we cannot be certain in what order the GameObject class's `IPoolableComponent` interfaces will have their `Spawned()` methods invoked. It is unlikely that another `IPoolableComponent` will change the object's velocity during despawning, but it is possible that a different `IPoolableComponent` attached to the same object might want to set the Rigidbody's initial velocity to some important value during its own `Spawned()` method. Ergo, performing the velocity reset during the `ResetPooledRigidbodyComponent` class's `Spawned()` method could potentially conflict with other Components and cause some very confusing bugs.

In fact, creating Poolable Components that are not self-contained, and tend to tinker with other Components like this, is one of the biggest dangers of implementing a pooling system. We should minimize such implementations, and routinely verify them when we're trying to debug strange issues in our game.

For the sake of illustration, here is the definition of a simple Poolable Component that replaces the `TestMessageListener` class we defined back in *Chapter 2, Scripting Strategies*. This Component automatically handles some basic tasks every time the object is spawned and despawned:

```
public class PoolableTestMessageListener : MonoBehaviour,
IPoolableComponent {
    public void Spawned() {
        MessagingSystem.Instance.AttachListener
        (typeof(MyCustomMessage), this.HandleMyCustomMessage);
    }

bool HandleMyCustomMessage(BaseMessage msg) {
        MyCustomMessage castMsg = msg as MyCustomMessage;
        Debug.Log (string.Format("Got the message! {0}, {1}",
        castMsg._intValue, castMsg._floatValue));
        return true;
    }

    public void Despawned() {
        if (MessagingSystem.IsAlive) {
MessagingSystem.Instance.DetachListener(typeof(MyCustomMessage),
this.HandleMyCustomMessage);
        }
    }
}
```

The Prefab pooling system

Hopefully, we now have an understanding of what we need from our pooling system, so all that's left is to implement it. The requirements are as follows:

- It must accept requests to spawn a GameObject from a Prefab, an initial position, and an initial rotation:
  - If a despawned version already exists, it should respawn the first available one
  - If it does not exist, then it should instantiate a new GameObject from the Prefab
  - In either case, the `Spawned()` method should be invoked on all `IPoolableComponent` interfaces attached to the GameObject

- It must accept requests to despawn a specific GameObject:
  - If the object is managed by the pooling system, it should deactivate it and call the `Despawned()` method on all `IPoolableComponent` interfaces attached to the GameObject
  - If the object is not managed by the pooling system, it should send an error

The requirements are fairly straightforward, but the implementation requires some investigation if we wish to make the solution performance-friendly. Firstly, a typical Singleton would be a good choice for the main entry point, since we want this system to be globally accessible from anywhere:

```
public static class PrefabPoolingSystem {
}
```

The main task for object spawning involves accepting a Prefab reference, and figuring if we have any despawned GameObjects that were originally instantiated from the same reference. To do this, we will essentially want our pooling system to keep track of two different lists for any given Prefab reference: a list of active (spawned) GameObjects, and a list of inactive (despawned) objects that were instantiated from it. This data would be best abstracted into a separate class, which we will name `PrefabPool`.

In order to maximize the performance of this system (and hence make the largest gains possible, relative to just allocating and deallocating objects from memory all of the time), we will want to use some fast data structures in order to acquire the corresponding `PrefabPool` objects whenever a spawn or despawn request comes in.

Because spawning involves being given a Prefab, we will want one data structure that can quickly map Prefabs to the `PrefabPool` that manages them. And because despawning involves being given a GameObject, we will want another data structure that can quickly map spawned GameObjects to the `PrefabPool` that originally spawned them. A Dictionary is a good choice for both of these needs.

Let's define these maps in our pooling system:

```
public static class PrefabPoolingSystem {
    static Dictionary<GameObject,PrefabPool> _prefabToPoolMap =
    new Dictionary<GameObject,PrefabPool>();
    static Dictionary<GameObject,PrefabPool> _goToPoolMap = new
    Dictionary<GameObject,PrefabPool>();
}
```

Next we'll define what happens when we spawn an object:

```
public static GameObject Spawn(GameObject prefab, Vector3
position, Quaternion rotation) {
    if (!_prefabToPoolMap.ContainsKey (prefab)) {
        _prefabToPoolMap.Add (prefab, new PrefabPool());
    }
    PrefabPool pool = _prefabToPoolMap[prefab];
    GameObject go = pool.Spawn(prefab, position, rotation);
    _goToPoolMap.Add (go, pool);
    return go;
}
```

The `Spawn()` method will be given a Prefab reference, an initial position, and an initial rotation. We need to figure out which `PrefabPool` the Prefab belongs to (if any), ask it to spawn a new GameObject using the data provided, and then return the spawned object to the requestor. We first check our "Prefab-to-Pool" map, to see if a pool already exists for this Prefab. If not, we quickly create one. In either case, we then ask the `PrefabPool` to spawn us a new object. The `PrefabPool` will either end up respawning an object that was despawned earlier, or instantiate a new one (if there aren't any inactive instances left).

Either way, this class doesn't particularly care. It just wants the instance generated by the `PrefabPool` class so that it can be entered into the "GameObject-to-Pool" map and returned to the requestor.

For convenience, we can also define an overload which places the object at the world's center (useful for GameObjects that aren't visible, and just need to exist somewhere):

```
public static GameObject Spawn(GameObject prefab) {
    return Spawn (prefab, Vector3.zero, Quaternion.identity);
}
```

Note that no actual spawning and despawning are taking place, yet. This task will eventually be handled within the `PrefabPool` class.

Despawning involves being given a GameObject, and then figuring out which `PrefabPool` is managing it. This could be achieved by iterating through our `PrefabPool` classes and checking if they contain the given `GameObject`. But if we end up generating a lot of `PrefabPools`, then this iterative process can take a while. We will always end up with as many `PrefabPool` classes as we have Prefabs (at least so long as we manage all of them through the pooling system). Most projects tend to have dozens, hundreds, if not thousands of different Prefabs.

So, the GameObject-to-Pool map is maintained to ensure that we always have rapid access to the PrefabPool that originally spawned the object. It can also be used to quickly verify if the given GameObject is even managed by the pooling system to begin with. Here is the method definition for the despawning method, which takes care of these tasks:

```
public static bool Despawn(GameObject obj) {
    if (!_goToPoolMap.ContainsKey(obj)) {
        Debug.LogError (string.Format ("Object {0} not managed by
        pool system!", obj.name));
        return false;
    }

    PrefabPool pool = _goToPoolMap[obj];
    if (pool.Despawn (obj)) {
        _goToPoolMap.Remove (obj);
        return true;
    }
    return false;
}
```

 Note that the Despawn() method of both PrefabPoolingSystem and PrefabPool returns a Boolean that can be used to verify whether or not the object was successfully despawned.

As a result, thanks to the two maps we're maintaining, we can quickly access the PrefabPool that manages the given reference, and this solution will scale for any number of Prefab that the system manages.

Prefab pools

Now that we have a system that can handle multiple Prefab pools automatically, the only thing left is to define the behavior of the pools. As mentioned previously, we will want the PrefabPool class to maintain two data structures: one for active (spawned) objects that have been instantiated from the given Prefab and another for inactive (despawned) objects.

Technically, the PrefabPoolingSystem class already maintains a map of which Prefab is governed by which PrefabPool, so we can actually save a little memory by making the PrefabPool a slave to the PrefabPoolingSystem class, by not having it keep track of which Prefab it is managing. Consequently, the two data structures are the only member variables the PrefabPool needs to keep track of.

However, for each spawned GameObject, it must also maintain a list of all of its IPoolableComponent references in order to invoke the Spawned() and Despawned() methods on them. Acquiring these references can be a costly operation to perform at runtime, so it would be best to cache the data in a simple struct:

```
public struct PoolablePrefabData {
    public GameObject go;
    public IPoolableComponent[] poolableComponents;
}
```

This struct will contain a reference to the GameObject, and the precached list of its IPoolableComponents.

Now we can define the member data of our PrefabPool class:

```
public class PrefabPool {
    Dictionary<GameObject,PoolablePrefabData> _activeList = new
    Dictionary<GameObject,PoolablePrefabData>();
    Queue<PoolablePrefabData> _inactiveList = new
    Queue<PoolablePrefabData>();
}
```

The data structure for the active list should be a dictionary in order to do a quick lookup for the corresponding PoolablePrefabData from any given GameObject reference. This will be useful during object despawning.

Meanwhile, the inactive data structure is defined as a Queue, but it will work equally well as a List, a Stack, or really any data structure that needs to regularly expand or contract, and where we only need to pop items from one end of the list, since it does not matter which object it is. It only matters that we retrieve one of them. A Queue is useful in this case because we can both retrieve and remove the object from the data structure in a single call.

Object spawning

Let's define what it means to spawn a GameObject in the context of our pooling system: at some point, PrefabPool will get a request to spawn a GameObject from a given Prefab, at a particular position and rotation. The first thing we should check is whether or not we have any inactive instances of the Prefab. If so, then we can pop the next available one from the Queue and respawn it. If not, then we need to instantiate a new GameObject from the Prefab using GameObject.Instantiate(). At this moment, we should also create a PoolablePrefabData object to store the GameObject reference, and acquire the list of all IPoolableComponents that are attached to it.

Either way, we can now activate the GameObject, set its position and rotation, and call the Spawned() method on all of its IPoolableComponents. Once the object has been respawned, we can add it to the list of active objects and return it to the requestor.

Here is the definition of the Spawn() method that defines this behavior:

```
public GameObject Spawn(GameObject prefab, Vector3 position,
Quaternion rotation) {
    PoolablePrefabData data;
    if (_inactiveList.Count > 0) {
        data = _inactiveList.Dequeue();
    } else {
        // instantiate a new object
        GameObject newGO = GameObject.Instantiate(prefab,
        position, rotation) as GameObject;
        data = new PoolablePrefabData();
        data.go = newGO;
        data.poolableComponents =
        newGO.GetComponents<IPoolableComponent>();
    }

    data.go.SetActive (true);
    data.go.transform.position = position;
    data.go.transform.rotation = rotation;
    for(int i = 0; i < data.poolableComponents.Length; ++i) {
        data.poolableComponents[i].Spawned ();
    }
    _activeList.Add (data.go, data);

    return data.go;
}
```

Instance prespawning

Because we are using GameObject.Instantiate() whenever the pool has run out of despawned instances, this system does not completely rid us of runtime object instantiation and hence, heap memory allocation. It's important to prespawn the expected number of instances that we will need during the lifetime of the current Scene, so that we don't need to instantiate more during runtime.

It would be wasteful to prespawn 100 explosion particle effects, if the most we will ever expect to see in the Scene at any given time is three or four. Conversely, spawning too few instances will cause excessive runtime memory allocations, and the goal of this system is to push the majority of allocation to the start of a Scene's lifetime. We need to be careful about how many instances we maintain in memory so that we don't waste more memory space than necessary.

Let's define a method in our `PrefabPoolingSystem` class that we can use to quickly prespawn a given number of objects from a Prefab. This essentially involves spawning *N* objects, and then immediately despawning them all:

```
public static void Prespawn(GameObject prefab, int numToSpawn) {
    List<GameObject> spawnedObjects = new List<GameObject>();

    for(int i = 0; i < numToSpawn; i++) {
        spawnedObjects.Add (Spawn (prefab));
    }

    for(int i = 0; i < numToSpawn; i++) {
        Despawn(spawnedObjects[i]);
    }

    spawnedObjects.Clear ();
}
```

We would use this method during Scene initialization, to prespawn a collection of objects to use in the level. For example:

```
public class OrcPreSpawner : MonoBehaviour
    [SerializeField] GameObject _orcPrefab;
    [SerializeField] int _numToSpawn = 20;
    void Start() {
        PrefabPoolingSystem.Prespawn(_orcPrefab, _numToSpawn);
    }
}
```

Object despawning

Finally, there is the act of despawning the objects. As mentioned previously, this primarily involves deactivating the object, but we also need to take care of various bookkeeping tasks and invoking `Despawned()` on all of its `IPoolableComponent` references.

Here is the method definition for the `PrefabPool` class's `Despawn()` method:

```
public bool Despawn(GameObject objToDespawn) {
    if (!_activeList.ContainsKey(objToDespawn)) {
        Debug.LogError ("This Object is not managed by this object
                        pool!");
        return false;
    }

    PoolablePrefabData data = _activeList[objToDespawn];

    for(int i = 0; i < data.poolableComponents.Length; ++i) {
        data.poolableComponents[i].Despawned ();
    }
    data.go.SetActive (false);

    _activeList.Remove (objToDespawn);
    _inactiveList.Enqueue(data);
    return true;
}
```

First we verify the object is being managed by the pool, and then we grab the corresponding `PoolablePrefabData` in order to access the list of `IPoolableComponent` references. Once `Despawned()` has been invoked on all of them, we deactivate the object, remove it from the active list, and push it into the inactive queue so that it can be respawned later.

Prefab pool testing

The following class definition allows us to perform a simple hands-on test with the `PrefabPoolingSystem` class. It will support three Prefabs, and prespawn five instances during application initialization. We can press the 1, 2, or 3 keys to spawn an instance of each type, and then press Q, W, or E to despawn a random instance of each type.

```
public class PoolTester : MonoBehaviour {

    [SerializeField] GameObject _prefab1;
```

```
    [SerializeField] GameObject _prefab2;
    [SerializeField] GameObject _prefab3;

    List<GameObject> _go1 = new List<GameObject>();
    List<GameObject> _go2 = new List<GameObject>();
    List<GameObject> _go3 = new List<GameObject>();

    void Start() {
        PrefabPoolSystem_AsSingleton.Prespawn(_prefab1, 5);
        PrefabPoolSystem_AsSingleton.Prespawn(_prefab2, 5);
        PrefabPoolSystem_AsSingleton.Prespawn(_prefab3, 5);
    }

    void Update () {
        if (Input.GetKeyDown(KeyCode.Alpha1))
            {SpawnObject(_prefab1, _go1);}
        if (Input.GetKeyDown(KeyCode.Alpha2))
            {SpawnObject(_prefab2, _go2);}
        if (Input.GetKeyDown(KeyCode.Alpha3))
            {SpawnObject(_prefab3, _go3);}
        if (Input.GetKeyDown(KeyCode.Q)) { DespawnRandomObject
            (_go1); }
        if (Input.GetKeyDown(KeyCode.W)) { DespawnRandomObject
            (_go2); }
        if (Input.GetKeyDown(KeyCode.E)) { DespawnRandomObject
            (_go3); }
    }

    void SpawnObject(GameObject prefab, List<GameObject> list) {
        GameObject obj = PrefabPoolingSystem.Spawn (prefab,
        Random.insideUnitSphere * 8f, Quaternion.identity);
        list.Add (obj);
    }

    void DespawnRandomObject(List<GameObject> list) {
        if (list.Count == 0) {
            // Nothing to despawn
            return;
        }

        int i = Random.Range (0, list.Count);
        PrefabPoolingSystem.Despawn(list[i]);
        list.RemoveAt(i);
    }
}
```

Once we spawn more than five instances of any of the Prefabs, it will need to instantiate a new one in memory, costing us some memory allocation. But, if we observe the Memory Area in the Profiler, while we only spawn and despawn instances that already exist, then we will notice that absolutely no new allocations take place.

Prefab pooling and Scene loading

There is one subtle caveat to this system that has not yet been mentioned: the `PrefabPoolingSystem` class will outlast Scene lifetime since it is a static class. This means that, when a new Scene is loaded, the pooling system's dictionaries will attempt to maintain references to any pooled instances from the previous Scene, but Unity forcibly destroys these objects regardless of the fact that we are still keeping references to them (unless they were set to `DontDestroyOnLoad()`!), and so the dictionaries will be full of `null` references. This would cause some serious problems for the next Scene.

We should therefore create a method in `PrefabPoolingSystem` that resets the pooling system in preparation for this likely event. The following method should be called before a new Scene is loaded, so that it is ready for any early calls to `Prespawn()` in the next Scene:

```
public static void Reset() {
    _prefabToPoolMap.Clear ();
    _goToPoolMap.Clear ();
}
```

Note that, if we also invoke a garbage collection during Scene transitions, there's no need to explicitly empty the `PrefabPools` these dictionaries were referencing. Since these were the only references to the `PrefabPool` objects, they will be deallocated during the next garbage collection. If we aren't invoking garbage collection between Scenes, then the `PrefabPool` and `PooledPrefabData` objects will remain in memory until that time.

Prefab pooling summary

We have finally solved the problem of runtime memory allocations for GameObjects and Prefabs but, as a quick reminder, we need to be aware of the following caveats:

- We need to be careful about properly resetting important data in respawned objects (such as Rigidbody velocity)

- We must ensure we don't prespawn too few, or too many, instances of a Prefab

- We should be careful of the order of execution of `Spawned()` and `Despawned()` methods on `IPoolableComponents`
- We must call `Reset()` on `PrefabPoolingSystem` before Scene loading

There are several other features we could implement. These will be left as academic exercises if we wish to extend this system in the future:

- Any `IPoolableComponents` added to the GameObject after initialization will not be invoked. We could fix this by changing `PrefabPool` to keep acquiring `IPoolableComponents` every time `Spawned()` and `Despawned()` are invoked, at the cost of additional overhead during spawning/despawning.

- `IPoolableComponents` attached to children of the Prefab's root will not be counted. This could be fixed by changing `PrefabPool` to use `GetComponentsInChildren<T>`, at the cost of additional overhead if we're using Prefabs with deep hierarchies.

- Prefab instances that already exist in the Scene will not be managed by the pooling system. We could create a Component that needs to be attached to such objects and that notifies the `PrefabPoolingSystem` class of its existence and passes the reference into the corresponding `PrefabPool`.

- We could implement a way for `IPoolableComponents` to set a priority during acquisition, and directly control the order of execution for their `Spawned()` and `Despawned()` methods.

- We could add counters that keep track of how long objects have been sitting in the Inactive list relative to total Scene lifetime, and print out the data during shutdown. This could tell us whether or not we're prespawning too many instances of a given Prefab.

- This system will not interact kindly with Prefab instances that set themselves to `DontDestroyOnLoad()`. It might be wise to add a Boolean to every `Spawn()` call to say whether the object should persist or not, and keep them in a separate data structure that is not cleared out during `Reset()`.

- We could change `Spawn()` to accept an argument that allows the requestor to pass custom data to the `Spawned()` function of `IPoolableObject` for initialization purposes. This could use a system similar to how custom message objects were derived from the `BaseMessage` class for our Messaging System back in *Chapter 2, Scripting Strategies*.

The future of Mono and Unity

As we know, Unity does not use the latest and greatest Mono project code from http://www.mono-project.com, but an internally-customized version with some internal bug fixes.

 The actual Mono tweaks made by Unity Technologies can be found in the following GitHub repository:

https://github.com/Unity-Technologies/mono/

As an unfortunate consequence of how various components of the Mono Framework are licensed, Unity Technologies has only been able to update Mono on an infrequent basis. The occasions on which this task were accomplished was with the release of Unity 4, when they upgraded to Mono 2.6, and shortly afterwards version 2.6.5 back in mid-2010, which supports .NET 2.0/3.5 features. But, at the time of publication, the latest version of Mono, version 4.0, was released in May 2015, and supports .NET 4.5 features. This puts Unity's implementation about 5 years behind in terms of C# language and .NET framework features, which has drawn the ire of many Unity developers.

Unity Technologies has suggested there might be a Mono upgrade sometime in the lifecycle of Unity 5, but the last official update on this subject was back in August 2014. The Unity roadmap (https://unity3d.com/unity/roadmap) places it in the "Long and Uncertain" timeline, and Unity v5.2 was released in early September 2015, which did not include this upgrade. So, it is difficult to say when Mono will be receiving its much-needed upgrade. Unity Technologies has also been working with Microsoft to bring replacements to some Mono Components (such as upgraded versions of the static, JIT, and AOT compilers, as well as the CLR).

 Microsoft's announcement on the future of .NET:

http://blogs.msdn.com/b/dotnet/archive/2014/04/03/the-next-generation-of-net.aspx

Meanwhile, Unity Technologies has been working on the problem of long-term independence from these third-party dependencies for a while. With the release of Unity 5 they unveiled a new approach for script code compilation, which started as a way to provide improved scripting support for WebGL-based Unity applications, but has also been adopted as the main solution to these woes: IL2CPP.

Unity Technologies' IL2CPP announcement:

`http://blogs.unity3d.com/2014/05/20/the-future-of-scripting-in-unity/`

IL2CPP is shorthand for **Intermediate Language To C++,** and comes with its own .NET runtime that can be rolled out to multiple platforms. The basic idea is that C# script code will be converted into an intermediate language and then converted again to C++ during the build process. The resulting C++ will be pushed through one of several available platform-specific compilers to support cross-platform capability, taking away the burden of having to create and manage their own compilers.

This process will be mostly disguised from the user, and naturally there will be a loss of control as the code is pushed through multiple "code filters" with varying levels of optimizations. It remains to be seen if they allow some hooks to control the compilation process for advanced developers. The Editor is still expected to run on the C# .NET runtime for faster development iteration.

The suggested benefits of this approach include performance enhancements (since even near-native code generated by the JIT compiler still pales in comparison to statically-compiled native C++), faster porting and feature development for the Unity Engine, and improved garbage collection. The first platform to get the IL2CPP treatment in Unity 5 is WebGL, and will eventually be pushed to other platforms as the system matures, and becomes more reliable.

For more information on IL2CPP check out the various blog posts from Unity Technologies on the subject. The following post contains lots of information, as well as further links on important topics:

`http://blogs.unity3d.com/2015/05/06/an-introduction-to-ilcpp-internals/`

Why doesn't Unity Technologies just provide a C++ API for Unity? One can only speculate, but it's a pretty safe assumption that Unity supports a very large user base of developers who would be uncomfortable working in C++ directly. Losing the accessibility of C# and UnityScript would result in a very different product. Long-term, it would likely split the customer base into two camps, which rarely bodes well since whichever one brings in the most revenue will become the one that is supported to a greater degree, leaving the other to rot (as an interesting analogy, games typically suffer from the same problem, as expansions and map packs tend to segregate the multiplayer user base).

In addition, there are many .NET languages that share the same intermediate code after compilation (CIL), and they have a common binary interface, which makes it orders of magnitude easier to support cross-platform development and multiple libraries than with C++. Presumably, IL2CPP is a compromise for these concerns.

So, to make a long story short, there are a great many changes going on with the underlying Unity Engine and it's too early to say whether the IL2CPP approach will work sufficiently well on all platforms to keep feature parity and ease of deployment. One thing is for sure; the next couple of years of Unity development will bring some interesting transitions!

Summary

We've covered a humungous amount of theory and language concepts in this chapter, which have hopefully shed some light on how the internals of the Unity Engine and C# language work. These tools try their best to spare us from the burden of complex memory management, but there is still a whole host of concerns we need to keep in mind as we develop our game. Between the compilation processes, multiple memory domains, the complexities of Value types versus Reference types, passing by value versus passing by reference, boxing, object pooling, and various quirks within the Unity API, we have a lot of things to worry about. But, with enough practice, we will learn to overcome them without needing to keep referring to giant tomes such as this!

This chapter effectively concludes all of the techniques we can bestow that explicitly aim to improve application performance. Workflow optimizations are always useful things to keep in mind, however, as there are a lot of neat little nuances to the Unity Engine that aren't well known or clearly documented, and that only become apparent through experience and community involvement. As such, the next chapter will be full of hints and tips for improving how to manage our project and Scenes more effectively, how to make the most of the Editor, and hopefully save ourselves enough development time to actually implement all of the optimization techniques we've talked about through this entire book.

8

Tactical Tips and Tricks

There are a lot of little nuances to using the Unity Engine that can help improve our project workflow. However, quite a lot of the Editor's functionality is not well documented, well known, or just not something we think about until after the fact that it could have been applied perfectly to solve a particular problem we were having 6 months ago.

The Internet is crammed full of blogs and forum posts that try to help other Unity developers learn about these useful features, but they only tend to focus on a handful of tips at a time. There don't seem to be any online resources that group together many of them in one place. As a result, intermediate and advanced users probably have bookmarked managers bursting at the seams with links to these tips that they run into at one point or another, but which sit and rot until it comes time to do some spring cleaning.

So, because this book is primarily for intermediate and advanced users, it felt like it was worth throwing in a short chapter to bring tons of these tips and tricks together in one location. It works as a reference list in the hope of saving us a lot of future development effort.

Editor hotkey tips

The Editor is rife with hotkeys that can aid rapid development. It's worth checking out the documentation. But let's be honest, nobody reads the manual until they need something from it. Here are some of the most useful, yet lesser-known hotkeys available when playing with the Unity Editor.

 In all cases, the Windows hotkey is listed. If the OSX hotkey requires a different set of keystrokes, then it will be shown in parentheses.

GameObjects

GameObjects can be duplicated by selecting them in the hierarchy and pressing *Ctrl + D* (Cmd + D).

New, empty GameObjects can be created using *Ctrl + Shift + N* (Cmd + Shift + N).

Press Ctrl + *Shift + A* (Cmd + Shift + A) to quickly open the **Add Component** menu. From there, you can type in the name of the Component you wish to add.

Scene View

Pressing *Shift + F* or double-tapping the *F* key will follow an object in the Scene View, which can be helpful for tracking high-velocity objects or figuring out why objects might be falling out of our Scene.

Holding *Alt* and left-click dragging with the mouse will make the Scene View camera orbit the currently selected object (as opposed to looking around it). Holding *Alt* and right-click dragging will zoom the camera in/out.

Holding *Ctrl* and left-click dragging will cause the selected object to snap to the grid as it moves. The same can be done for rotation by holding *Ctrl* as we adjust the rotation widgets around the object. Selecting **Edit | Snap Settings...** opens a window where we can edit the grid that objects snap to on a per-axis basis.

We can force objects to snap by vertex, holding the *V* key as we move the object around. The selected object will attach itself to the nearest vertex, to the cursor of the nearest object. This is very useful for aligning level pieces into place, such as platforms and other tile-based systems, without needing to hand-adjust position vectors.

At one point, in Unity versions 4.2 to 4.6, it was possible to hold *Shift* with a Collider object selected to reveal little hooks through which we could adjust the Collider through the Scene View. This was removed in recent versions of Unity due to conflicts with other controls. We must use the **Edit Collider** button within the Collider component to access this feature going forward.

Arrays

We can duplicate array elements that have been exposed in the **Inspector** View by selecting them and pressing *Ctrl + D* (Cmd + D). This will copy the element and insert it into the array immediately after the current selection.

We can remove entries from an array of references (for example, an array of GameObjects) by pressing *Shift + Delete* (Cmd + *Delete*). This will strip away the element and condense the array. Note that the first press will clear the reference setting it to null, but the second press will remove the element. Removing elements in arrays of primitive types (ints, floats, and so forth) can be accomplished by simply pressing *Delete* without the *Shift* key (Cmd) modifier.

We can use the *W*, *A*, *S*, *D* keys while right-click dragging on the Scene View to fly around with the camera, in a typical first-person camera control style. The *Q* and *E* keys can be used to translate the camera on the vertical axis, respectively.

Interface

We can hold *Alt* and click on any hierarchy arrow (the small grey arrow to the left of any parent object name) to expand the object's full hierarchy and not just the next layer. This works on GameObjects in the **Hierarchy** View, folders and Prefabs within the **Project** View, lists in the **Inspector** View, and so on.

We can save and restore selections from objects in the **Hierarchy** or **Project** Views in typical RTS game style! Make the selection and press *Ctrl + Alt + <0-9>* (Cmd + *Alt + <0-9>*) to save the selection. Press *Ctrl + Shift + <0-9>* (Cmd + *Shift + <0-9>*) to restore it. This is exceptionally useful if we find ourselves selecting the same handful of objects over and over again while we make adjustments.

Pressing *Shift* + Spacebar will expand the current window to fill the entire Editor screen. Pressing it again will shrink the window and restore it to its previous location.

Pressing *Ctrl + Shift + P* (Cmd + *Shift + P*) will toggle the **Pause** button while in Play Mode.

Other

We can quickly access the documentation of any Unity keyword or class, by highlighting it in MonoDevelop and pressing *Ctrl + '* (Cmd + '). This will open the default browser and perform a search on the Unity documentation for the given keyword or class.

 Note that users with European keyboards may also need to hold down the *Shift* key.

With the recent release of **Visual Studio Tools for Unity** (**VSTU**), it is possible to access the documentation in the same way through Visual Studio by pressing *Ctrl + Alt + M*, followed by *Ctrl + H* (no equivalent OSX hotkey, obviously).

Editor interface tips

The following collection of tips relates to the Editor and its interface controls.

General

We can prioritize which Scripts will have their Update and Fixed Update methods called before others, by navigating to **Edit | Project Settings | Script Execution Order**. With the exception of some time-sensitive systems, such as audio processing, if we find ourselves trying to solve complex problems using this feature, it implies that we've got some fragile and tight coupling between our Components. From a software design perspective, this can be a warning sign that we might need to approach the problem from another angle. However, it can be helpful to have particular objects get their `Update()` and `LateUpdate()` functions called before other objects, in order to do some bookkeeping.

Integrating Unity projects with a Source Control solution can be a little tricky. The first step is to force the project to generate `.meta` files for assets; if we don't do this, then anyone pulling data into their local Unity project must regenerate their own metadata files. This can easily cause conflicts, so it is essential that everyone uses the same versions. Visible metadata files can be enabled by navigating to **Edit | Project Settings | Editor | Version Control | Mode | Visible Meta Files**. All of the `.meta` files will now be visible within the file structure and available for upload into Source Control.

It can also be helpful to convert certain asset data into a Text-only format, rather than binary data, to allow manual editing of data files. This turns many data files into the much more human-readable YAML format. For instance, if we're using `ScriptableObjects` to store custom data, we can use a text editor to search and edit these files without having to do it all through the Unity Editor and serialization system. This can save a lot of time, especially when hunting for a particular data value or when multiediting across different derived types. This option can be enabled by navigating to **Edit | Project Settings | Editor | Asset Serialization | Mode | Force Text**.

The Editor has a log file, which can be accessed by opening the Console window (where log messages are printed out to), clicking on the "hamburger icon" (made from three horizontal lines) at the top-right, and selecting **Open Editor Log**. If we recently built our project, it will contain a breakdown of compressed file sizes of all assets that were packed into the executable and ordered by size. This is an extremely helpful way of figuring out which assets are consuming the majority of our application footprint (hint: it's almost always Texture files), and which files are taking up more space than we would expect.

Additional windows can be added to the Editor by right-clicking on the title of an existing window and selecting **Add Tab**. This also allows us to add *duplicate* windows, such as having more than one **Inspector** View open at a time:

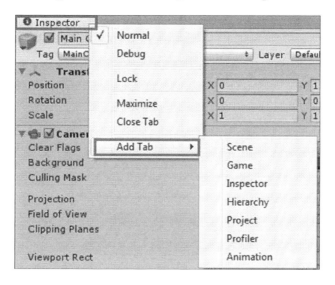

Having duplicate views can be kind of redundant, unless we use the "lock icon" to lock the given view to its current selection. When we select an object, all **Inspector** Views will update to show the object's data, except for any locked **Inspector** Views, which continue to show the data of the object they were locked to.

Common tricks that make use of window locking include the following:

- Using two of the same View (**Inspector**, **Animation**, and so forth) to compare two objects side-by-side or easily copy data from one to another

- Using a duplicate **Project** View to move large data sets around

- Testing what happens to any dependent objects if an object is tweaked during runtime

- Selecting multiple objects in the **Project** View, then dragging-and-dropping them into a serialized array in the **Inspector** View without losing the original selection

The Inspector View

We can enter calculations into numeric inspector fields. For example, typing `4*128` into an `int` field will resolve the value to `512`, sparing us from having to pull out a calculator or do the math in our head.

Array elements can be duplicated and deleted from a list (in the same fashion as the hotkeys mentioned previously) by right-clicking on the root element and selecting **Duplicate Array Element** or **Delete Array Element**.

A Component's context menu can be accessed through both the small cog icon in the upper-right or by right-clicking on the name of the Component. Every Component's context menu contains a **Reset** option, which resets all values back to their default, sparing us from having to reset values manually. This is useful when working with Transform Components, as this option will set the object's position and rotation to `(0,0,0)` and its scale to `(1,1,1)`.

It's commonly known that, if a GameObject was spawned from a Prefab, then the entire object can be reverted back to its initial Prefab state using the **Revert** button at the top of the **Inspector** View. However, it's less well known that individual values can be reverted by right-clicking on the name of the value and selecting **Revert Value to Prefab**. This restores the selected value, leaving the rest untouched.

The **Inspector** View has a debug mode that can be accessed by clicking on the hamburger icon next to the lock icon and selecting **Debug**. This will disable all custom Inspector drawing and reveal all raw data within the given GameObject and its components, even private data fields. Private fields are grayed-out and cannot be modified through the **Inspector** View, but this gives us a useful way of examining private data and other hidden values during Play Mode. The **Debug** view also reveals internal ObjectIDs, which can be useful if we're doing "interesting" things with Unity's serialization system and want to resolve conflicts.

If we have an array of data elements serialized in the **Inspector** View, then they are typically labeled Element <N> where <N> is the array index. This can make it tricky to find a specific element if our array elements are a series of serialized classes or structs, which tend to have multiple children themselves. However, if the *very first field* in the object is a string, then the elements will be named after the value of the string field.

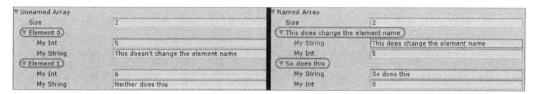

When a mesh object is selected, the **Preview** window at the bottom of the **Inspector** View is often fairly small, making it hard to see details in the mesh and how it will look when it appears in our Scene. But, if we right-click on the top bar of the **Preview** window, it will be detached and enlarged, making it much easier to see our mesh. We don't have to worry about setting the detached window back to its original home because, if the detached window is closed, then the **Preview** window will return to the bottom of the **Inspector** View.

The Project View

The **Project** View's search bar allows us to filter for objects of a particular type by clicking on the small icon to the right of the search bar. This provides a list of different types we can filter by, revealing all objects of that type within the entire project. However, selecting these options simply fills the search bar with a string of the t:<type> format, which applies the appropriate filter.

Thus, we can simply type the equivalent strings into the search bar for the sake of speed. For instance, typing t:prefab will filter for all Prefabs, no matter where they can be found in the hierarchy; t:texture will reveal textures, t:scene will reveal Scenes, and so on. Adding multiple search filters in the search bar will include objects of all types (it does not reveal objects which only satisfy both filters). These filters are modifiers in addition to name-based filtering, so adding a plain text string will cause a name-based search through the filtered objects. For example, t:texture normalmap will find all texture files that include the word normalmap in their name.

If we're making use of AssetBundles and the built-in labeling system, the **Project** View's search bar also allows us to hunt down bundled objects by their label using l:<label type>.

If a `MonoBehaviour` script contains serialized references (using `[SerializeField]` or `public`) to Unity Assets, such as Meshes and Textures, then we can assign default values directly into the script itself. Select the script file in the **Project** View and the **Inspector** View should contain a field for the asset for us to drag-and-drop the default assignment into.

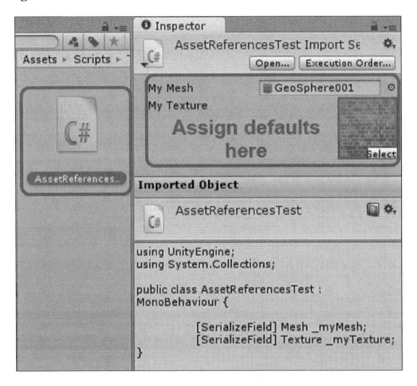

By default, the **Project** View splits files and folders into two columns and treats them separately. If we prefer the **Project** View to have a typical hierarchy folder and file structure, then we can set it to **One Column Layout** in its context menu (the hamburger icon at the top right). This can be a great space saver in some Editor layouts.

Right-clicking on any object in the **Project** View and selecting **Select Dependencies** will reveal all objects upon which this asset relies in order to exist, such as Textures, Meshes, `MonoBehaviour` script files, and so on. For Scene files, it will list all entities referenced within that Scene. This is helpful if we're trying to perform some asset cleanup.

The Hierarchy View

A lesser-known feature of the **Hierarchy** View is the ability to perform component-based filtering within the currently active Scene. Confusingly, it uses the same syntax as performing type-based filtering in the **Project** View and can therefore be accomplished by typing `t:<component name>`. For example, typing `t:light` into the **Hierarchy** View search bar will reveal all objects in the Scene that contain a Light component.

Upper- or lower-case characters are unimportant, but the string must match the full component name in order for the search to complete. Components that derive from the given type will also be revealed, so typing `t:renderer` will reveal all objects with derived components such as Mesh Renderers, Skinned Mesh Renderers, and so on.

The Scene and Game Views

The Scene View camera is not visible from the Game View, but it is generally a lot easier to move around and place through the use of the hotkeys mentioned previously. The Editor allows us to align the selected object to the same position and rotation of the Scene camera by navigating to **GameObject | Align with View** (*Ctrl + Shift + F* / Cmd + *Shift + F*). This means that we can use the camera controls to place the Scene camera where we would like our object to be, and place the object there by aligning it to the camera.

Similarly, we can align the Scene view to the selected object by navigating to the **GameObject | Align View to Selected** option. This is useful for checking if the given object is pointing in the right direction.

We can perform similar component-based filtering on the Scene View, as we can with the **Hierarchy** View, using the `t:<component>` syntax within its search bar.

At the very top right of the Unity Editor is a drop down labeled **Layers**. This contains a Layer-based filtering and locking system for the Scene View. Toggling on the "eye" icon will show/hide all objects of that Layer within the Scene View. Toggling the lock icon will allow or prevent objects of the given layer from being selected. This is helpful for things such as preventing someone from accidentally selecting and moving background objects that have already been situated in the perfect location.

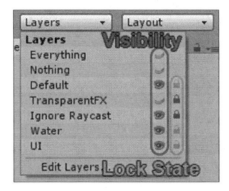

A commonly known and useful feature of the Editor is that GameObjects can be given special icons or labels to make them easier to find in the Scene View. This is particularly helpful for objects with no renderer but that we wish to find easily. For instance, objects such as Lights and Cameras have built-in icons that identify them in our Scene View more easily.

However, the same gizmos can be revealed within the **Game** View by clicking on the **Gizmos** button at the top right of the **Game** View. The drop down for this option determines what gizmos will be visible when this option is enabled.

Play Mode

Since Play Mode changes are not automatically saved, it is wise to modify the tint color applied during Play Mode to make it blatantly obvious which mode we're current working with. This value can be set by navigating to **Edit** | **Preferences** | **Colors** | **Playmode tint**.

Changes can be saved from Play Mode by simply using the clipboard. If we're tweaking an object in Play Mode and we're happy with its settings, then we can copy the object into the clipboard using *Ctrl + C* (Cmd + C), and paste it back into the Scene once Play Mode ends with *Ctrl + V* (Cmd + V). All settings on the object at the time of the copy will be kept. The same can be done with individual values or entire components using the **Copy Component** and **Paste Component** options in the component's context menu. However, the clipboard can only contain data for one object, component, *or* value, at a time.

Another approach, which allows us to save the data of multiple objects during Play Mode, is to create Prefabs from them by dragging and dropping them into the **Project** Window at runtime, once we're happy with the settings. If the original object was derived from a Prefab, and we wish to update it across all instances, then we only need to overwrite the old Prefab with the new one we created by dragging and dropping the copy on top of the original. Note that this also works during Play Mode runtime, but it can be dangerous since there is no dialog pop-up to confirm the overwrite. Be very careful not to overwrite the wrong Prefab.

We can use the **Frame Skip** button (the button to the right of the Pause button in the Editor) to iterate one frame at a time. This can be useful for watching frame-by-frame physics or gameplay behavior. Keep in mind that this causes both one Fixed Update and one Update to be called each step, in equal counts, which may not exactly reflect actual runtime behavior where we tend to have unequal calls to these methods.

If the Pause button is enabled when Play Mode begins, then the game will be paused just after the very first frame, giving us a chance to observe any anomalies that occurred from initialization of our Scene.

Scripting tips

The following tips are useful features to know when scripting.

General

We can modify various templates of new Script, Shader, and Compute Shader files. This can be helpful to remove the empty Update stubs which, as we learned, can cause unnecessary runtime overhead. These files can be found in the following locations:

- Windows: `<Unity install>\Editor\Data\Resources\ScriptTemplates\`
- OSX: `/Applications/Unity/Editor/Data/Resources/ScriptTemplates/`

The recent release of Unity Version 5.1 introduced the `Assert` class and allows for assert-based debugging, which some developers are more comfortable with as opposed to exception-based debugging. Check the Unity documentation for more information on Asserts: `http://docs.unity3d.com/ScriptReference/Assertions.Assert.html`

Calling `Debug.Break()` is functionally equivalent to pausing the Editor during Play Mode, which can be useful for catching awkward graphical behavior, or as a more convenient alternative to the absurd hotkey required to pause the Scene (*Ctrl + Shift + P*).

Attributes

Attributes are very useful meta-level tags that can be given to almost any target in C#. They are most commonly used on member data (fields) and classes, allowing us to flag them with special properties so that they can be processed differently. Intermediate and advanced Unity developers will find it worthwhile to read the C# documentation on attributes and use their imagination to come up with their own attributes that help accelerate their workflow. There are quite a few attributes built in to the Unity engine that can be exceptionally useful when used in the right place.

 Advanced users will note that attributes can also be given to enums, delegates, methods, parameters, events, modules, and even assemblies.

Variable attributes

Public variables are fairly dangerous things to add to our components, as anything can come along and change the value at runtime, making it hard to trace bugs, as well as requiring special hand holding to prevent the variable from being given an invalid value. However, `public` variables are usually the first way that Unity developers learn to expose variables in the **Inspector** View. In some cases, the `public` variable is absolutely intended to be public, but we don't wish it to be seen in the **Inspector**. In such a case, the `[HideInInspector]` attribute can be used to hide the variable from the **Inspector**, whenever necessary.

However, the preferred approach is to make our variables private or protected and allow Editor-based development by exposing values through the `[SerializeField]` attribute. This attribute allows private and protected variables to be revealed in the **Inspector** for designers to manipulate, without risking other components accidentally changing the variable at runtime.

The `[Range]` attribute can be added to an integer or floating-point field to convert it into a slider in the **Inspector** View. We can give minimum and maximum values, limiting the range that the value can contain.

Normally, if a variable is renamed, even if we do a refactor through our IDE (whether its MonoDevelop or Visual Studio) then the values are lost as soon as Unity recompiles the MonoBehaviour and makes the appropriate changes to any instances of the component. However, the `[FormerlySerializedAs]` attribute is incredibly helpful if we wish to rename a variable that has been previously serialized, as it will copy the data from the variable named within the attribute into the given variable during compilation time. No more lost data due to renaming stuff!

Note that it is *not* safe to remove the `[FormerlySerializedAs]` attribute after the conversion is completed, unless the variable has been manually changed and resaved since completion. The ".prefab" data file will still contain the old variable name, and so it still needs the `[FormerlySerializedField]` attribute to figure out where to place the data the next time the file is loaded (for example, when the Editor is closed and reopened). Thus, this is a helpful attribute, but extended use does tend to clutter up our codebase a lot.

Class attributes

The `[SelectionBase]` attribute will mark any GameObject the component is attached to as the root of selection for the Scene View. This is especially useful if we have meshes that are children of other objects, as we might want the parent object to be selected with the first click, instead of the object with the Mesh Renderer component.

We can use the `[RequireComponent]` attribute to force designers to attach vital components to the same GameObject if they attempt to attach this component. This ensures any dependencies that our codebase relies on will be satisfied by designers, without having to write out a whole bunch of documentation for them.

The `[ExecuteInEditMode]` attribute will force the object's `Update()`, `OnGUI()`, and `OnRenderObject()` methods to be called even during Edit Mode. However, there are caveats:

- The `Update()` method is only called if something changes in the Scene
- `OnGUI()` is only called during Game View events, not for other views such as the Scene View
- `OnRenderObject()` is called during any repaint event for the Scene and Game Views

However, this gives such objects a different set of event hooks and entry points compared to typical Editor scripts, so this attribute still has its uses.

Logging

We can add rich text tags to debug strings. Tags such as `<size>`, `<b>` (bold), `<i>` (italics), and `<color>` all work on debug strings. This can be helpful for differentiating the different kinds of log messages and highlighting specific elements.

```
Debug.Log ("<color=red>[ERROR]</color>This is a <i>very</i>
<size=14><b>specific</b></size> kind of log message");
```

The MonoBehaviour class has a print() method for convenience, which does the same thing as Debug.Log().

It can help to create a custom logger class, which automatically appends \n\n to the end of every log message. This will push and hide away the unnecessary UnityEngine.Debug:Log(Object) clutter that tends to fill the Console window.

Useful links

Unity technologies provide many useful tutorials on the usage of various scripting features, which are primarily targeted at beginner and intermediate-level developers. The tutorials can be found at https://unity3d.com/learn/tutorials/topics/scripting.

There's a helpful post on Unity Answers, which provides a reference list that covers many of the different scripting and compilation errors we might run across during development, which can be found at http://answers.unity3d.com/questions/723845/what-are-the-c-error-messages.html.

ScriptableObjects are very useful objects and an excellent way of storing game data in a form that does not need to be instantiated at runtime. They work like any other class in that they can contain methods and variables, can be serialized, allow polymorphism, and so on. The only tricky part is they can only be created through scripting, and must be loaded into memory at any time using Resources.Load(). But this allows us to control which ScriptableObjects are present in memory at any given time, giving us more control over runtime memory consumption. Explaining the nuances of ScriptableObjects here would take too much space, but Unity technologies have provided a good introductory examination of ScriptableObjects in the following tutorial video:

https://unity3d.com/learn/tutorials/modules/beginner/live-training-archive/scriptable-objects

> Note that, despite the category of the ScriptableObject video, it's generally considered more of an intermediate-level topic. Beginners would be best served by focusing on becoming comfortable with Prefabs, before turning things on their head through ScriptableObjects and the important serialization topics that need to be understood.

Nested Coroutines are another interesting and useful area of scripting that is not well documented. But, the following third-party blog post, which covers a lot of the interesting details, should be considered when working with Nested Coroutines:

`http://www.zingweb.com/blog/2013/02/05/unity-coroutine-wrapper`

We can figure out when a particular feature was added to the Unity API by checking the API history page at `http://docs.unity3d.com/ScriptReference/40_ history.html`.

Custom editors/menus tips

We can set custom hotkeys for MenuItems. For example, we can make the *K* key trigger our Menu item method, by defining the `MenuItem` attribute as follows:

```
[MenuItem("My Menu/Menu Item _k")]
```

We can also include modifier keys such as *Ctrl* (Cmd), *Shift*, and *Alt* using the %, #, and & characters, respectively.

MenuItems also have two overloads, which allows us to set two additional parameters: a Boolean that determines whether the menu item requires a validation method, and an integer that determines the menu item's priority in the hierarchy.

Check the documentation for MenuItems for a complete list of available hotkey modifiers, special keys, and how to create validation methods:

`http://docs.unity3d.com/ScriptReference/MenuItem.html`

It is possible to "ping" an object in the Hierarchy, similar to what happens when we click on a GameObject reference in the **Inspector** View, by calling `EditorGUIUtility.PingObject()`.

The original implementation of the Editor class, and the way that most people learned how to write Editor scripts, originally involved writing all logic and content drawing in the same class. However, `PropertyDrawers` are an effective way of delegating Inspector drawing to a different class from the main Editor class. This effectively separates input and validation behavior from display behavior, allowing more fine-tuned control of rendering on a per-field basis and more effective reuse of code. We can even use Property Drawers to override default Unity drawing for built-in objects, such as Vectors and Quaternions.

`PropertyDrawers` make use of `SerializedProperties` to accomplish serialization of individual fields, and they should be preferred when writing editor scripts, since they make use of built-in undo, redo, and multiedit functionality. Data validation can be a little problematic, and the best solution is to use `OnValidate()` calls on setter properties for fields. A session at Unite 2013 by Unity Technologies developer Tim Cooper, which explains the benefits and pitfalls of various serialization and validation approaches in great detail at `https://www.youtube.com/watch?v=Ozc_hXzp_KU`.

We can add entries to Component context menus and even the context menus of individual fields with the `[ContextMenu]` and `[ContextMenuItem]` attributes. This allows an easy way to customize Inspector behavior for our Components without needing to write broad Editor classes or custom Inspectors.

Advanced users may find it useful to store custom data within Unity metadata files through the `AssetImporter.userData` variable. There are also a multitude of opportunities to make use of Reflection of the Unity codebase. Ryan Hipple's session at Unite 2014 outlines a huge number of neat little hacks and tricks one achieve with Reflection in the Unity Editor:

`https://www.youtube.com/watch?v=SyR4OYZpVqQ`

An undocumented feature was introduced in Unity v4.5, **Reorderable Lists**. These allow us to have an Inspector View of a generic `List<T>`, which can be easily reordered by dragging and dropping the elements around. However, this feature appears to be unfinished, as it requires a custom Editor class to make use of them properly. The following post on Unity Answers explains how to use Reorderable Lists fairly succinctly:

`http://answers.unity3d.com/questions/826062/re-orderable-object-lists-in-inspector.html`

External tips

The following tips and tricks relate to topics outside the Unity Editor itself that can help Unity development workflow enormously.

Googling Unity-related problems or concerns can go a lot faster if we start the search with `"site:unity3d.com"`.

If the Unity Editor crashes, for whatever reason, then we can potentially restore our Scene by renaming the following file to include the `.unity` extension (for Scene files), and copying it into our `Assets` folder:

```
\<project folder>\Temp\_EditModeScene
```

If we're developing on Windows, then there's very little reason not to use Visual Studio at this point. MonoDevelop has been dragged along kicking and screaming for many years, and many developers have been switching over to the more feature-rich Visual Studio Community edition for most of their development workflow needs, particularly with incredibly helpful plugins such as Resharper.

For some developers, the only reason to boot up MonoDevelop has been for runtime debugging of code, but with the recent release of Visual Studio Tools for Unity (VSTU), Visual Studio now offers better integration with the Unity Editor. It even allows our C# code to be runtime-debugged through Visual Studio itself. Unless we have particular hangups about the interface or the fact that it's made by the big, bad Microsoft, we should want to give Visual Studio Community a try as it accelerate our script code development in ways we hadn't expected.

Check out the following video for more information on Visual Studio and its integration with Unity through VSTU:

```
https://channel9.msdn.com/Events/Visual-Studio/Visual-Studio-2015-
Final-Release-Event/Building-Unity-games-in-Visual-Studio
```

There is a great resource for game programming patterns (or rather, typical programming patterns explained in a way that is pertinent to game development) and it is completely free and available online:

```
http://gameprogrammingpatterns.com/contents.html
```

Keep an eye on any session videos that come from Unite conferences, whenever they happen (or better yet, try to attend them). There's usually a couple of panels at each conference held by experienced developers sharing lots of cool and interesting things they've been able to accomplish with the Engine and Editor. In addition to this, make sure to keep involved in the Unity community, either through the forums on unity3d.com, Twitter, reddit, Stack Overflow and Unity Answers, or at whatever social gathering places pop out of the woodwork in the coming years.

Every single tip that was included in this book started out as an idea or tidbit of knowledge that someone shared somewhere at some point. So, the best way to keep up-to-date on the best tips, tricks, and techniques is to keep our fingers on the pulse of where Unity is heading by staying involved in its community.

Other tips

Finally, the following section contains tips that didn't quite fit into other categories.

It's always a good idea to organize our Scenes using empty GameObjects and name them something sensible. The only drawback to this method is that the empty object's Transform is included during position or rotation changes and gets included during recalculations. Proper object referencing, Transform change caching, and/or use of `localPosition`/`localRotation` solves the problem adequately. In almost all cases, the benefits to workflow from Scene organization are significantly more valuable than such trivial performance losses.

Animator Override Controllers were introduced way back in Unity v4.3, but tend to be forgotten or rarely mentioned. They are an alternative to standard Animation Controllers that allow us to reference an existing Animation Controller, and then override specific states to use different animation files. This allows for much faster workflows since we don't need to duplicate and tweak Animation Controllers multiple times; we only need to change a handful of animation states.

When Unity 5 is launched, it automatically opens the **Project Wizard**, allowing us to open a recent project. However, if we prefer the default behavior from Unity 4, which is to automatically open the previous project, we can edit this behavior by navigating to **Edit | Preferences | General | Load Previous Project** on startup. Note that this setting has a different name under Unity 4 and works in the opposite fashion. You can see this by navigating to **Edit | Preferences | General | Always Show Project Wizard**. Note that if the **Project Wizard** is enabled, we can also open multiple instances of Unity Editor simultaneously.

The amazing customizability of the Unity Editor and its ever-growing feature set means there are absolutely tons of little opportunities to improve workflows and more are being discovered or invented every single day. The Asset Store marketplace is absolutely rife with assets, which try to solve some kind of problem that modern developers are having trouble with, which makes it a great place to browse if we're looking for ideas or, if we're willing, drop some money to save us a ton of hassle. Because these assets tend to sell to a broad audience, this tends to keep prices low, and we can pick up some amazingly useful tools and scripts for surprisingly little cost. In almost all cases, it would take us a significant number of hours to develop the same solution ourselves. If we consider our time as valuable, then scanning the Asset Store on occasion can be a very cost-effective approach to development.

Summary

This brings us to the book's conclusion, and hopefully you enjoyed the ride. To reiterate perhaps the most important tip in this book, always make sure to verify the source of the performance bottleneck via profiling before making a single change. The last thing we want to waste time on is chasing ghosts in the code base, when five minutes of profiler testing can save us an entire day of work. Also, in a lot of cases, the solution requires a cost-benefitting analysis to determine if we're not sacrificing too much in any other area at the risk of adding further bottlenecks. Make sure to have a reasonable understanding of the root cause of the bottleneck, to avoid putting other performance metrics at risk.

Performance enhancement can be a lot of fun since, due to the complexity of modern computer hardware, small tweaks can yield big rewards. There are many techniques that can be implemented to improve application performance or speed up our workflows. Some of these are hard to fully realize without the experience and skills necessary to spend a reasonable amount of time implementing them. In most cases the fixes are relatively simple, once we find the source of the problem. So, go forth and use your repository of knowledge to make your games the best they can be!

Index

Execution Order
    URL 26
external tips
    about 258, 259
    other tips 260

F

fill rate, back end bottlenecks
    about 164
    Occlusion Culling 167, 168
    overdraw 165, 166
    shader optimization 168
    Shaders intended for mobile platforms,
        using 169
Find() method
    avoiding, at runtime 44-46
First In First Out (FIFO) queue 81
FixedUpdate() method 126
Fixed Update Timestep 124
foreach loops 217
Forward Rendering
    URL 182
fragment Shader 153
Frame Debugger 156
front end bottlenecks
    about 161
    GPU Skinning, disabling 163
    Level Of Detail (LOD) 161, 162
    tessellation, reducing 163

G

GameObject null reference check
    performing 77
game programming patterns
    URL 259
garbage collection, managed memory
    about 198
    at runtime 200, 201
    memory fragmentation 199, 200
    tactics 202
    threaded Garbage collection 201
Garbage Collector
    finalizer thread 201
    main thread 201

global messaging system
    about 54
    custom message, implementing 60
    globally accessible object 55
    implementing 57, 58
    message cleanup 62, 63
    message processing 56
    message, processing 58, 59
    message, queuing 58, 59
    message registration 60, 61
    message, sending 61
    registration 55
    wrapping up 64
GPU Profiling 153-156
greedy methods 11

H

heap 197
hotkey tips, Editor
    about 243
    arrays 244, 245
    GameObjects 244
    interface 245
    Scene View 244
    Unity keyword, accessing 245

I

immutable Reference types
    about 210
    string concatenation 211-213
    strings 210, 211
interface tips, Editor
    about 246
    Game View 251, 252
    general 246-248
    Hierarchy View 251
    Inspector View 248, 249
    Play Mode 252, 253
    Project View 249, 250
    Scene View 251, 252
Intermediate Language To C++ (IL2CPP)
    about 241
    URL 241

N

name property
retrieving, avoiding 68-70
Native Domain 195
Nested Coroutines
URL 257

O

OnGUI() method 32
Operating System (OS) 191
Order of Execution
URL 125
overdraw 165

P

pass by reference 206
passing by value 206
performance analysis
approaches 13
performance-enhancing techniques
baked animations, considering 119
meshes, combining 120
necessary data, calculating 119
necessary data, importing 119
Optimize Meshes option 120
polygon count, reducing 117
Physics Engine
about 123
using 123
Physics Engine internals
about 124
Collider types 129, 130
collision detection 128, 129
Collision Matrix 131
Dynamic Colliders 128
Fixed Update loop 125, 126
Maximum Allowed Timestep 126
object casting 132
physics 124, 125
physics updates 127
ray casting 132

Rigidbody active state 131, 132
Rigidbody sleeping states 131, 132
runtime changes 127
Static Colliders 128
time 124, 125
physics performance optimizations
about 132
cast and bounding-volume checks,
minimizing 140, 141
Collision Matrix, optimizing 135, 136
complex Mesh Colliders, avoiding 141, 142
discrete collision detection, preferring 136
FixedUpdate frequency,
modifying 137, 138
Maximum Allowed Timestep,
adjusting 139
physics objects, allowing to sleep 145, 146
physics, using 149
ragdolls, optimizing 147
scene setup 132
Solver Iteration Count, modifying 146, 147
Static Colliders, using 135
upgrading, to Unity 5 150
polygon count
Read-Write Enabled flag, using 118
reducing 117
Tweak Mesh Compression 117, 118
prefab pooling
about 223-233
and scene loading 238
instance prespawning 234, 235
object despawning 236
object spawning 233
Poolable Component 226-229
summary 238, 239
system requirements 229-232
testing 236-238
Procedural Materials
about 116
URL 117
Profiler.enableBinaryLog method 26
Profiler.enabled method 25
Profiler.logFile method 26
Profiling and Analysis 33

U

Unity
  batching systems 80
  documentation, URL 113
  future 240-242
  URL 28, 241
Unity 3D 2
Unity 5.0 2
Unity API 217
Unity Editor
  about 2
  profiling 4
  reflection, URL 258
Unity memory domains
  about 195
  managed memory 197
  native memory 196
Unity Profiler
  about 2, 34
  connecting, to Android device 6
  connecting, to iOS device 6
  data, loading 25-33
  data, saving 25-29
  launching 3
  Standalone Instances 3, 4
  Unity Editor 3, 4

Unity Webplayer connection,
    connecting 4, 5
  window 7
Unity Profiler window
  about 7
  controls 8
Unity Webplayer 3
UnloadAudioData() method 98
unused scripts and objects
  disabling 65
  disabling, by distance 66, 67
  disabling, by visibility 65, 66

V

value types
  about 203-205
  structs 207-209
Vertical Sync (VSync) 17
Visual Studio
  URL 259
Visual Studio Tools for Unity (VSTU) 245
VRAM limits, back end bottlenecks
  about 179
  texture preloading 179
  texture thrashing 180

Thank you for buying
Unity 5 Game Optimization

About Packt Publishing

Packt, pronounced 'packed', published its first book, *Mastering phpMyAdmin for Effective MySQL Management*, in April 2004, and subsequently continued to specialize in publishing highly focused books on specific technologies and solutions.

Our books and publications share the experiences of your fellow IT professionals in adapting and customizing today's systems, applications, and frameworks. Our solution-based books give you the knowledge and power to customize the software and technologies you're using to get the job done. Packt books are more specific and less general than the IT books you have seen in the past. Our unique business model allows us to bring you more focused information, giving you more of what you need to know, and less of what you don't.

Packt is a modern yet unique publishing company that focuses on producing quality, cutting-edge books for communities of developers, administrators, and newbies alike. For more information, please visit our website at www.packtpub.com.

Writing for Packt

We welcome all inquiries from people who are interested in authoring. Book proposals should be sent to author@packtpub.com. If your book idea is still at an early stage and you would like to discuss it first before writing a formal book proposal, then please contact us; one of our commissioning editors will get in touch with you.

We're not just looking for published authors; if you have strong technical skills but no writing experience, our experienced editors can help you develop a writing career, or simply get some additional reward for your expertise.

Unity 4.x Cookbook

ISBN: 978-1-84969-042-3   Paperback: 386 pages

Over 100 recipes to spice up your Unity skills

1. A wide range of topics are covered, ranging in complexity, offering something for every Unity 4 game developer.

2. Every recipe provides step-by-step instructions, followed by an explanation of how it all works, and alternative approaches or refinements.

3. Book developed with the latest version of Unity (4.x).

Mastering Unity 4 Scripting [Video]

ISBN: 978-1-84969-614-2   Duration: 01:39 hours

Master Unity 4 gameplay scripting with this dynamic video course

1. Master Unity scripting using C# through step-by-step demonstrations.

2. Create enemy AI systems.

3. Script character animations.

4. Program directional and conditional sound effects as well as background music.

Please check **www.PacktPub.com** for information on our titles

Unity 4.x Game Development by Example Beginner's Guide

ISBN: 978-1-84969-526-8   Paperback: 572 pages

A seat-of-your-pants manual for building fun, groovy little games quickly with Unity 4.x

1. Learn the basics of the Unity 3D game engine by building five small, functional game projects.

2. Explore simplification and iteration techniques that will make you more successful as a game developer.

3. Take Unity for a spin with a refreshingly humorous approach to technical manuals.

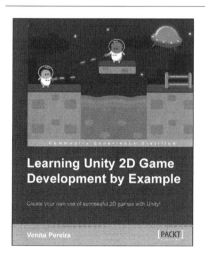

Learning Unity 2D Game Development by Example

ISBN: 978-1-78355-904-6   Paperback: 266 pages

Create your own line of successful 2D games with Unity!

1. Dive into 2D game development with no previous experience.

2. Learn how to use the new Unity 2D toolset.

3. Create and deploy your very own 2D game with confidence.

Please check **www.PacktPub.com** for information on our titles

52135923R00165

Made in the USA
Lexington, KY
17 May 2016